D1071152

# VINYL AGE

MAX BRZEZINSKI

# VINYL AGE

## A GUIDE TO RECORD COLLECTING NOW

BLACK DOG
& LEVENTHAL
PUBLISHERS
NEW YORK

Copyright © 2020 by Carolina Soul, LLC
Illustrations by Matthew Tauch

Cover design by Matthew Tauch
Cover copyright © 2020 by Hachette Book Group, Inc.

Hachette Book Group supports the right to free expression and the value of copyright. The purpose of copyright is to encourage writers and artists to produce the creative works that enrich our culture.

The scanning, uploading, and distribution of this book without permission is a theft of the author's intellectual property. If you would like permission to use material from the book (other than for review purposes), please contact permissions@hbgusa.com. Thank you for your support of the author's rights.

Black Dog & Leventhal Publishers
Hachette Book Group
1290 Avenue of the Americas
New York, NY 10104

www.hachettebookgroup.com
www.blackdogandleventhal.com

First Edition: November 2020

Black Dog & Leventhal Publishers is an imprint of Perseus Books, LLC, a subsidiary of Hachette Book Group, Inc. The Black Dog & Leventhal Publishers name and logo are trademarks of Hachette Book Group, Inc.

The publisher is not responsible for websites (or their content) that are not owned by the publisher.

The Hachette Speakers Bureau provides a wide range of authors for speaking events. To find out more, go to www.HachetteSpeakersBureau.com or call (866) 376-6591.

Print book interior design by Carlos Esparza

Library of Congress Cataloging-in-Publication Data

Names: Brzezinski, Max, author. | Carolina Soul Records (Durham, North Carolina), author.
Title: Vinyl age : a guide to record collecting now / Max Brzezinski and Carolina Soul Records.
Description: First edition. | New York : Black Dog & Leventhal, 2020. | Includes bibliographical references and index. | Summary: "From Carolina Soul Records, one of the world's largest record sellers, comes the definitive guide to every aspect of online record collecting in the digital era. This illustrated guide is packed with information for every type of collector, from crate diggers to hi-end collectors of rare vinyl" —Provided by publisher.
Identifiers: LCCN 2019059823 (print) | LCCN 2019059824 (ebook) | ISBN 9780316419710 (hardcover) | ISBN 9780316419697 (ebook) Subjects: LCSH: Sound recordings—Collectors and collecting. | Popular music genres.
Classification: LCC ML111.5 .B805 2020 (print) | LCC ML111.5 (ebook) | DDC 780.26/6075—dc23
LC record available at https://lccn.loc.gov/2019059823
LC ebook record available at https://lccn.loc.gov/2019059824

ISBNs: 978-0-316-41971-0 (hardcover); 978-0-316-41969-7 (ebook)

Printed in China

IM

10 9 8 7 6 5 4 3 2 1

*For Malcolm & Sarah*

# CONTENTS

# FOREWORD

"Did you go to school for this?"

I'd never been asked that before. I'd also never thought about whether a degree program for record buying could or should exist. As a record dealer, I've lost count of the number of folks who have invited me into their homes to encourage me to make an offer on their record collections. On each of these "house calls," chances were good that I'd find myself in a colorful conversation, and all bets were off as to whether it would even be about music. On this particular occasion, I was sitting in the seller's living room, surrounded by their records, and peering at a desirable disc that I was holding horizontally to see if it was warped. In doing so, I evidently looked very studious or very silly.

"No, no I didn't," I responded to their question with a bit of a laugh. But this made me think: How can one learn about buying and collecting vinyl records?

One way is to engage in buying and selling over many years. My friend Gary Burgess, who has dealt in vinyl for at least two decades, makes periodic references to his "education": the innumerable records he's bought, and continues to buy—whether from flea markets, thrift stores, retiring collectors, or other dealers—that fall short of his hopes for what they could be in terms of collectability and monetary value, in terms of sound, or both. (They often go hand in hand, after all.) If asked how he knows so much, he invariably responds that he's "paid for a lot of lessons." He's right—so much of what you might simply call intuition is cultivated through an iterative trial-and-error process, earned one record at a time. Truly, there's no substitute for experience; it's a mighty teacher, even if it isn't the most efficient one.

In my beginning collecting days, the early 2000s, I discovered a few key resources: friends and fellow volunteers at WXYC (my college radio station), local DJs and collectors, magazines, and internet message boards dedicated to funk, soul, and crate digging in general. But I craved more, and it turned out that a Burgesslike method worked well for me: purchasing records used and new, researching their value, listening to them, figuring out what I liked, and so on and so forth. Now that the internet has grown up, it offers a staggering array of record-related websites. This makes me feel both envious of newer collectors and overwhelmed on their behalf. If I were new to the game now, I'm not sure I'd know where to begin. Anyone looking to learn about vinyl for the first time, or learn more about vinyl, can benefit from a means of cutting through the sheer volume of info out there.

That's where *Vinyl Age* comes in. Within these pages, you'll find that Max Brzezinski, Carolina Soul's marketing director, has crafted an insightful and thought-provoking work. He's done so to give us, the readers, the benefit of someone else's experience, to accelerate the vinyl learning curve so we can more quickly build our own philosophies, quickening the assembly and maintenance of a record collection that is most meaningful for each of us.

There are many ways to build a record collection that you're passionate about. The best way, of course, is the one that feels right for you. I can tell you that even in my own home there isn't a consensus on the ultimate approach. My wife, Hollie, has collected records for years and fits into Max's description as a record "omnivore": In her somewhat extensive collection you'll find a variety of wildly divergent genres and styles. The vast majority are pieces that she acquired at yard sales, thrift shops, and library sales for $1 or less. She didn't set out to accumulate a collection of great monetary worth; instead she revels in the constellation of sounds she might never have experienced if not for happenstance and affordability. For her, sticking to a low price point means that she feels free to take a chance on records that seem interesting, and she also feels just as free to eventually discard those that do not speak to her, while savoring the ones that truly do.

I'm more of what Max has termed as a "fundamentalist." I've worked hard at collecting mostly within a single niche area: I've assembled a robust representation of independently released soul music from North and South Carolina in the 1960s through 1980s. This body of music has captivated me since I was twenty-one years old, volunteering at WXYC. The excitement of finding something obscure yet amazing, and doing so in my own backyard, initially drew me in. I loved the process of learning about the rich network of unheralded musicians that operated in the region where I grew up. Even today, I still serendipitously encounter local records that I haven't seen before and that deserve a wider audience. I love this music so much that it seemed to be the most appropriate name for the business that I eventually founded and still operate today, Carolina Soul.

Over the last decade, Carolina Soul has grown out of my focused interests into a brick-and-mortar storefront in Durham, North Carolina, and an online storefront that routinely sends multiple genres and formats to collectors all around the world. In brief, going into business allowed me to work in a field that I was passionate about and enabled me to continue collecting within my niche area while selling my other finds to support the endeavor. In my early days of dealing, I would search out local sellers who might be offering a local record and I would look through everything else they had and make purchases, with an eye toward both education and resale. At home, I would sort through the purchases and figure out what to keep and what to sell. As is still the case now, my main avenue then for selling was through eBay auctions. I would personally describe, grade, photograph, and prepare sample recordings of each item, and then list them one by one on eBay. Eventually, I brought friends on board to help with the sales process. Along the way, we opened up our auctions to consignments from our personal connections, meaning we'd sell their records on their behalf. Today, the majority of our eBay sales are consignments, and these come to us from the public at large.

Consignment has been one of our greatest joys, and one of our greatest acquisition methods. The relationships we've built through consignment, and the material that we might never have seen otherwise, have been very exciting. Some of the most intriguing one-of-a-kind material has come to us on consignment: reggae dubplates, unreleased Miles Davis acetates, unreleased studio reel-to-reel tapes, promotional glossy photos, rockabilly 45s, and "radio spots" (promotional records used to advertise movies on the radio in the pre-digital era).Through the windows of these relationships, we have even more impressions of collecting types and how they can and probably will evolve over time, if given long enough. And that's once again to show that there are no "right ways" to approach this world.

I believe that the issues raised in this book are truly worth thinking about. Some of it you may agree with, some of it you might not; regardless, you will have a fuller thought framework when it comes to buying and owning vinyl, and I believe that this is the book's true gift to us, the readers. Whether you're new to record collecting or, like me, have turned buying records into a profession, this book will encourage you to consider not only your approach, but also the assumptions that underlie it. If you are newer to record collecting, virtually all of this book will be particularly valuable for you. Max gives a great orientation to the record market that can serve as a shortcut to deciding how you might best approach various acquisition channels. He references some of the internet resources I personally use on a daily basis. If you've been collecting for some time now, I believe you will also find topics in these pages that will challenge you to consider your relationship with records. For example, in chapter 5, Max examines the experience of listening to vinyl, considering ways to appreciate music beyond the dimensions of space and time. I wonder what sound journeys this chapter will inspire. I certainly hope you'll reach out and let us know!

Record collecting is an activity best experienced on one's own terms. *Vinyl Age* will not decide for you what your approach and philosophy should be, but it will help inform the considerations you might make as part of your personal journey. The framework that Max develops here will be relevant to you whether you've yet to purchase your first record or whether your first record was acquired decades ago.

At the end of the day, when it comes to learning to collect, and continuing to collect, there's no singular right way. Just start, and keep going. Bon voyage.

Jason Perlmutter
Founder/Owner
Carolina Soul Records
April 2020

# INTRODUCTION

## WHY VINYL NOW?

A vinyl record is a magic commodity. Despite being bought and sold every day like copper or coffee, the true value of a record always exceeds its cash price. More now than ever, vinyl collectors attribute deep spiritual, intellectual, and emotional meaning to their records. In the hearts and minds of those who love vinyl, a record can never be just another "little nameless object" to be "gripped and flipped." Rather, records are the bearer of what Albert Ayler called "the healing force of the universe." Nevertheless, even the most die-hard vinyl fundamentalist knows that vinyl markets are soaring. Since 2007, new vinyl sales have gone up every year; many rare records now consistently sell for four and five figures. *Forbes* conservatively estimates that 30 million new and used records were sold in the year 2017 alone.[1] Carolina Soul Records sells roughly 7,000 records a month (see Fig. 1: Unit Vinyl Sales), many for historically high prices.

Currently, the vinyl record holds two very different types of value at the same time: the first earthly and economic; the second spiritual and aesthetic. As a commodity, the record is traded like any other good; as a work of art, it is music's "king format,"[2] a medium for our profoundest thoughts and passions. As a result, one collector's "grail" is another's financial instrument. This means investments of money and passion into vinyl are both at an all-time high.

What has brought about this surge in vinyl value? Many commonplace answers spring to mind: the record's nostalgic, retro appeal; the gratifying tactile pleasures of playing vinyl on a turntable; the display value of a record collection and the way it allows a music fan to show off their taste via their physical possessions; the "warmer" sound of analog compared to digital.

While these factors all contributed to vinyl's return, it's the internet that broke the path for the analog revival. Without an online platform, the causes above would never have been sufficient to bring vinyl back. On eBay and Discogs, you can now find millions of records for sale, from multiplatinum megahits like *Thriller* and *Dark Side of the Moon* to ultra-obscure private press records like Black Ryder's "Black Ryder" (not on label, 1982) and Ice's "Reality" (not on label, 1980). Both the breadth and depth of vinyl now available online are unprecedented. For the first time, the scarcest, most locally rooted piece of vinyl can be bought from anywhere around the world alongside the most common. The collector is no longer at the mercy of their hometown brick-and-mortar's stock—even those living in record deserts, whether in Ohio or Oman, can (for the right price) buy almost any record they want.

In the pre-internet (1980s and before) and nascent internet eras (early 1990s), it took considerably more work to research records, particularly non-mainstream ones. For example, if you were into punk 7" records back in the day, you might have scoured the pages of *Slash*, *Forced Exposure*, *Maximum Rocknroll*, and local zines to find records. As a result, you developed your collection slowly, record by record, mail order by mail order. You had to buy records on faith, or in response to a stray print review. Now, between YouTube, Soulseek, and paid streaming services, you can hear millions of tracks, including vinyl rips, of once impossible to hear 7", 12", LP, and even 78 rpm records. While you still can't buy and hear everything, there's exponentially more available now than just a few decades ago. The sheer number of digital files online has revealed how many analog records there are out there in the wild.

Now, if you wake up one morning and want to learn about obscure punk 7" records, you can download twenty volumes of the *Killed by Death* compilations in ten minutes. If a track on these KBD comps catches your fancy, say Gasoline's "Killer Man" (Egg [France], 1977), you can immediately look up the original (OG) pressing on sites like Discogs and Popsike. There, you can find reliable sales histories for the first-release of the 7". If you are willing to spend between $45 and $325 for an OG copy of "Killer Man," you can then buy one that day. Before the internet, it would have taken a master digger to track down this record. Now, it's within the grasp of anybody with a service provider.

For the casual music fan, the rise of hipster reissue labels in the late 1990s and early 2000s was one of the first signs of how exciting the internet could be for record collectors. Labels like Soul Jazz (est. 1992), Jazzman (est. 1998), Strut (est. 1999), Numero Group (est. 2002), Now-Again (est. 2002), Sublime Frequencies (est. 2003), and Mississippi Records (est. 2005) were among the first to capitalize on the internet's expansion of the archive of records. These labels compiled and re-pressed out-of-the-way music they themselves often first heard about online on music blogs, peer-to-peer file sharing sites, invite-only torrent groups, and message boards. These labels' reissues popularized records previously only accessible to the most dedicated old-school diggers.

Genre-wise, these reissues reflected the larger polyphony of the online music world. They were one of the first big signs that rock music was no longer the center of the record universe. Soul Jazz and Jazzman specialized in soul and jazz reissues, Strut focused on dance and club records, Numero and Now-Again concentrated on funk and soul, Sublime Frequencies mined world music, and Mississippi reissued Americana. Not only did these labels dislodge rock from its baby boomer pride of place, they also signaled their distance from the taste norms of the non-rock genres they themselves were reissuing. For example, Jazzman was the first to sell "spiritual" jazz compilations. Strut and others put out "mutant" and "left-field" disco and dance records. Numero tagged its brand of soul "eccentric." Sublime Frequencies and Mississippi Records packaged their world and Americana in DIY sleeves to emphasize their cool and contrast themselves with the staid associations that came with vernacular music.[3] Taken as a whole, these compilations showed that record collectors raised by the internet were becoming increasingly interested in the subgenres of every musical tradition. One side effect of this hyper-specialization has been a shift of attention from established classics of an era to its lesser-known titles. Now, it's not uncommon to encounter avid soul collectors who have little time for Aretha Franklin and Otis Redding, or deep "outsider" singer-songwriter fans with scant interest in Bob Dylan or Joni Mitchell. For collectors of all genres, rare and obscure records often feel fresher than the overfamiliar "classics" of previous generations. Even within the output of established artists, collectors now make fine-grained distinctions that tend to favor lesser-known works. For example: Joni Mitchell's *Hejira* instead of *Blue*; Dylan's *Street Legal* over *Blonde on Blonde*; Aretha's "Who's Zoomin' Who?" over "Respect," and so on. As access to cool records increases, it takes more and more to gain credibility as a "true head." Simultaneously, the internet has inspired both more name-dropping obscurantism and more genuinely deep exploration of what's possible.

In the process, the internet and its reissue culture have also fostered the development of new genre classifications and collecting subcultures. New materials required new organizational concepts. The new subgenre terms range from the sublime (yacht rock) to the ambiguous (random rap) to the ridiculous (bonerz). Online boards devoted to vinyl collecting (for example, Soul Source UK, Waxidermy, and Terminal Boredom) and Facebook collecting groups (for example, Now Playing and its offshoots) have enabled folks to refine their record tastes and think about musical classification in new ways. While a head in the '60s and '70s only had to keep up with one or two major genres like rock or soul to be considered on the cutting edge, now there are hundreds of microgenres to educate oneself on.

The internet incubated the revival of vinyl and transformed its culture in the process. At the same time, though, collectors cherish records in large part because they allow flight from the connected life. The record has a spiritualized aura again, partially because it allows us to escape the everyday. While contemporary streaming services push music into every pore of our lives, the vinyl listening experience stands apart from it all. The more streams and files function as banal parts of the digital everyday, the more the record comes to seem like a heavenly possession.[4] The internet brought vinyl back economically, but in many ways life on the internet is inimical to record culture. In fact, listening to and collecting records provides access to zones of experience unavailable online.

For one, unlike a digital stream, a record's a solid object. You can't hold a Spotify playlist in your hands. With subscription music services, you don't own your collection; you rent content. If you stop paying your monthly bill or the wrong server goes down, you lose access to your entire collection. With a record, on the other hand, you get a total musical work, with large original sleeve art, liner notes, photographs, inserts, labels, and record in one package. Using a streaming service, you must depend on the organizational defaults of that service—whether the playlist system of Spotify or the "auto-play" function of YouTube.

By contrast, you can sort your record collection however you want. You decide what belongs, and because each record costs something, you must be mindful of your selection criteria. Compared to a record collection, the sea of musical data online is an undifferentiated mass of material. What's more, with a record, you get to decide what you hear. The vinyl listening experience is active—while the auto-play function on streaming sites can lead to new discoveries of the RIYL (recommended if you like) variety, the function of these programs is mostly out of the user's control. Online services have cut out the face-to-face, social dimension of record collecting. Compared to swapping records with friends or even to reading radio station record reviews, learning about music from corporate algorithms can be a bloodlessly impersonal, alienating affair.

Collecting vinyl allows you to develop your own taste, your own thoughts and feelings about what music is important. Anyone who's ever been on Twitter knows it can be a negative, toxic space for discussion. Online music culture, on the other hand, has become increasingly "poptomistic"—it's become increasingly common to see fans and music writers alike promote the most popular music as the most worthy of praise and attention. As a result, current artists on major labels with the highest sales tend to be celebrated, while everything else is ignored. In contrast to online poptomism, record collecting allows the collector to exercise judgment over what does and does not belong in their collection. It lets you develop a personal canon of music distinct from standards of online music journalism. It also frees you from the need to cycle rapidly from one disposable fad to the next in the name of staying current. This is not to say that contemporary records by Future, Rihanna, and Frank Ocean aren't amazing—only that music wasn't born yesterday, and these records have hundreds of thousands of peers in the vinyl archive.

In a widely circulated tweet, music writer Geeta Dayal recently pointed to another appealing thing about vinyl, the disconnection it affords from online surveillance:

> It's [vinyl] not networked. No service is tracking my listening, serving ads, or monetizing my experience. No one knows what I'm listening to, except me.[5]

In other words, a record player's an air-gapped, black-box device. To extend Dayal's point, it's useful to remember that turntables are usually found in homes and not in workplaces. This means that listening to a record on vinyl is one of the few musical experiences left that allows imaginative escape from the world outside. In contrast, digital music is more and more being used as a coping mechanism to distract from the daily grind: to dampen the boredom of office work, to endure manual labor, or to take the edge off a long commute. Even in our leisure, we use music as background to other activities. By contrast, listening to a vinyl record in ideal conditions allows for a more attentive, liberating listening experience. Concentrating on a record means internalizing its rhythms and musical ideas, which are necessarily opposed to the ones of everyday life. When you have the luxury of taking a record in, you become absorbed in another way of thinking and feeling, and another sense of time. Having a "room of one's own" in front of the turntable allows you to disconnect from what is and get in touch with what could be. While such a room requires leisure time and money to enjoy, it's still far cheaper than collecting Rembrandts or First Folios of Shakespeare. Plus, if you know how to dig, there are still steals to be had at thrift stores, at pawn shops, and in corners of the internet.

The disconnection from the "real world" a turntable offers makes it conducive to what musician Pauline Oliveros has called "deep listening." Oliveros defines deep listening as "a practice that is intended to heighten and expand consciousness of sound in as many dimensions of awareness and attentional dynamics as humanly possible."[6] While deep listening is sometimes bandied about in an elitist way, it is an experience open to all. Vinyl is just one proven way into close, "deep" listening, not the only one.[7]

And in contrast to the blankness of an MP3 or FLAC, material history inheres in a record and its sleeve. From the moment it's released, a record begins absorbing its surroundings. Each one includes markers of where it has been, whether this comes in the form of cool, beautiful, or strange ephemera—pencil and pen notations on covers, drawings, love letters and pornography stuffed in jackets, or in more banal signs of wear—scuffs, warps, or taped-over splits. All are signs of a record's past lives and the lives of its previous owners.

Many records have even become collectible as works of visual art. For example, David Stone Martin's minimal jazz 10" designs, the mysterious Harvey's uncanny gospel landscapes, Marte Röling's jazz portraits for Fontana, Reid Miles's modernist forms for Blue Note, and Wilfred Limonious's outlandish dancehall cartoons are all sought after by collectors. And this is not to mention sleeves made by already internationally famous artists like Jean-Michel Basquiat, Andy Warhol, Ernie Barnes, Jasper Johns, and R. Crumb. The recent outpouring of appreciation that followed legendary cover designers Pedro Bell's (Parliament-Funkadelic) and Vaughan Oliver's (the 4AD label) passings is a testament to the importance of a distinct cover design. It's no wonder, then, that vinyl has become increasingly interesting to both social historians and art collectors. For example, in 2010, Duke University's Nasher Museum of Art mounted the first exhibition "to explore the culture of vinyl records in the history of contemporary art."[8] This was another sign that vinyl had become an art object and was creeping into tonier realms than old-school diggers could have imagined. But it's also a testimony to the material appeal of the vinyl record: it's hard to imagine a comparable exhibition being put on in tribute to the WAV file.

But the history embedded in records comes not only in the form of charming memorabilia and artistic treasure. Records are also primary documents of music's more unseemly moments: for example, its participation in histories of racism and sexism. Album sleeves from the '50s and '60s often extended white supremacy. They did this explicitly, as with Mr. Bones's blackface cover for *Hey Mister Banjo* (Palace, 195x—*x* is used throughout when the specific year is unknown), or implicitly, whitewashing the covers of records like *Lightnin' Hopkins Strums the*

*Blues* (Score, 1958) or James Brown's *Good, Good Twistin'* (King, 1962). The cover for *Lightnin' Hopkins Strums the Blues* features a lily-white hand in a checked shirt "strumming" a guitar, while *Good, Good Twistin'* shows two rather old-looking white "teens" stuck in mid "dance," presumably at a sock hop. Both covers erased black artists to make their records marketable to white consumers during segregation. And lest we think racism in collecting is a thing of the past, there is still a market for white power records in genres like black metal (Burzum LPs), hardcore (Skrewdriver LPs), and outlaw country (David Allan Coe's *Underground Album*, D.A.C., 1982). Or consider the original covers for Blind Faith's *Blind Faith* (Polydor, 1969) and Scorpions' *Virgin Killer* (RCA, 1976). They feature pervy nude photographs of prepubescent girls—a fact that has done nothing to dampen their appeal for certain collectors.

So when we say above that records are fascinating for the way they embody the history of their times, this means not just the good but also the bad and ugly sides of that history. And in many ways, they reveal the way these histories live on. In any case, obviously no such sense of history, personal or public, inspiring or disgusting, inheres in immaterial streams and downloads—though I am sure some Gen Xers and millennials feel nostalgia for their old external hard drives.

The same sense of history found on the covers and labels can also be found in the way they sound. Since vinyl was the dominant musical format from the 1950s until the 1980s, the first pressings of most known releases came on vinyl. This means that the first pressing was the one to which critics and fans first became attached: its sound was the basis for the initial response to the work. First pressings started life as just one version among many possible, the result of various accidents of production, engineering, and mastering. But because they were first, they now have an outsized effect on the received meaning of the music they carry. So if you want to understand why Miles Davis's *Kind of Blue* (Columbia, 1959) became arguably the most famous jazz LP of all time, you should track down an original "6-eye" mono pressing to hear what those at the time first heard, rather than a later stereo pressing. This is not because the first pressing always sounds best, but because its particular sound has historical significance. In fact, early pressings sometimes sound terrible: landmark early house 12" records on Chicago's Trax Records were pressed on low-quality recycled vinyl. Many classic hip-hop albums were crammed with too many songs per side, which resulted in thin-sounding tracks. But these defects became features as the records made a place in musical history.

On the other hand, many great records were made when vinyl was the dominant format and were mastered specifically for turntable use. Purist audiophiles insist too strongly on the significance of minor differences between pressings, but it is true that some sound better than others. While what counts as a "hot stamper"[9] will always be highly subjective, specific engineers, pressing plants, and source tapes did sometimes produce unique-sounding variant pressings. Different countries sometimes also released quite different-sounding and different-looking versions of a record. So, while audiophile fundamentalists often make exaggerated, pretentious claims about sound quality,[10] it's undeniable that record collecting allows you to "A-B" compare many permutations of the same sound recording. By contrast, finding your favorite version of a record using digital music alone would be impossible.

For most record collectors, streams and downloads have become merely functional. Collectors now use digital services to decide whether a record is worth buying or not. In the internet era, the stream and MP3 allow for a trial run of a piece of music before the purchase of its vinyl OG copy. Even before the internet, record collectors "minted up" copies of their collection by replacing them with cleaner ones in better condition. Now, this minting up process often begins with streams or downloads before a collector ever touches a real record. Digital music today represents a flat means to an end, a stepping-stone to the eventual "hard-filing" (adding a record to your permanent collection) of a pristine vinyl copy.

Above, we've run through many of the reasons people are getting deeply into records again. This book is a guide for anyone looking to do the same. In what follows, we'll be mapping the land and guiding you through its territories—both analyzing how the contemporary record world works and teaching practical collecting skills. While the internet has made it easier than ever to skim the surfaces of record life, it's made going deep harder than ever. As Stephen Graham writes, a collector still needs to "go to the underground, instead of it coming to you [...] even if that 'going to' now largely consists of web searches and Facebook likes as opposed to sending out mail orders or traveling to a record shop."[11]

I'll review several methods and skills essential to digging in the internet era—how to research, find, buy, evaluate, and understand records in the twenty-first century. I'll explain the ins and outs of various trends, subcultures, and microgenres that make the record world spin. I'll demystify the sometimes useful, sometimes absurd, but always entertaining ways collectors relate (or fail to relate) to one another. And I'll suggest ways to parse the difference between historical trends and more faddish trends. After you've read this book, no one will ever front on you using cryptic acronyms like WOL (short for "writing on label"), DNAP ("does not affect play"), or RVG (the initials of Rudy Van Gelder, the legendary jazz engineer). From how not to get ripped off online or in brick-and-mortar record stores to the differences in sound between crossover and '70s soul, from setting up an eSnipe to understanding the resurgence of gospel and new age, I'll take you through it all.

LANIER & CO.

CURTIS MAYFIELD: HONESTY

MOTOWN

BERNARD-PURDIE

SHAFT

YOU'RE WHAT'S MISSING IN MY LIFE

CHUCK JACKSON · TEARDROPS KEEP FALLIN' ON MY HEART

'CROWN PRINCE OF DANCE' / RUFUS THOMAS

G. C. CAMERON

JESUS CHRIST GREATEST HITS — THE OD SQUAD featuring LEONARD CASTON

ARY MCA2-11929

BOOGIE TO THE TOP

KUDU RECORDS

THE STAPLE SINGERS — BE WHAT YOU ARE

STEREO

© ℗ 1978 CREED TAYLOR INC.

MAD

WEBSTER LEWIS

FUNKADELIC

Fred Wesley and the J.B.'s / Damn Right I Am Somebody

LET ME BE THE ONE

THE BEST OF

LEWAND RECORDS

SING

JAE MASON/TENDER MAN

CURTIS MAYFIELD/SUPERFLY

SUDDENLY

WARNER

# CHAPTER 1

# Playing the Record Game

As highlighted in our introduction, the internet has revolutionized record collecting. It has simultaneously erased old barriers to access and erected new ones. While reviving vinyl's relevance, the internet has also turned parts of the record game into a highly speculative stock market where fortune favors the rich. It has superseded the simple world of handwritten want lists and printed price guides and put a complex new system in its place. For both new collectors and those looking to get deeper into records, it's easier than ever to see what's out there. But it's also become more challenging than ever to collect records at the highest level. This chapter will map the new economic and cultural landscape of contemporary record collecting. Using charts drawn from Carolina Soul's private sales data, I'll detail the rules of the new record game, the challenges it presents to those looking to play it, and strategies for overcoming these challenges.

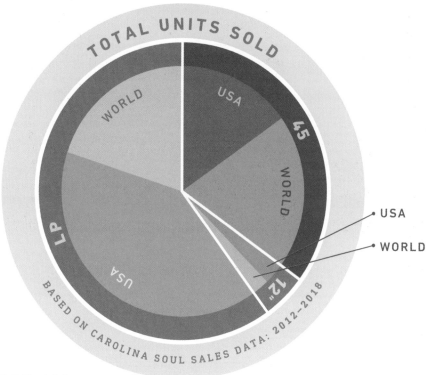

Fig. 1. Unit Vinyl Sales

## A RISE IN PRICES

One glaring effect of the internet on record collecting is a general rise in prices. From *Rumours* to rare Rex Harley, any given piece of vinyl is probably more expensive now than it would have been in, say, 1995. Although the record's no longer the dominant music format, interest in vinyl both new and old has undeniably produced a seller's market. By opening the record archive up to an international buying pool, eBay auctions have tended to redistribute vinyl wealth upward toward the 1 percent and away from everyone else. In turn, this has made rare record collecting more a game of the privileged than ever. As a result, some folks feel priced out, while others have been discouraged from even getting into records in the first place. While less expensive records are still more accessible to the average collector, the rise in record prices across the board has put the squeeze on all but the wealthiest buyers.

At the deepest level, this raises ethical questions about where records are *going*—both literally and figuratively. Can a system that takes records away from their local owners and puts them in the hands of a minority of rich international collectors possibly be just and fair? What's more, most valuable records now go to high-income countries like the US, the UK, and Japan, with very few going to countries in Africa or South Asia (see Fig. 2). Wouldn't it be better if radio stations, museums, schools, and universities could keep record collections whole, rather than the market scattering them around the world? These questions, however, point to structural problems without immediate, quick-fix solutions. They will require large-scale changes by the entire market, maybe even in the structure of capitalism itself. In the meantime, though, the situation is far from hopeless—the record game operates on many levels, and some are more exciting than ever. But if you don't know the rules of a game, you're doomed to lose out. And before you can play the record game well, you need to understand how it works—one method is provided below.

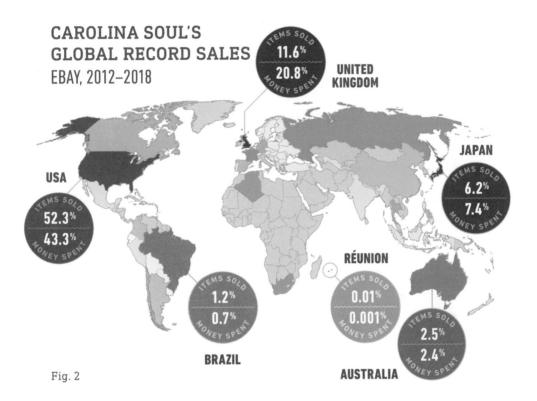

**CAROLINA SOUL'S GLOBAL RECORD SALES**
EBAY, 2012–2018

UNITED KINGDOM
ITEMS SOLD **11.6%**
**20.8%** MONEY SPENT

JAPAN
ITEMS SOLD **6.2%**
**7.4%** MONEY SPENT

USA
ITEMS SOLD **52.3%**
**43.3%** MONEY SPENT

RÉUNION
ITEMS SOLD **0.01%**
**0.001%** MONEY SPENT

BRAZIL
ITEMS SOLD **1.2%**
**0.7%** MONEY SPENT

AUSTRALIA
ITEMS SOLD **2.5%**
**2.4%** MONEY SPENT

Fig. 2

**TASTE**

Knowledge of the record game is necessary both to succeed within it and to go beyond it. Even seemingly negative trends can be played to your advantage. For example, now that rare records have gone up in price, you can flip ones you don't want in order to buy those you need. As it's still possible to dig up such valuable records in the vinyl wilds, you can play the speculative game to expand your personal collection. All it takes is a little know-how, a willingness to travel, and an openness to getting your hands dirty.

This is just one example of a theme that I'll expand upon below: wealth can't buy taste. The most expensive records are not de facto the best. If you look at the best eBay sale aggregator, Popsike, you can sort completed record auctions by highest price. The records at the top of this list, the ones with the most outrageous price tags, are an aesthetic mixed bag—some are great, some just average, and some actively annoying, while still others are rare souvenirs of no particular musical interest. See Appendix 1.

The same goes for Carolina Soul's private list of top sellers—a high price is no guarantee of aesthetic quality. For example, compare two of the company's highest-priced Northern soul auction results: a vinyl promo. Does this mean the Larry Clinton is approximately 3.3 times the record of Saints? Of course not. In fact, I personally find the gliding elegance of "I'll Let You Slide" superior to Clinton's work on "She's Wanted." Yet the internet—by archiving, organizing, and making sales data publicly available—has seduced many into mistaking a high price for a marker of superior musical quality. This is because, at first glance, a price list seems objective, a way out of the subjective wilds of judgment and evaluation.

But data can't save us. For example, in the case of the expensive Northern soul 45s above, remember that for any given genre, sales data reflect the taste of a small, wealthy niche audience, numbering only a few hundred people worldwide. It's far from a value-neutral expression of the vox populi. Given that the buying data reveals only the tendencies and predilections of specific classes of buyers, it's important to hang on to your own sense of judgment. You can use data as a tool to flip records, as a whetstone to sharpen your own taste, and to find out about music you haven't heard. But there is no set list of classics to which you must automatically pay obeisance. Record data is fun and useful, but it does not reflect a standard on which to build a canon any more than *Rolling Stone*'s "500 Greatest Albums of All Time."

In other words, in the big-data internet era, remember that economic value and aesthetic value are never synonymous. Prices are moot when it comes to all the important questions about a record on its meaning, affective power, and historical significance. Some one-dollar records are amazing, while many expensive ones are dull. In this, as in so many other cases, you cannot trust the "rationality" of the market. Now that the internet has thrown records into a

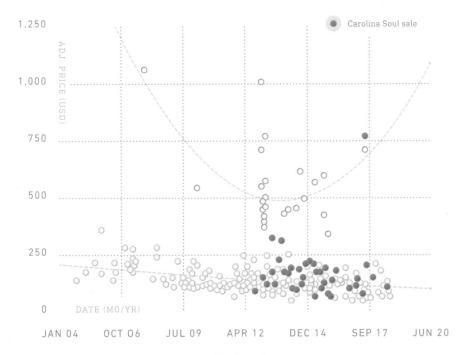

Fig. 3. Ann Sexton, "You've Been Gone Too Long"

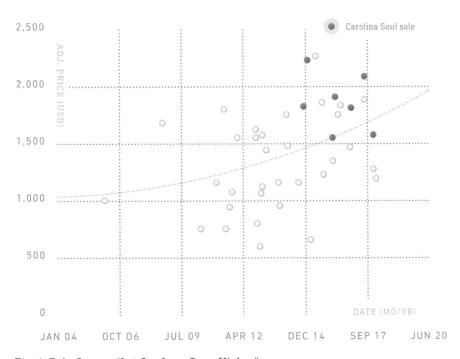

Fig. 4. Eula Cooper, "Let Our Love Grow Higher"

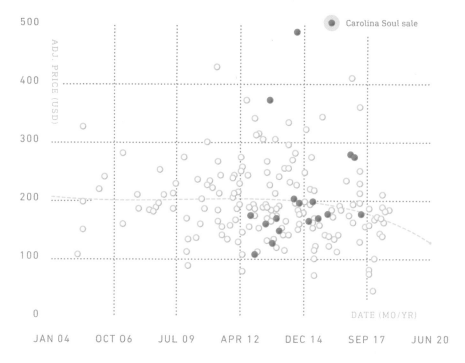

500

ADJ. PRICE (USD)

400

300

200

100

0

● Carolina Soul sale

DATE (MO/YR)

JAN 04    OCT 06    JUL 09    APR 12    DEC 14    SEP 17    JUN 20

Fig. 5. The Honey Drippers, "Impeach the President"

stock exchange, they've become subject to a host of irrational crazes and manias worthy of the Dutch tulip trade.

The internet has also put the price of individual records in flux. This means that a record you love can dramatically plummet or jump up in financial value. Take, for example, Ann Sexton's soul perennial "You've Been Gone Too Long," two of three versions of which have been dropping in dollar value (see Fig. 3). According to Carolina Soul data maven Nate Smith, this is because "the market was spooked for the most sought after version on Impel when in early 2013, quantity surfaced and 14 copies were sold on eBay over the course of just one month. The most common pressing, the Seventy Seven yellow label version, has suffered an even more dramatic decline in value, –50%, because people have been pumping copies onto eBay steadily since the early 2000s." In response, one might be led subconsciously to reconsider Ann Sexton's 45 in light of this market revaluation. You might start thinking of "You've Been Gone Too Long" as a more "common" sounding record than you once thought, equating its higher quantity with lower quality. But while your experience of listening to Ann Sexton encompasses a complex range of personal associations, thoughts, and feelings, the record's going rate on eBay is a simple number. On the flip side, when a record rises in value like Eula Cooper's "Let Our Love Grow Higher" has (see Fig. 4), you may find yourself second-guessing your previous take on the record, straining to hear what others now seem to hear. Or in the case of a record that has maintained a steady value, like the Honey Drippers' "Impeach the President" (see Fig. 5), you may assume it's a classic simply because it seems impervious to fluctuations in the market. But you must remember the market is just one source of information, and a narrow and faulty one even in the best of times. Charting prices is essential and a useful research tool if you want to flip records, but resist

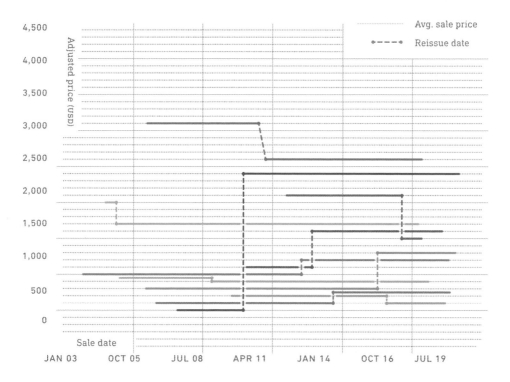

Fig. 6. Reissue Effects on OG Release Prices

GAINED VALUE

- **Equatics "Doin It"** (no label)
  REISSUE: Now-Again, Feb 2010
  RE-PRESS: Jul 2017

- **M'Boom "Re:Percussion"** (Strata-East)
  REISSUE: Think!, Oct 2012

- **Stark Reality "Discovers Hoagy Carmichael's Music Shop"** (AJP)
  REISSUE: Now-Again, May 2015

- **Patterson Twins "Let Me Be Your Lover"** (Commercial)
  REISSUE: Think!, Sep 2013

- **Rhythm Machine "S/T"** (self-titled Lulu)
  REISSUE: Now-Again, Jul 2012

LOST VALUE

- **Milton Wright "Spaced"** (Alston)
  REISSUE: Jazzman Oct 2008

- **Edge Of Daybreak "Eyes Of Love"** (Bohannon's)
  REISSUE: Numero Group, Oct 2015

- **Brief Encounter "S/T"** (Seventy-Seven)
  REISSUE: P-Vine, Oct 2010 and Jazzman, Jan 2011

- **Freddie Terrell's Soul Expedition "S/T"** (Lefevre Sound)
  REISSUE: Jazzman, Jan 2005

- **Tommy McGee "Positive-Negative"** (MTMG)
  REISSUE: Numero Group, May 2016

the temptation to conflate the voice of money with the voice of a record itself, because in reality the two speak different languages.

As mentioned in the introduction, reissue labels were the first to capitalize on the internet's expansion of popular musical horizons. Labels like Now-Again and Numero Group in the US, Jazzman in the UK, and P-Vine in Japan started reissuing records previously known only to "heads" or not at all. Fig. 6 explores the effect of such reissues on the value of original pressings. As you can see, half of the original pressings studied lost some value after their reissue, while the other half saw a rise in value. In other words, it's unclear whether reissues have an inhibitive or enticing effect on buyers. Whatever the case, it seems clear that reissues and originals can coexist in the marketplace without the risk of one replacing the other.

Just as you shouldn't take the market as a reflection of universal taste, don't take reissues as a reflection of the underground's taste. Take the reissue canon, too, with a grain of salt. Though respected reissue labels have brought many cool records back into wider circulation, their catalogs do not directly reflect the will of the independent music community or of hardcore diggers. What gets reissued is often an accident of copyright, the condition of master tapes, and specific dealings between labels and artists. Musical greatness or historical significance is no automatic guarantee of a prestigious reissue, while a subpar record is sometimes cynically reissued as a "lost classic" just because a deal made financial sense for its reissue label.

## NAVIGATING TASTE COMMUNITIES

To establish your taste in records contra the market (including the reissue market), you needn't go it alone. There are a variety of face-to-face and virtual communities out there, each with its own record canon methods of interpreting and using vinyl. Joining in the life of such communities will help you resist internalizing market prices as your aesthetic values. The internet has spawned a dizzying number of small taste cultures, micro-scenes, and boutique associations focused on particular subgenres. And despite the homogenizing effects of gentrification on culture, local music scenes still exist everywhere. Some are bigger and/or more interesting than others, but all challenge the objectivity of the price system in their practices. Engaging with them will help you learn and clarify your own taste.

In "real life," find local record stores and determine their genre specialties; find niche clubs and take in their house sound. Tune in to college and community radio stations and/or volunteer there—these are spaces to learn. In Carolina Soul's area, North Carolina's Triangle (Durham, Raleigh, and Chapel Hill), each local institution carves up music in a different way. While there's some overlap, each scene has its own style. The four major independent radio stations—WXDU, WXYC, WHUP, and WKNC—attract different types of DJs and are almost always immediately distinguishable from one another. All their sounds draw heavily from their vinyl music libraries, and each one will expose you to a different vibe. Likewise, each record store in the Triangle has a distinctly different focus. For example, the records in Carolina Soul's store in Durham skew toward black popular music from the 1950s to the 1980s, while the stock of All Day Records in nearby Carrboro leans heavily toward more contemporary dance and electronic records. Sorry State Records in Raleigh specializes in punk, hardcore, and metal. Local labels like Merge and Paradise of Bachelors put out primarily indie rock and boutique folk, respectively—and so have different canons and record cultures. The more music communities you can find, the more raw material you will have to draw on in order to decide what's important for you. If you enter into these communities with openness and love, you will find models for new ways of hearing cool records. Not only will it help you find these records, but it's also genuinely rewarding to make friendships and intellectual connections with people. In communities of friends, people trade and gift records all the time.

If you're introverted and all this proposed social interaction sounds overwhelming, there's always online record life. You can use social media (Facebook, Twitter, Instagram) and online message boards (for example, Soul Source for soul and Terminal Boredom for punk), although the latter have somewhat faded in importance in recent years. Facebook has invite-only and public groups (like Now Playing) in which you can trade records, and socialize with other record collectors. Record Instagram is another way to explore new music. While it tends to be a little more braggy than other sites, it's still a rich research tool. While people come to these groups for all sorts of reasons, and they're easily infiltrated by what hippies used to call "breadheads," such communities couldn't exist without people who find much more in the music than a way to make a buck. After all, despite the boom in prices, the profit margins for records will never equal the outrageous ones of corporations and finance firms.

On the internet, music writing and radio have also been subject to fragmentation and diversification. While older websites like Pitchfork and Rolling Stone sometimes continue to write as if they possess an omniscient grasp of the scene, smaller genre-specific sites and independent streaming radio stations are better sources to learn about new movements and trends. Rather than look to large corporate websites for the key to all mythologies, find ones that connect with you and your community's particular interests. For example, if you want to dig deeper into contemporary dance and electronic, start reading Resident Advisor. For the history of psych, loner, and generally out-there countercultural music, look into the archives of sites like Perfect Sound Forever and the WFMU blog. There are niche publications online for almost every genre, so just start poking around. Go down YouTube rabbit holes and test out what the algorithm churns up. And maybe above all, listen to independent online radio. Freeform stations like NTS (London and now LA), Red Light Radio (Amsterdam), Intergalactic FM (The Hague), and WFMU (Jersey City) play tons of vinyl, run for twenty-four hours a day, and will expose you to new artists and subgenres hourly if you give them a chance. NTS in particular, because it permanently archives all its shows, is a treasure trove (and where Carolina Soul has had its own show for more than four years now).

And if you feel like taking a break from your newfound communities, don't be afraid to explore streaming and downloading. These can be joylessly utilitarian ways to engage with music, but they can also be invaluable resources. You can test records out before you buy them, something not possible even as late as the 1990s. And the fact that more people are digging these days means more obscure, rare, and even previously unknown records have popped up on eBay and Discogs in recent years. While these sites have contributed to many of the challenges facing collectors today, they can be used for your own purposes. You don't have to have $10,000 to spend on a single record in order to follow Carolina Soul's eBay listings (or Funkyou!'s or Paperstax's) and find out about rare, obscure, and classic vinyl. Many times, you can find these recordings on Soulseek, Spotify, and the like. There are many ways to hear even the rarest records outside of splashing outrageous amounts of cash. While the algorithms of Spotify and YouTube are pernicious, they aren't evil (for listeners: their scandalously low royalty rates is another matter). Even they can be used against the grain to find out about a wide variety of rare and obscure vinyl.

## BUYING RECORDS NOW

However, if you want to actually buy records for your collection rather than download or stream them, there are some skills you'll need to have. As online and in-person buying require different strategies, I'll run through them separately below, starting with brick-and-mortars. If you're in a record store, first figure out if they're using Discogs sales data to price their records. You can check by looking up a record they're selling on Discogs and comparing prices. If they are pricing online, you'll be less likely to find deals—their prices will either duplicate those online or inflate them. If a store isn't pricing against the internet market (something less common as time goes on), you'll have a better chance of finding valuable records undervalued. But watch out—occasionally the reverse will occur. Older dealers will cling to decades-old valuations for records that have long since fallen or even cratered in value online. In any case, the more you know about internet prices, the better you will do in brick-and-mortars.

Even if a store is looking prices up online, they will often have dollar bins and sections of records that go beyond their area of expertise. These are a good place to find deals. Maybe a store manager knows a lot about rap, funk, and soul but not so much about contemporary classical and new age—in this case, there's more of a chance they won't price these genres accurately. Maybe they know LPs and 45s but not 12" records. In either case, if their prices are too high, you can bargain with them from a position of strength. And if you find records that are priced too low, you can, of course, just buy them without the need to haggle at all.

Additionally, online data for some genres is less robust than for others. This can also result in blind spots in a store's pricing system. For example, if you're a fan of doo-wop and gospel singles, you can be pretty sure store prices for these records will be somewhat arbitrary—Discogs and Popsike don't have very good sales data on these genres. When it comes to doo-wop, this is because only particular pressings with specific dead-wax markings are valuable, and many collectors don't trust the average amateur Discogs seller to accurately identify such details. When it comes to gospel singles, many of the rare records were pressed in such low quantities that there haven't been enough sales online to build up a reliable sample of transactions. In these genres, buy records that sound good, because a lack of data means nothing about either its aesthetic quality or long-term market value. These things change, of course, as more sales data becomes available. Until recently, for example, it used to be difficult to find vintage jazz LP sales information (it's another genre where particular pressing details are vital for pricing), but this is no longer the case.

If you are looking to get closer to the source, you can bypass record stores completely and find private individuals with records. There are many strategies for doing so. You can run direct-mail campaigns, send out postcards, and await responses. You can cold-call names from old record labels in the hopes of finding band members, producers, studio owners, or music publishers. The online version of direct mail, Google Ads search engine optimization (SEO) can be used to solicit records in pinpointed geographic regions. You can make road trips to areas and scenes associated with particular labels and genres and then go door to door. You can put up signs and flyers in places which had music scenes.

And when you start going on such buying trips, one house or studio visit will often lead to another—word of mouth is still a valuable resource in the internet age—which means you need to treat the people you are buying records from fairly and decently. Above all, this means paying them fair prices for their records and not taking advantage of them. This also means treating them with respect and honor, not least because they are often the people who made and supported the music you are buying before you even knew it existed. If you don't do these things, you might be engaging in what historians of capitalism are beginning to call "predatory inclusion"—bringing marginalized groups into the financial system at their own detriment. As the record industry has a long, sordid history of cheating poor people—particularly nonwhite people—out of money, the last thing you should be doing is perpetuating such a system. While the slogan "There's no ethical consumption under capitalism" applies to the record world, this is no excuse for outright exploitation. There's still a difference between paying fair prices and scandalously low ones.

On the other hand, you do sometimes run into folks who think all records are now insanely valuable. This is sadly false—most records aren't auction-worthy (a good rule of thumb for an auctionable record is one valued at $4 or more with more than thirty-five wants or at $8 or more [regardless of want numbers] on Discogs). When dealing with these optimists, gently remind them that some records are just not valuable. Some were pressed in the millions and so are easily available, while others have an "uncollectable" sound few want.

In the 1990s to the mid-2000s, flea markets, thrift and vintage stores, record fairs, and estate and garage sales were great places to score vinyl. But as more and more people have gotten back into records, these have become much less dependable sources. Particularly in "hipster" cities, resale stores are pretty picked over. While you can have more luck in shops off the beaten path, fewer places actually are *off* the beaten path—every community, no matter how remote, has the internet and a post office, and so can price things for the global market rather than the local one. This is not to say "come-ups" don't still happen in such locales, only that they are rarer and take more legwork than they did just ten years ago.

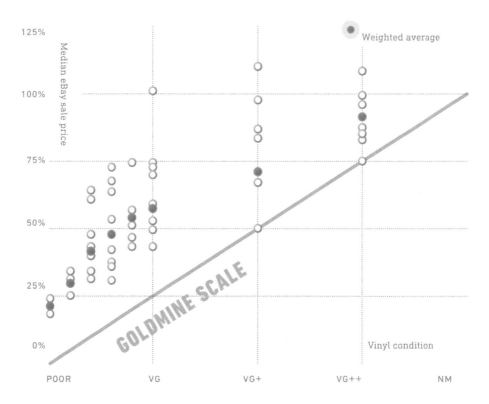

Fig. 7. The Goldmine Grading Scale vs. Carolina Soul's Contemporary Sales Data

## GRADING RECORDS

Next, if you're going to buy records, you need to know how to grade them—to evaluate the physical condition of vinyl itself. The fundamentals are few: look for scratches with a bright light; hold a record to eye level lengthwise to see if it's flat and not warped; look for discoloration and a loss of glossiness, two signs of heat damage. Go to any record auction we run on eBay and you'll find our grading standards, which are based on the *Goldmine* method of visually grading records (as opposed to the UK's *Record Collector's* method). In the *Goldmine* system, grades range from M (mint) to P (poor), but almost no one actually uses M or P in practice. In between these poles, there is NM (near mint, sometimes called M-), VG++ (very good++), VG+, VG, VG–, G+ (good plus), G, and F (fair). Dealers have long used *Goldmine*-based rules of thumb to estimate the effect of a record's condition on market value: A VG++ copy bears 75 percent the value of a NM one, a VG+ copy 50 percent, a VG 25 percent, and a Poor copy more or less 0 percent. Finally, a G copy under this rubric is usually assumed to be worth 10 percent of NM.

While this remains a handy trick for approximating value based on condition, Carolina Soul's analysis of the numbers tells a different story (see Fig. 7). This shouldn't come as a huge surprise, considering Goldmine's price data is unaligned with current internet prices. Using aggregate data from Popsike (for auctions over $15) and Roots Vinyl Guide (for auctions under $15), Carolina Soul found that buyers are much more willing to spend big money for lower-graded records than the *Goldmine* rule of thumb has led people to believe. Online buyers treat records graded VG++ comparably to NM, paying on average 90+ percent of NM values for VG++ vinyl. Records in the G+ to VG range still go for 50–60 percent of NM value, which is also much higher than the *Goldmine* method would predict. And while fewer data points exist for F and P records, in general buyers seem comfortable paying 30 percent of a NM price for a copy graded F. This is surprising, considering that the scratches or warps on records graded F often make them unlistenable.

If you're looking to sell, this means you can be more confident listing off-condition records (assuming you have a fair return policy). If you're a buyer, it's a bit more complicated. On the one hand, you should think twice about following the crowd and spending a lot on a copy that may not sound very good at all. On the other hand, it should reassure you that if you are dissatisfied with the sound quality of a record you own, you can probably find someone else who will want to buy it at a value similar to or higher than the price you paid for it. Even beat-up copies of desirable records hold their value.

It should be clear that learning how to read eBay and Discogs listings is essential to buying and selling records. Built in the 1990s, eBay is a frustratingly programmed site in desperate need of an overhaul. It can be hard to get all the information you want, but the basics are simple. Use eBay to find and follow good sellers. A good seller will have a lot of positive feedback, grade consistently and conservatively, list a lot of records every week, use a VPI machine to clean their records, and store and ship their wares professionally. If they put out a weekly mailing list, subscribe to it. If they are on social media, follow them. This way, you can keep up with their rapidly changing inventory each week.

If you are trying to buy records on eBay and keep losing auctions, get a bid sniper like eSnipe. Bid snipers are online services that allow you to set a maximum bid for an auction ahead of time. A bid sniper will place a bid up to your maximum in the last possible second of an auction. If someone is manually watching an auction to key in their maximum bid, a bid sniper will always box them out at the end, before they can beat your max bid. Not only does this allow you to beat manual bidders to the punch, it also prevents you from getting caught up in auction frenzy and overbidding.

Other than eBay, Discogs is the major place to buy records online. Unlike eBay, Discogs does not run time-dependent auctions. Rather, sellers post items as set sales and wait for someone to buy them. Started in the 1990s by electronic dance fans who wanted to catalog their personal record collections online, Discogs has since grown into a large selling platform. But it's maintained the casual Gen X vibe with which it started. As a result, the quality of sellers can vary considerably. It's a good place to buy all records except truly rare and exceptional ones—for these, eBay is still king (though more rare records are showing up on Discogs these days). But you're more likely to find a good price for staples and even moderately rare records on Discogs than in an eBay auction, where prices often skyrocket.

Even more important than Discogs' utility as a place of commerce, however, are its educational functions. The wealth of discographic and pressing information it holds, while fallible, is invaluable—it is the record world's Wikipedia. It's a user-created database for an incredibly heterogenous mixture of information about records and the people who made them. And its marketplace statistics function makes it the most reliable tool to gauge the going price of any given record. Want to know who designed the cover for Poco's *Legend*? A quick Discogs search will tell you it's *SNL* comedian Phil Hartman. Want to know what the Captain from Captain and Tennille worked on when "Love Will Keep Us Together" was just a twinkling in his eye? Discogs will lead you to his rarer than rare psych drone LP *Me and My Brother* (1971), recorded under his given name, Daryl Dragon (with brother Dennis), on "out" jazz label ESP-Disk'/West. For trivia like this, as well as more important info like the list of Arthur Russell's collaborators on *Another Thought*, Discogs is essential.

On Discogs you can find out who played what, who released what when, and as many granular facts on pressing histories, cover versions, and run times as you need. You can see the entire catalog of almost every record label and sort it chronologically. Before Discogs, one had to cobble together this information from a variety of sources like the Allmusic guide and many heavy discographic reference books. Now it's all in a single clearinghouse—as such, it's impossible to overestimate Discogs's value as a record research tool.

Some online tools are more specialized. Differences in pressing features of jazz LPs from the Impulse!/Blue Note/Prestige era of the 1950s and '60s account for price differences in the thousands of dollars. Seemingly negligible considerations in the appraisal of jazz records, particularly of the Blue Note label, then, can turn out to be extremely significant. Answers to questions like the following can be decisive: "Is RVG stamped or etched into the dead wax?" "Is a small glyph of an ear scratched into the dead wax?" "Does a record bear a flat edge? Is it serrated, beaded, or rounded?" "What address is listed on a record's label, and does it match the one listed on the back cover?" "Does the label bear a circular indentation called a deep groove or not?" The blog London Jazz Collector provides an in-depth guide to such Blue Note arcana. And for hundreds of labels, the site cVinyl offers an expansive visual guide to variations in issues of records, from A&M to Westbound. These sites, in conjunction with Discogs, then, will allow you to master a skill that used to be quite specialized. With the rise of the internet, you generally no longer need to be intimidated by the acronyms and inside baseball terms thrown around by older record collectors. This specialized language, the old record game's bureaucratic in-speak, once functioned to keep outsiders at bay. But now it's easily decipherable by anyone with an internet connection or friends in the know. In any case, it's now inferable through context and seems outdated in the mouths of those who use it to gatekeep.

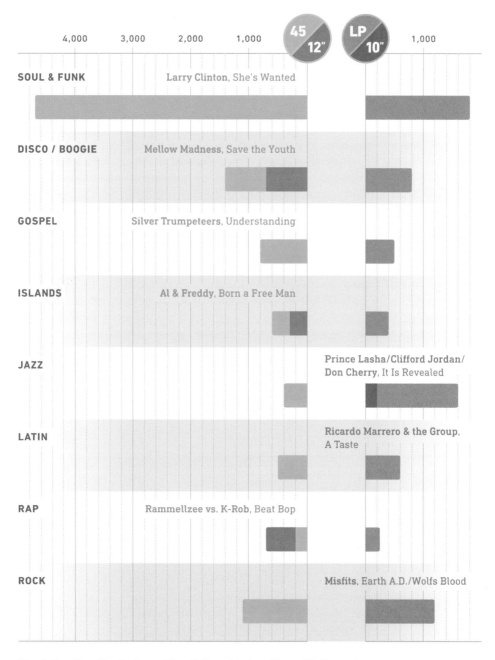

Fig. 8. Carolina Soul's Genre Top-Sellers, Broken Down By Format

## GENRE/FORMAT PAIRINGS

Another helpful insight into record buying comes from understanding the connection between genre and format (see Fig. 8). Album-length LPs, 12" singles, and 45 rpm singles are at the center of certain genre scenes but marginal to others. Soul, for example, is a 45-centric genre. Northern, crossover, '70s, and modern soul styles top our 45 sales charts. Primarily faster dance records, 45 singles fueled DJ scenes across Europe and made them highly sought-after by collectors. Connoisseurs of vintage doo-wop, R&B, and blues also prefer the 45 format, but for a different reason. These styles from the 1940s and '50s predate the heyday of the LP, and so it makes logical sense that their collectors would want the dominant format of their era. Folk and jazz, on the other hand, are album-centric genres, while rock tends to be popular in both formats. The longer run time of LPs allowed for extended instrumental breaks, improvisations, and the use of overarching concepts, which these genres are known for. And, to quote Nate Smith on the 12" single, "the top rap records tend to be on the DJ/scratch-friendly 12" format, along with other OG club DJ-preferred styles such as disco, boogie, modern soul and electro, which dominated Carolina Soul's highest sales list on 12"."

These are the dominant format/genre pairings to be aware of when hunting for records. However, minor subcurrents lurk under these major ones. For example, rap 45 singles like Big Daddy Kane's "Raw" (Cold Chillin', 1988) are quite valuable these days because of the overall dominance of the 12" in the genre. Because the 45 was a minor format for the golden era of rap, the relatively few in existence are rare and now fetch major prices.

## BEWARE OF FETISHISM

Another effect of the vinyl revival has been to spawn several start-ups looking to capitalize on a trend. For example, record subscription services try to sell customers nonessential records and related products, banking on the general aura of vinyl. As opposed to essential records preferred by most collectors—whether they be expensive original pressings, affordable later pressings, reissues or archival releases with hard-to-source material—grifters often repackage records that are already widely available both in brick-and-mortars and online. Such online subscription services overcharge for "deluxe" (usually just colored vinyl) presses of common and relatively well-known records. They add extraneous and corny bells and whistles, like cocktail recipes and stencils, in order to justify their high prices and distract from the overall redundancy of their wares. For the price of the one record you get per month from the most popular subscription service, you could buy five or six higher-quality OG records using the methods detailed above.

Such services are less a revival of the BMG and Columbia House "eight CDs for a penny model" than they seem. They provide far less music for a higher price, marketing on the boutique "magic" of the medium itself as a status object for buyers. And unlike BMG and Columbia House, they choose your records for you. Since a large part of the fun of records comes from building a collection from the ground up according to your own taste, the personal shopper model feels pretty rote and passionless. What's more, these services short-circuit actually existing, vibrant taste cultures and music communities described above. Rather than learn about records from friends and colleagues (in real life and online), with these services, you are supposed to passively wait for one record a month, deemed important by a faceless corporation. If this model were to become dominant, it would further desocialize records and break apart communities in favor of the sort of astroturfing of "community" you find on these subscription services' websites. My advice is that you avoid any service that takes the process of discovering music out of your own and your community's hands.

The record subscription model is just one part of a larger trend of vinyl fetishism—the ritualistic treatment of the record as an inherently magical object. This "magic" underwrites the relatively high prices these services charge for single records. Under the sway of such fetishism, the music itself and the experience of it become secondary to ownership of the magical object. When a particular record becomes a fetish object, a grail, as collectors are wont to call it, finding and buying that record becomes the terminal step in one's relationship to it. After you buy a grail, you can of course post pictures of it online, display it prominently around your house, and even listen to it, but possession is nine-tenths of the appeal for such sacred objects. When you own a record, especially a grail, you needn't develop your own emotional relationship to it or interpretation of it. You own it, therefore you have mastered its contents passively. The fetishized record comes pre-felt and pre-interpreted by everyone who has previously built it up into a fetish object. While some have argued that such vinyl fetishism is "positive" in that it inspires passionate use and hard work from DJs-cum-collectors, my view is that it stops people from actively listening, forming their own opinions, and using the records in a creative way.

The ultimate embodiment of vinyl fetishism is the sealed collector. When they were originally released decades ago, LPs and 12" records were factory sealed in plastic shrink. Sealed collectors buy such records exclusively and, in other words, explicitly not to play them. There are plenty of sound financial and musical reasons for a music fan to buy a sealed record, not the least because they're clean (although still susceptible to warp) and so tend to sound great. But we're talking here about buying sealed records just to keep them on the shelf. This is the apotheosis of the magic object model for vinyl—the belief that the record, beyond its use and exchange values, holds inherent worth. In Fig. 9, we can see that the median price for a sealed record is on average 23 percent higher than that of a NM copy. Further breaking down the data by genre, we find that sealed classic rock and blues LPs go for 69 percent above NM rates, while non–classic rock and blues titles are only 15 percent higher. This is strong evidence that the biggest believers in the magic of a sealed record are the rich white baby boomers who predominantly buy rock and blues albums, and that this fetishism may not persist in the long term. In other words, there's hope that the fetishism that accounts for this nearly 70 percent bump in value may soon be a thing of the past.

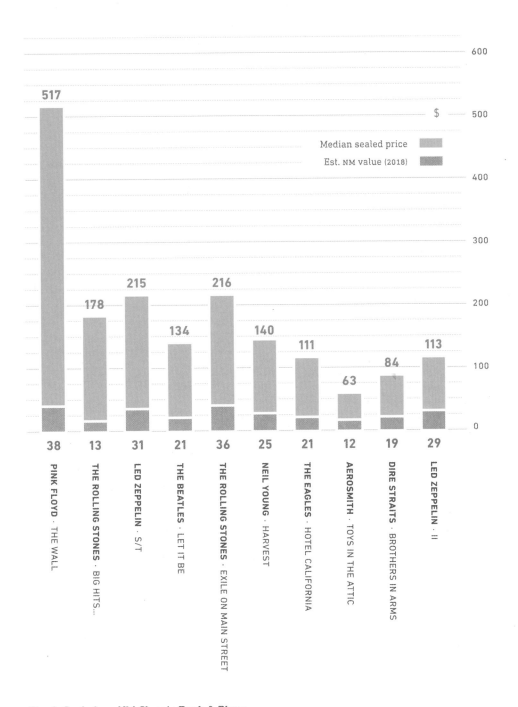

Fig. 9. Sealed vs. NM Classic Rock & Blues

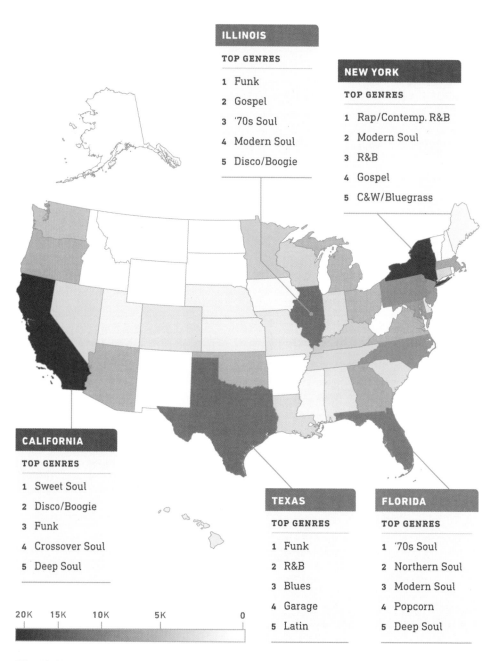

**ILLINOIS**

TOP GENRES

1 Funk
2 Gospel
3 '70s Soul
4 Modern Soul
5 Disco/Boogie

**NEW YORK**

TOP GENRES

1 Rap/Contemp. R&B
2 Modern Soul
3 R&B
4 Gospel
5 C&W/Bluegrass

**CALIFORNIA**

TOP GENRES

1 Sweet Soul
2 Disco/Boogie
3 Funk
4 Crossover Soul
5 Deep Soul

**TEXAS**

TOP GENRES

1 Funk
2 R&B
3 Blues
4 Garage
5 Latin

**FLORIDA**

TOP GENRES

1 '70s Soul
2 Northern Soul
3 Modern Soul
4 Popcorn
5 Deep Soul

20K   15K   10K   5K   0

Fig. 10. U.S. Record Sales, 2012–2018

## THE VALUE OF REGIONAL VARIATION

In the new record environment, there's a strong trend toward taking questions of judgment and value out of the hands of everyday listeners while placing faith in the market, middlemen, and dealers. While these influencers have become more powerful, the means to resist them and do your own thing, described above, have also strengthened. You can still do it yourself when it comes to vinyl—develop your own taste, find records for cheap, and participate in grassroots record communities.

It should inspire you that beneath each large-scale trend described above lurk many smaller ones that point toward regional variation and the persistence of local knowledge and taste. For example, Carolina Soul data reveals both that scenes with long traditions have endured and that some new ones have emerged. New Jersey buys doo-wop 45s far above the national average, Arkansas buys a disproportionally high amount of rockabilly records, Texans plump for funk music at higher percentages than those in the other 49 states, and Californians are way into sweet soul. If you know a bit of music history, these trends make sense: Each of these states was foundational to the creation and endurance of their still-favored genres in the first place. This is evidence of musical continuity. On the other hand, the data reveal that some surprising new trends are also developing—Rhode Island goes hard for reggae, North Dakota for punk and post-punk, and Massachusetts for black gospel.

# TOP GENRES BY NATION
## 2012–2018

The same patterns show up internationally. Popcorn soul is Belgium's answer to the UK's inventions Northern and crossover soul—a specialized reinterpretation of particular American 45s to make a new collectors' scene. It's no surprise, then, that this genre is disproportionately purchased by Belgians even today. Country, classic rock, and oldies, staples of Americana and US mainstream music culture, are unsurprisingly less popular abroad. Brazil, a country that has produced some of the most unique and exciting rhythms of the modern era, is intuitively a large consumer of other innovative dance traditions, like Miami bass and electro. But as in the state-by-state breakdowns, there are also some beguiling national patterns that need further exploration—the causes of Netherlands' affinity for surf records, Australia's love of dancehall, and France's statistically outlying affection for reggae all remain fascinating mysteries. All this is proof that musical variety and difference are still out there.

## PAST AND PRESENT

Current record trends mix long-standing regional traditions with newly emerging taste patterns. Wherever they are, record buyers seem pulled by two seemingly contrary tendencies: a nostalgia for the recordings of the past and a desperate need to keep up with the trends of the current moment. The first phenomenon has been most aptly described by music critic Simon Reynolds as "retromania."[1] According to Reynolds, our listening is defined by a nostalgic desire to rework past musical forms. This, he argues, is holding back the emergence of truly new music. One of the symptoms of retromania, Reynolds suggests, is the rebirth of vinyl as an au courant format.

The second tendency, sometimes called "poptimism," is perhaps better termed musical presentism. Both its detractors and celebrants describe poptimism as revelry in contemporary popular music's liberating political potential. Ironically, like so many movements before it, poptimism rejects the works of the past as both aesthetically outdated and politically suspect. Rather, poptimists chose to revel in the pleasures of pop music, equating this with populism.

Most music writers treat these diagnoses as mutually exclusive. We are either obsessed with the past to the detriment of the present (retromaniacs) or too immersed in music of the present to understand its connection to the past (poptimists). But these two theories, rather than contradicting one another, seem better understood as two sides of the same coin.

They are both symptoms, I'd argue, of the internet's decontextualization and dehistoricization of music. As discussed earlier, the internet is a useful resource for raw data on records—prices; discographical information; trivia; names of songs, artists, and albums; and a whole host of miscellaneous bits and bytes. But it presents all this data in an absolutely chaotic fashion, without any historical or aesthetic narrative about the connection between data points. The result is that the average internet-reared music fan knows a lot more information about records than their parents, but has a harder time contextualizing works. I'd argue that what nostalgia and presentism share is a rejection of musical analysis and contextualization in favor of fantasy, whether about the past or the present. Both nostalgia and presentism cordon off a period of time, and its records, from analysis in order to revel in their particulars without thinking deeply about them.

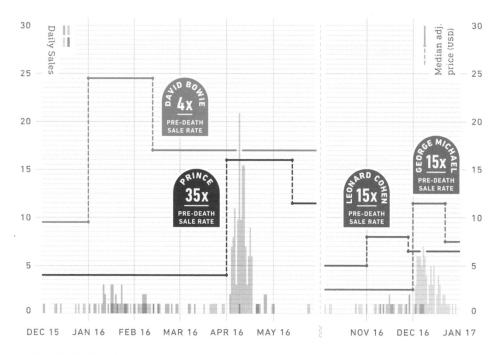

Fig. 11. The Death Effect

One relevant phenomenon that shows these two contradictory poles uniting is what we call the "death effect." It's well known that when an artist dies, there's a run on their records. After a spate of famous deaths in 2016, it felt like every seller my colleagues met on a house call had set aside records featuring the recently passed David Bowie, Glenn Frey, Maurice White, Phife, Merle Haggard, Prince, Leonard Cohen, Leon Russell, Sharon Jones, or George Michael, assuming that these would have skyrocketed in value because of the artist's death. These folks' intuition was borne out by the data. "In the span of three to six weeks post death," Nate Smith says, "the market will see a spike in both sales' frequency and price." George Michael's *Faith* nearly tripled in value after he died, and Prince's records sold at thirty-five times the rate they did before his death. But while these deaths fostered small but long-lasting bumps in their artists' value, most records fall back down to their pre-death values after the glow of the moment fades. In other words, these were presentist bouts of nostalgia.

The spike in consumer desire that comes with an artist's death is at once backward-looking and present-oriented—at the moment of an artist's death, we fantasize that their works become classic and that we can now listen to them without thinking. But rather than part of a long-lasting tribute, the brevity of such collective fantasies proves them to be further instances of poptimism. The charts also speak to the surface-level nature of the death effect: *Purple Rain* and *Faith* jumped much higher in price than *Low* and *Songs of Love and Hate* because the former were already the most well known and "career defining" before their artist's death. As both nostalgists and poptimists, we want to enjoy what's already known as good rather than explore a less famous release.

Yet there are hopeful currents implicit in both movements. The two need only to be deepened and connected with one another in order to build a more sophisticated and rewarding method for collecting and listening. Poptimists are right in arguing that we in the present should judge the past according to the present's needs, and in putting aesthetic pleasure at the center of their listening. But the nostalgic are correct in emphasizing the enduring importance of the past's records. We should neither reject history in favor of the allure of the present nor knock the pleasure out of listening with dry-as-dust retreads of the past. Rather, we should go back into the record archive to find music that spurs pleasure now, while at the same time deepening our understanding of today's music as a product of history.

OUNG

E DOOBIES VOLUME II

CHECKER 3002 • LITTLE MILTON • SINGS BIG BLUES

THE OL' BLUES SINGER

580

Banquet

℗ 1976 A&M

680

London

# CHAPTER 2

# Developing a Collecting Method

As of October 2019, 6.4 million vinyl records have been logged into Discogs, including 2.7 million LPs, 2.1 million 45s, and 1.3 million 12"s. Discogs is the world's largest music database, but its listings cannot possibly account for every record ever made. Even so, the numbers are daunting—no listener, no matter how monomaniacal, could ever hope to listen to 6.4 million records. And even if they somehow could, it would probably be a miserable experience—no favorites could be replayed, memories of a record heard among the first million would be washed away by the next 5 million, and so on.

The sublime cache of records out there tantalizes. We can neither give up on the dream of mastering the archive nor hope to achieve such mastery. So what follows is a description of methods that have sprung up in response to our new sense of vinyl excess. Below, I map the most prominent ways collectors have chosen to carve up the vinyl archive. But none of these should be taken as a gold standard. As you'll see, we note their weaknesses alongside their strengths. Each method has its own native shortcomings—its own contradictions, compromises, and blind spots. But as no collector can own, let alone listen to, all that's available, everyone must specialize. And while unavoidable, specialization means making choices—to follow certain genres and exclude others, to embrace some enabling ideas and beliefs while rejecting their opposite numbers. Without such strategies, the record archive remains an unmotivated, monstrous mass of plastic and paper. Below, then, is an assessment of methods to best help you find your way through the record archive—in other words, to make vinyl fun, meaningful, and useful. These methods concern five major areas of contemporary record collecting— format, depth, circulation, use, and genre.

## FORMAT: TRUE BELIEF, APOSTASY, AND AGNOSTICISM

First, it's important to decide your relation to vinyl as a format, independent of any consideration of specific genres, artists, and labels. Most collectors don't do this in the early days of their digging. But over time, every collector develops a belief system about vinyl. Because they've done so unconsciously, they may not even realize they have a vinyl "ideology," or understand how it informs their collecting. So, the more clearly you can articulate your thoughts and feelings about the medium of vinyl itself, the easier it will be to break your own path as a collector. In my experience, I've encountered three major vinyl ideologies: the fervor of true belief, the bitterness of apostasy (abandoning the faith), and the interrogative probing of agnosticism.

## TRUE BELIEF

Record collecting's present and past are shot through with examples of true belief in vinyl's numinous power. The 45-worshipping Northern soul scene hangs together to this day under the motto "Keep the Faith," while attendees of David Mancuso's legendary Loft parties still describe the records played there in religious terms. I've already noted the spiritual undertones of the term "grails" to describe rare records, and the belief in vinyl magic accounting for the large difference in price between nearly identical near mint and sealed records. It could even be argued that beneath the scientific trappings of vinyl audiophiles' obsession with fidelity there lurks an unconsidered religious desire for the purity of first origins, for an original among a sea of copies.

True believers consider vinyl the only proper format for music. This position is inaccessible to logical argument: It requires a leap of faith and functions as a sort of theological first principle. And while it may seem vulgar to analyze such a faith-based position, it seems to me that true belief in the vinyl format has both some things to recommend it and some drawbacks.

On the positive side, true belief results in a coherent and enduring focus on only records. Cassettes, reel-to-reels, CDs, digital files, and streams can be bracketed from view. With this concentration, you can dedicate yourself to building a vinyl-only collection. You needn't waste your energy looking for anything but records. This approach has a simplicity and boundedness that allows you to treat your records as part of a unified whole, rather than a heterogenous grouping of recordings in a chaos of formats. It provides you with a material set of objects you can place on shelves, organize according to design, and listen to consecutively without shifting gears. For those who grew up when vinyl was king, true belief enables the collector to feel the continuity between past and present. And you can more easily use an all-vinyl collection because you can form a satisfactory mental map of it in its entirety and gain a familiarity with its parts to make it easy and enjoyable to use.

But this attitude does have its blind spots. First, while vinyl is a generally great-sounding medium, this is not always the case. I've already mentioned the low-quality vinyl used for pressings of iconic Chicago house tunes on Trax and the tendency of some labels to jam too many songs onto an LP, resulting in thin-sounding records. Sometimes, CDs and tapes sound better than vinyl pressings—this is especially the case for genres like private-issue new age, which boomed in the 1980s and '90s, when vinyl was a decidedly residual format for most new music. A pristine CD will usually sound much better than a deeply scratched and warped record of that same recording. Finally, for many, the best listening experiences come while driving, or walking with headphones. Though the 1950s and '60s saw many companies try and fail to sell in-dash 45 players for cars, vinyl is a fundamentally terrible format for mobile listening. The same quality that allows focus and deep listening in the home is an obvious weakness in different listening contexts. Try taking a walk while using a Numark portable turntable—it'll test even the most devout vinyl zealot's faith.

## APOSTASY

Among the vinyl apostates, however, you'll find no worrying over their lost faith. Apostasy, the repudiation of one's past beliefs, has taken hold among some in the record-collecting community. Spend a little time online or in your local music scene, and you'll find a minority of folks who've turned their back on vinyl entirely. Their rejection of the format can largely be understood as a reaction to vinyl's move to the internet. Vinyl being an analog format, some Luddites gave up when it became necessary to use a computer to get the best records. Others understandably have become frustrated by the increase in prices of records they used to be able to buy for cheap. Some resent the influx of dabblers and newbies into a hobby they'd pursued for a long time, viewing such newcomers as late-adopting gentrifiers. For them, vinyl lived and died—all that's left is a bitter aftertaste.

This view is inspiringly negative. It can be appreciated for its hard-nosed resistance to marketing hype touting the magic of frivolous reissues, 180-gram re-presses, and other unnecessary vinyl merchandise. There's a pragmatic appeal to such apostates' turn to cheaper formats, and their argument that format shouldn't get in the way of listening has an intuitive, DIY appeal. But vinyl apostasy can easily turn into nihilism. If you swear off vinyl completely, you are essentially giving up on millions of recordings you can't find in any other format. Many records can still be found for cheap, while many others can now be flipped for higher prices. This being the case, people who turn their back on vinyl are often glamorizing their own resentment as principle. Such vinyl apostasy is strongest when it recommends clear-sighted skepticism of all trends and fads, weakest when it terminates in condescension to younger and less experienced record collectors.

## AGNOSTICISM

Finally, we come to vinyl agnosticism. This approach is a testing, questing approach that treats vinyl as one important musical format among many. As this implies, it takes a more pragmatic approach to records than either true belief or apostasy. This approach makes room for the magic produced by particular records, not the format as a whole. In other words, magic isn't built into all records; instead the listener finds it in the process of only listening to certain recordings. If you are a vinyl agnostic, it's only these records you buy and keep, hard-filing them into a permanent place in your stacks. In general, vinyl agnostics choose to collect records for a broader array of reasons than true believers who automatically "need" everything on vinyl. In addition to the records that produce aesthetic delight, a vinyl agnostic might buy a record for its historical significance, for sentimental reasons, or to flip it or trade it with friends. But vinyl is not the be-all and end-all for this approach.

This position has some advantages—it requires the collector to be thoughtful and selective. It values certain records in certain contexts, without making black-and-white judgments on the vinyl format in toto. Using this approach also has its drawbacks—your collection may be scattered over multiple incompatible formats, you may miss out on trends in hardcore vinyl-only scenes, and you may have a permanent feeling of rootlessness without a home format to collect in.

## DEPTH: VOCATION, CONNOISSEURSHIP, AND HOBBYISM

Next comes the question of how deep into vinyl you want to go with your collecting. Your answer to this question will partially depend on your commitment level and privilege. Some consider record collecting a calling, others see it as a game for prestige, still others treat it as a hobby (while for me and my colleagues at Carolina Soul, it's a profession). Each of these orientations conceives of records in a radically different way, and so its practitioners tend to pursue different types of records with different methods. And unlike what we've already discussed regarding format, one's commitment level is strongly impacted by one's material circumstances. The basic considerations of how much free time and money are available to us set the parameters within which we decide how far we can go into the vinyl game. For example, if you are in debt and working more than one job, you can't just decide to be a connoisseur of rare soul 45s. Or you can, but achieving that goal will be much harder for you than for the son of a financier or some famous actor. Depending on your circumstances, one of the three approaches may be more accessible to you than others.

## VOCATION

A vocation is a calling. It is work you want to do for ideals beyond profit. Insofar as it is motivated by the pursuit of truth and beauty, it may seem quaint to the more cynical. In the vinyl world, we use the term "heads" to describe those called to records. This term, reminiscent of the 1960s, is the highest form of praise you can give in some collecting circles. A head is someone who truly knows what's up—not just which records are valuable, but which ones have true aesthetic value. Heads go deep and intimately know records many have never even heard. To be a head, you need to know the music inside and out. Rattling off the names of trendy records without saying much about how they sound or what makes them special won't cut it. As you would expect, becoming a head takes time. It means a lot of digging and thoughtful listening. As a result, there aren't a lot of young ones out there. It's also, like most honorifics, not something you can decide to call yourself. If you go around calling yourself a head among folks that know vinyl, it's bound to have the opposite effect of what you intended.

A head is the opposite of a hack. They immerse themselves in their favored genres, exploring the rare records, the established classics, and everything in between. They are never satisfied with the records they know and that others know. Rather, they are on a permanent quest to revolutionize their listening. Those who approach records and music as a vocation view it as a means to what the poet John Keats called "soul-making": to use the frisson of the aesthetic to experiment on themselves, to expand their understanding of what's possible to say and do in the world. Treating record collecting as a calling means finding and sharing unknown records and generating new insights into old ones. To do all this requires dedication to a slow process of researching, listening, and living with records.

It should be clear from this description that not everyone can become a record head nor should they necessarily aspire to do so. I'm not sure you even *can* aspire to become a head; it's more something you become over time in the eyes of others. And as I've mentioned, it's easier to become one if you have time and money to explore. As a holdover of the 1960s, the ideal of headdom perhaps unsurprisingly is also a gendered concept. You rarely hear female or trans collectors described as heads. If not used carefully, it easily falls into cliché: the wise old man in a flowing robe, dictating to his followers from on high. So be careful—the road to becoming a record expert should be approached with humility and in the spirit of permanent education, with the goal of sharing music. If it's not, it easily becomes just another ego trip for the beautiful-soul type who thinks he's too deep for the real world because he's heard Cold Sun's *Dark Shadows*.

## CONNOISSEURSHIP

As opposed to collectors who see records as a vocation, the record connoisseur buys rare records the way Jay-Z buys Basquiats: to practice what Thorstein Veblen called "conspicuous consumption,"[1] to have something others do not and to confer distinction on themselves in its flaunting. Or, alternately, to squirrel away in secret records they desire, to have and hide from the rest of the world's collectors, in what we might call acts of inconspicuous consumption. In either case, connoisseurs like rare, obscure, and unknown records primarily because of the status they bring as baubles of cultural capital.

It would be an oversimplification to say that this is all connoisseurship entails. Individual connoisseurs can be as intent and thoughtful as any listener. But in general, this approach depends on the internalization of the rare record price system we warned against in chapter 1. As such, connoisseurs tend to ignore re-presses in favor of harder-to-source originals, and prefer scarce records to common ones, and niche records and labels over ones that found wide popularity in their time. If a record connoisseur steps outside of the tastes held by their small coterie of experts, it is as much in a spirit of financial speculation as of aesthetic discovery. As with visual art, the connoisseur is looking to capitalize on the next big thing before it becomes more popularly known.

As the downsides to such an approach should be clear, it may seem connoisseurship has nothing to offer beyond the promise of personal enrichment. But record connoisseurship's focus on rarity has churned up a lot of genuinely amazing, previously unknown records. So indirectly, connoisseurs provide an incentive for others to discover these records and share them with the public. This may lead to vinyl rips showing up online and cheap reissues coming out—great rare records sometimes trickle down into more affordable formats over time. As with Carolina Soul, it's most likely the case that connoisseurs keep the lights on at Funkyou!, Craig Moerer Records, Paperstax, John Manship Records, and other large record sellers. While connoisseurship taken to its logical endpoint hollows out the experiential possibilities of record collecting into an empty game for prestige, there's no denying it fuels a large part of today's vinyl economy.

## HOBBYISM

Finally, there are those who seek to keep up with broader vinyl trends. These are the vinyl hobbyists. While the term may suggest to some a slightly pejorative connotation of amateurism, I use it here because most collectors probably do consider themselves record hobbyists, rather than latter-day vinyl monks or elitist connoisseurs. What's more, treating collecting as a hobby has many benefits. It avoids self-seriousness and puts the emphasis on listening to records and genres that are contemporarily relevant, at least as defined by the indie music press, radio stations, and "major" small record labels. Hobbyists generally want to stay up to date—as you would expect for people just getting into records, they're generally a younger bunch. Because the tastes of hobbyists are relatively open, they haven't yet congealed into the fixed patterns you sometimes find in heads and connoisseurs.

Hobbyists tend to buy a lot of reissues and the established "big" records in a genre. They might cast their net as wide as Discogs and their local brick-and-mortars, but not to eBay. As music lovers just starting to get deeper into records, they understandably don't know much of the world of rare and original pressings—or if they do, they may feel too intimidated to go after them. Sometimes you hear grizzled old record dogs dismiss such hobbyists as "entry-level" collectors, but this seems to grasp the problem the wrong way around. If someone listens to exactly the same records at forty as they did at eighteen (and thinks about them the same way), yes, this may seem "entry-level." But just as every collector starts as a hobbyist, so every hobbyist has the potential to become their own version of a head or connoisseur—someone with a more expert relation to the deeper potential of record collecting. Hobbyism is the unpretentious, passionate way we all start collecting records, out of genuine affection for music. Its youthful enthusiasm and narrow focus on the dominant records of the moment are the starting point of a work in progress and so are nothing to mock.

## CIRCULATION: HOARDING, GAMBLING, CONSERVATION/CURATION

As a collector, another matter you'll need to decide is how aggressively you want to circulate the records you own. In other words, there are many ways for you to conceptualize your record collection. Do you consider it, along with theorist Walter Benjamin, a way to save works of art from the marketplace?[2] Or do you treat it as an investment, pieces of property that you can flip and make a profit on when you need (something Benjamin, though now the patron saint of collectors, himself did from time to time). Do you treat it as a hoard, a collection to be constantly added to and never subtracted from? Or do you take a curatorial approach to your vinyl, treating your collection like a library does its books or a museum its art and artifacts?

## HOARDING

Record hoarders, as you would expect, continually take records on and rarely part with any of them. My colleagues have been on house calls where records had taken over entire living spaces. They've found records under bar cushions, on top of pool tables, in fish tanks, stored on dowel rods and broom handles. But some hoarders don't fit this reality-show stereotype—they keep their collections neatly on shelves, in acid-free sleeves, rigorously alphabetized. But despite appearances, these neat freaks share with the messier hoarders a desire to hold on to every record they come across. Like rabid bibliophiles, for record hoarders, every record holds potential.

The upside of hoarding is obvious—you never lose anything. Everything you've ever wanted in the past is still available for you to hear, provided you can still find it. A hoarder assumes they may have much different tastes in the future, so to get rid of anything would be to deprive their future selves of something they might need to hear later. Hoarding depends on the fear that any record you get rid of will one day be missed. And while the movie *High Fidelity* got so many things wrong about record collecting, one thing it got right is the way a record collection takes on autobiographical connotations over time. So if you are brave or foolhardy enough to keep all your records, the records on your shelves will take on a self-chronicling function. Trying to forget that summer you got really into the 2000s garage rock revival? If you're a hoarder, your record collection remembers. Want to revisit your adolescent days as a young goth? In a completist's collection, your Bauhaus, Joy Division, and Sisters of Mercy LPs will be right there waiting for you.

The downside to keeping everything means the records you truly love and want to listen to the most can get lost. If a collection gets too big, it can get "noisy" and distracting. It can be a drag to flip through twenty-five records you've lost your enthusiasm for to find the one you still love. And records you bought when you were a younger, less experienced collector don't always hold up. Except for outright masterpieces like Glenn Gould's *Goldberg Variations* or outright failures like A.R.E. Weapons' *A.R.E. Weapons,* when you first buy a record, it sits in a murky gray zone between fad and classic. It takes time to evaluate most records, and the same ones that appeal to you in the moment don't always endure. A hoarded record collection at its worst resembles a ruined garden, with the weeds obscuring the flowers.

## GAMBLING

The hoarder's dialectical opposite number is known by many names: flipper, speculator, gambler. This approach shares something with actual gamblers in Las Vegas—eternally bored figures constantly looking for some new thrill. Record gamblers put their vinyl into a constant state of flux. They are perpetually trading, selling, and flipping their old records, either to make a profit or to try out new sounds. By constantly reintroducing their collection to the market using Discogs, eBay, and private trading groups on Facebook, they keep their records in circulation. Churning and burning through previous infatuations, they are the promiscuous members of the vinyl world, always willing to throw aside a past love for a present fling. They have short attention spans and get tired of records once they feel they have assimilated them, or they simply enjoy the process of gambling itself. Whatever the reason, with this approach, records in one's collection pale in comparison to the vinyl not yet owned.

The main appeal of this line of collecting comes from the perpetual feeling of novelty it provides. Every day, you get to hear and hold a new record, one that you didn't have before. You are constantly learning about new labels, genres, and artists. You find out a little about a lot of records, and you get a great sense of the manifold forms that music can take. But as you never spend too much time with any one record, it's very easy to become a dilettante, a professional dabbler. What you gain in breadth you lose in depth. Unless you have incredible powers of recall and interpretative ability, you're going to forget a lot about the records you once owned and perpetually chase new records without ever having digested the ones you cast away in haste.

## CONSERVATION/CURATION

The middle course between hoarding and gambling is curation. Or, if the word "curation" raises your hackles, call it conservation. To continue the gardening conceit above, this approach treats a record collection like a well-tended, manicured garden. While a curated collection is pruned from time to time, it's rarely if ever radically made over. In this way, a collection grows gradually, with nonessential records discarded over long periods of time. The collector as curator builds their library deliberately, usually carefully indexing what they buy. Discogs has made keeping track of your collection much easier—many curatorial collectors enter their entire collections into Discogs for easy reference.

As the term "conservation" implies, the curatorial approach tends to be conservative. So, unless its curator has an unlimited amount of money, this means new records are added slowly, through modest purchasing. It can't grow and change its proportions dramatically the way a collection based on gambling or hoarding can. It is a stable, modest, and sane way to acquire records. As many record collectors also happen to be maniacs, it's not for everyone.

## USE: SELF-EXPERIMENTATION, MUSIC MAKING, AND CRITICISM

Though your purposes for collecting will change over time, it's important to clarify for yourself how you intend to use the records you acquire. If you don't consider what you are going to do with your records, you may end up regretting starting a collection at all (especially when you have to move house). Because there's a vague cool attached to the record itself, you may start buying vinyl with fuzzy notions of what you're going to do with it. But records only take on meaning in use; the sooner you figure out how you want to put your stacks in action, the more you'll get out of them.

## SELF-EXPERIMENTATION

The most intuitive use of records is the personal one. Most people collect records for their mood-altering properties. Listening to music in general, and records in particular, is often a transformative experience. Records are a great way to alter your thoughts and moods. If you're down, they can perk you up; if you're up, they can bring you down. If you're feeling complacent, the right record can shake you; if you're filled with rage, the right one can soothe you. A record collection holds manifold pathways to self-experimentation—it provides the means to transform how you think and feel. Without the side effects of drugs, a record collection for many is sort of a pharmacy—a source of therapeutic, exploratory means to self-discovery and intellectual experiment. Digging through a well-rounded record collection, you can find music that will bring you pleasure, fear, catharsis, melancholy, joy, or some mixture of all of these.

The final few chapters of this book go into detail about the experiential effects of records. In any case, if you are reading this book, you shouldn't need much convincing that records can expand your sense of the world. What may seem less obvious is the potential downside to this use of records. Unlike drugs, there's no danger of overdose or side effects. But used incorrectly, record collecting can turn into a selfish, navel-gazing endeavor. Like anything else, people can get addicted to self-experimentation and so lose the thread back to the outside world. Rather than use music to find new ways into social and public life, private enjoyment of records can become a means to reject the world. Tending to the cultivation of the self, it becomes easy to forget no one does anything alone. The immediacy and excitement records bring shouldn't seduce us into thinking our experiences alone are significant. At its best, self-experimentation with records results in new relations to the outside world, not merely solipsistic considerations of inner states.

## MUSIC MAKING

Another predominant use of old records is to make new ones. DJs and remixers directly use old records to make their own music. More indirectly, other musicians may use them as sources of inspiration and technical guidance. Such uses are inherently directed toward a public. As a result, musicians approach records in a more practical way, translating the musical past for the present. Of course, musicians also use records for self-experimentation, but the use of records to aid one's own music making requires a different emphasis. Rap producers are well known for using only snatches of a record to make their own track—for example, a brief open drum break or vocal sample. In the process, a whole work gets chunked into pieces to make something new. This is radically different than the sort of deep listening self-experimenters tend to do, where the emphasis is on long, continuous spates of listening so a record can flow. A rap producer values records for the beats they can mine from it and so has no need for a holistic approach to a record.

Other musicians look to the recorded past for inspiration. The recorded archive provides a wealth of models and cautionary examples, traditions and countertraditions. The more a musician explores the past, the more they can define themselves in the present. When musicians collect records, they find the raw materials for their own expression. Here they can find tones they wish to avoid, solos they wish to use (hopefully adding something of their own in the process), lyrical approaches to take on or reject, and so on. Historically, record collecting guides them to compare what was possible in the past with what's possible now—to make music for the present both by recognizing what in the past remains relevant and what no longer carries power. Singers and players in folk traditions depend on old records for their source material; students learning complicated jazz techniques play along to their LPs. For all musicians, records are the means to enter a tradition that predates their birth but also contain the knowledge of how to break with that tradition (sometimes radically).

Occasionally, musicians directly discuss records of the past in interviews or essays. They do this to contextualize their own music for present-day critics and fans. A rundown of a musician's favorite vinyl can often be a revealing look into how their own music is made. For example, when you read Wire frontman Colin Newman write about his abiding love for Todd Rundgren's *A Wizard, A True Star* (Bearsville, 1973), the progressive rock elements of Wire's own music suddenly come into focus. And sometimes more current music directly opens a dialogue with previous releases: a full understanding of Destroyer's "The Bad Arts" from the *Streethawk* LP (Misra, 2001) is impossible without knowing that it's a rewrite of Joy Division's "Disorder" (*Unknown Pleasures*, Factory, 1979). And from Kitty Wells's "It Wasn't God Who Made Honky-Tonk Angels" (Decca 10″, 1952) on through I-Roy's "Straight to Prince Jazzbo's Head" (Upsetters 45, 1975) straight to Pusha-T's "The Story of Adidon" (not on label, 2018), records have been and continue to be made as answers to other records. Sometimes we forget that musicians are often record collectors themselves! In fact, the key to grasping the music they make often comes through an understanding of what they've heard. Sometimes, however, a musician will immodestly or unwittingly invite comparison of their own music to that of legends. This rhetorical use of records can get a little uncomfortable for fans: If musicians aren't careful, they may draw down an invidious comparison between the records they make and the classics of their idols. It's a fine line sometimes between saying you love John Coltrane and that you think you *are* John Coltrane; that you love Dolly Parton's voice and that you can sing just as well. At times, it can seem as if some of today's musical acolytes want to drape themselves in the achievements of the past masters. But these are exceptions in musicians' use of vinyl. For the most part, a good record collection is a wellspring for a practicing player and/or songwriter—a model, a source of inspiration, and a fount of ideas and lyrics to which they can answer in their own work.

## MUSIC CRITICISM

Finally, some use records for what I call a critical purpose—to interpret, contextualize, and share what they know and think about records. The book you're now reading is one example of this use. Products of this approach include popular music histories, music journalism, popular and academic books, radio shows, and specialized music libraries. All these folks attempt to organize others' thoughts and feelings about records in constructive ways. They interpret music and try to figure out how it works. They make judgments on the meanings and impact of particular records and whole genres, attempting in the process to put them in historical context. Some focus on the social aspects of the music, others the formal, while many combine the two.

When done well, this use of records injects provocative questions and arguments into a sometimes anti-intellectual music world. The fact is, most musicians don't have time for critics and DJs. But that's because most music writing and a fair number of radio shows are terribly pretentious and miss the mark—not because they're somehow too intellectual. The smartest critical use of music can inspire you to listen closer, hear new things, and grasp records in their full historical context. That so little work of this type gets through is not for want of creative, thoughtful writers and DJs, but rather a function of widespread gatekeeping in academia, corporate media, and even college radio.

## GENRE: FUNDAMENTALISM AND OMNIVOROUSNESS

As I'll detail in the next two chapters, the internet has subdivided record collecting taste cultures into a thousand little scenes and subgenres. While it's become popular in recent years to dismiss genre as a mere marketing ploy to sell records, I believe the rule of genre has persisted and maybe even strengthened in the internet era. I think those who feel the internet has rendered genre obsolete mistake streaming's default form of listening—decontextualized, magpie flightiness—for the only one possible. But streaming has far from made genre irrelevant—even Spotify still relies heavily on genre tags for its playlists. And the fact that taste cultures have splintered and microgenres have exploded in number means an understanding of genre in record collecting is more vital a task than ever.

## FUNDAMENTALISM

One approach to this situation is what I call genre fundamentalism. As the name implies, the genre fundamentalist pursues only one genre of record and does so doggedly. One benefit of this approach is that a collector can achieve a rare sense of mastery and control. If you narrow your sights to a specific genre or subgenre, particular labels or scenes, you can be a completist. My friend David Griffiths has made buying trips to Dayton, Ohio, for years now. As a result, he has probably the world's most exhaustive collection of funk and soul 45s from Dayton and its surrounding environs. Carolina Soul founder Jason Perlmutter probably knows the name and label of more Carolina soul records than any other person living. The now-defunct print magazine *Maximum Rocknroll* has the world's most exhaustive collection of punk LPs and 7" records stashed away somewhere in the Bay Area. Northern soul fans collect a very well-defined subcategory of soul, and so can build up comprehensive archives. And since some labels put out only a few fascinating, desirable records before they closed their doors, it's possible to own many such labels' complete catalogs. When you tightly control the parameters of your interests and limit yourself to one genre, you can map out an entire musical subculture and really get to know it inside and out.

But this genre tunnel vision comes at a cost. What you gain in depth, you lose in breadth—you must shut out contemporary music as well as all other genres from the past to focus on just one. If you're not careful, you could become so specialized that you'll lose touch with the broader movements in music. Not only can this get monotonous, it can also blind you to the way genres crisscross one another. If you focus too tightly on dance boogie 12" records, for example, you'll miss the way the genre overlaps with a host of other genres from minimal wave to post-punk. Or if you limit your interest to vernacular music and its related folklore, you may write off many records as decadent "art music." If you are obsessed with funk breaks and rap LPs, it's easy to get lost in the past and so miss out on what contemporary rap has to offer.

## OMNIVOROUSNESS

At the other extreme, there are those romantic types who won't limit themselves by genre at all. These omnivores want to collect everything at once and refuse to narrow their focus to just one research interest. The desire here is to sample as many types of records as possible and make mental connections between them. Whole mental maps articulating the relationships between genres are put together by this type of collector, who wants to take in the full scale and scope of the record archive.

Hearing every single record in the world, is, of course, a practical impossibility. No one can own or hear everything. But as an enabling desire, it can produce great results. When the omnivorous approach to records works, it reveals interesting and fruitful connections between records not usually grouped together. In their collecting patterns, these omnivores are the free-form DJs of records—finding through lines between disparate records and genres to produce new combinations. The danger of this method is in its potential incoherence—when one tries to connect everything to everything else, contradictions and mismatches of style are bound to occur from time to time.

BURNING SPEAR / ROCKING TIME · BURNING SPEAR / HUG

TOOTS AND THE MAYTALS / FUNKY KIN

COME AGAIN

Pick A Dub

THE MIGHTY INVADERS · INVASION! · Aira Records

DENROY MORGAN

SLY DUNBAR · SLY-GO-VILLE

The Gladiators · Trenchtown Mix Up · Virgin Records V2062

BYRON LEE & THE DRAGONAIRES · DANCE THE SKA

SOUL REBELS BOB MARLEY and the WAILERS

IN THE BOMB SHELTER

MAX ROMEO WAR INA BABYLON

⊕⊕⊕⊕⊕⊕⊕⊕ - THE CONGOS ⊕⊕⊕⊕⊕⊕⊕⊕ · HEART OF THE CONGOS

# CHAPTER 3

# Collectors' Genres and Subgenres

As noted in Chapter 2, it's become fashionable for music critics to claim that genre is dead. Dismissing all classificatory terms as marketing gimmicks, they argue that genre concepts stand between us and a fuller, more adventurous listening experience. But while the internet has transformed the way we categorize music, it's a mistake to think computers have rendered genre irrelevant. It would be more accurate to say that the current era of music consumption, especially record collecting, is dominated by subgenres, microgenres, niches, and boutique movements. The broadest genres—for example, rock, soul, jazz, and dance—have been subdivided into hundreds of smaller, distinct categories. In general, collectors are now less interested in the overarching genres of old than the swerves within and away from established genres—power pop and doom metal rather than classic rock; sweet and modern soul rather than Motown; spiritual and free jazz rather than straight-ahead jazz; house and techno rather than disco (at least in its orchestral form). What's more, collectors prioritize genre cross-pollinations over single genre works: Carolina Soul auction an increasing number of records with multiple subgenres in their description. Some examples chosen at random from the company's recent listings include psych funk, islands modern soul, and electro bass rap. When categories are in flux, there will always be those who call change chaos. And record genres are in the process of transformation. Not only are there more subgenres and genre combinations to keep track of, but their meanings are still works in progress. If anything, the internet has revitalized the need for thinking about genre.

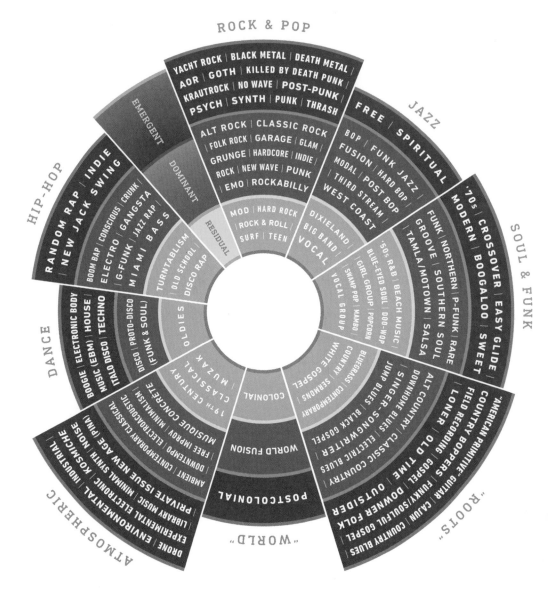

Fig. 12. Collectors' Genre Trends

In fact, discarding genre diminishes rather than liberates the listener. First, it robs records of their historical context. If you consider genre as just marketing, you ignore the fact that people have been using it to analyze music throughout the history of recorded music. As a result, our understanding of any given record is intertwined with the history of its genre. For example, think about writing a history of black music in the US without a working concept of the various meanings of "gospel" or "jazz." You just can't! And the fact that you can't is because music is made and listened to in response to genre conventions. In any case, no concept in the modern world is untouched by marketing—but that doesn't mean everything can be reduced to *just* marketing. For example, the periodic table was invented in czarist Russia, but no one would deny its usefulness to chemistry. And in fact, our genre concepts come from a welter of competing societal forces beyond marketing. Even genre and subgenre names bear this out: some are historical periodizing concepts ('70s soul), some are aesthetic descriptors (harsh noise), and others focus on the music's effect on listeners (rocksteady). Still others are geographical (Zamrock, short for Zambian rock), problematically race- or gender-specific (blue-eyed soul and girl group), functional (steel drum, turntablism), or figurative (sweet soul, black metal).

What's more, genre demarcates real musical differences. If its concepts didn't exist, it would be necessary to invent them in order to account for the clear sonic differences between, for example, Charley Patton's country blues and Laurie Spiegel's algorithmic electronic music, or Tony Allen's drumming and that of Javanese gamelan. Without an understanding of the aesthetic fundamentals of a genre, it becomes impossible to know the meaning of any given record in that genre's orbit. Finally, genre concepts bring about mental connections among artists, records, and performances. While genre can be misused in a reductive way (see the section on genre fundamentalism in the previous chapter), it is usually productive. For example, before the concept of Northern soul developed in late 1960s Britain, it didn't exist as a recognizable subgenre. The criteria early Northern DJs used to slice up American soul—to include faster tempos and chippier singing styles while excluding their alternatives—connected previously scattered records into a coherent conceptual grouping. Collectors and DJs are creative—they can organize music in new ways and produce concepts that give records new meaning.

But because we only understand records when they become part of history, new collectors' concepts are necessarily back-formations. They invent a meaning for records that are no longer contemporary and so have become accessible to recontextualization. When a record first comes out, it's impossible to judge its significance—to tell whether it will "hold up" or not. In the heat of the present moment, fads are nearly impossible to separate from lasting trends.

The reverse is also true. If you go too far back in recorded history, a genre's prevailing meanings feel set in stone. In other words, not all records are equally open to reuse and reinterpretation. To account for why, it's helpful to consider cultural studies pioneer Raymond Williams's conceptualization of dominant, residual, and emergent trends.[1] According to Williams, dominant cultural trends are those that assert themselves as natural and normal, true and beautiful. These are the ideals that hold the most sway over the popular imagination. In the case of records, these are the established genres and subgenres—'60s rock and soul, the Blue Note jazz era, and so on. Residual trends, in contrast, are those that are no longer immediately influential on popular culture but still play a strong symbolic role in the popular imagination. Residual record genres and subgenres include much of what we call vintage or antique: doo-wop, prewar country and blues, Dixieland jazz, for example. As mentioned earlier, such residual records come with a predetermined history baked in—it's harder to imagine new meanings and uses for these records than it is for dominant and emergent ones. Finally, emergent trends are those that are still in the process of formation. They challenge the legitimacy of dominant and residual trends. In the case of records, these are what I am calling new collectors' genres and microgenres— categories like random rap, private issue new age, spiritual jazz, and a legion of genre hybrids.

In the next chapter, I tell the story of eight major genre groupings—soul, "world," atmospheric, rock/pop, rap, dance, jazz, and vernacular—from the perspective of present collectors' interests. I will describe both what emergent subgenres offer and how they force us to reinterpret their broader genre's past (both dominant and residual, classic and vintage). I write from the perspective of these rising genres for a reason—history is useless if it doesn't relate the past to the needs of the present. If we were to center our discussions on the dominant genres and subgenres, we would most likely repeat what's already been said in *Rolling Stone*, *Pitchfork*, and Ken Burns's PBS music documentaries. In other words, retell the standard narrative. On the other hand, if we told the story with residual genres and subgenres at the fore, we would get lost in an antiquarian worship of the past, cherishing old records simply because they're old. Telling the story of record genres from the present backward and then forward again is a more active, creative approach to thinking about records. It treats the record archive as an unsettled zone of experimentation, a place to find new and obscure strands of the musical past suited to our dreams for the future. If record collecting is to persist into the adulthood of millennials, zoomers, and their children, vinyl culture can't get lost in the past. Genres need to be understood as living forces that actively form the present. The best collectors are not just conservators of past treasures; they produce new combinations of records and draw conceptual lines between them. When collectors reinvent genres and create subgenres, they open up new horizons for thought and experience.*

---

\*       A note on the subgenres listed in this chapter's headers: They are not exhaustive. Pulled from our eBay auction listings, they are a representative sampling of what rare record buyers seek out these days. We've left out some of the more arcane subgenres and focused on root terms to the exclusion of their many possible hybrids.

| | | |
|---|---|---|
| '50s R&B | | |
| Beach Music | | |
| Blue-Eyed Soul | Funk | |
| | Northern | |
| Doo-Wop | P-Funk | '70s |
| Girl Group | Rare Groove | Boogaloo |
| Mambo | Salsa | Crossover |
| Popcorn | Southern Soul | Easy Glide |
| Swamp Pop | Tamla/ Motown | Modern |
| Vocal Group | | Sweet |

# FUNK, SOUL, R&B

'60s Soul · '70s Soul · Beach Music · Blue-Eyed Soul · Country Funk · Crossover Soul · Deep Soul · Doo-Wop · Funk Breaks · Girl Group · Go-Go · Group Soul · Jazz Funk · Modern Soul · New Jack Swing · Northern Soul · P-Funk · Popcorn · Rare Groove · Southern Soul · Stage Band · Steppers · Swamp Pop · Sweet Soul · Tamla/ Motown · Vocal Group

Soul and funk records, particularly 45s, have been collectible since the 1960s. Their direct stylistic predecessors, R&B and doo-wop, have been sought out since the 1950s. While these genres' origins were American, the music quickly spread around the globe and was translated into different national contexts. In 1950s and '60s Jamaica, ska and rocksteady grew out of direct and indirect transformations of R&B and soul records played on US airwaves. And in the late 1960s, soul fans in the English north and Midlands created the subgenre tag "Northern soul" to describe the American soul 45s they favored in their clubs and homes. Northern was an English mod interpretation of the Tamla/Motown sound, driven by a hipster taste for rare and obscure records, danceable tempos, and (to American ears) slightly syrupy vocals. To this day, Northern 45s fetch higher prices than any other subgenre on the international record market. It's ironic, then, that the dominant subgenres of American soul 45s have been heavily shaped by the tastes of English DJs, collectors, and fans. And this influence is not just limited to records from the 1960s. As Northern moved into the 1970s, it produced microgenres under the larger subheading of Northern, including crossover, '70s, and modern soul. Forty-fives in these styles, too, continue to be highly collectible.

For American collectors, however, the dominant streams of soul and funk are still symbolized by the iconic labels Tamla/Motown, Atlantic, and Stax—the labels of the Supremes and Isleys, Aretha Franklin and Otis Redding. These are the artists and labels you still hear on the radio and mentioned in *Rolling Stone*'s best album lists. As opposed to the Northern scene, Americans tend to expect a little more grit and raw power in their soul and funk. Southern, sweet, and deep (though even this term is a coinage of OG English collector Dave Godin) soul and all funk subgenres tend toward grimier, less-polished vocals and recordings than Northern, crossover, '70s, and modern. But there is, of course, profound overlap between the categories of UK and US soul classifications. Together, they form the dominant genres of the moment. To put things simply, the 1960s soul sound (and 1970s funk sound) still dominates collectors' consciousness.

Which means the proto-soul sounds of the 1950s work residually. R&B and doo-wop are still highly respected as foundational genres, but the collectors actively seeking them are dwindling into a graying minority. Labels like King, Federal, Checker, and Chance, plus hundreds of smaller R&B and doo-wop labels, populate every R&B/rock 45 auction that Carolina Soul runs, but it's an open question whether the next generation of record collectors will continue to revere and pursue these labels. As a rule, the further you have to go back for a subgenre's original heyday, the harder it is for records in that category to break through to contemporary listeners as purely pleasurable music. And so as it becomes easier to respect 45s from the Flamingos or Five Keys as historically significant, it also gets harder to immerse oneself in their music.

If the 1960s subgenres dominate, and the 1950s subgenres haunt us as tradition, what new soul groupings are emerging? As you might expect from trends still in the process of formation, these are more heterodox and less tightly defined. Modern and '70s records have emerged as a viable alternative for those tiring of first-wave Northern. Sixties and '70s sweet soul, a long-standing staple of Latino California car culture, has taken on a newfound popularity among collectors more generally. And the straightforward funk we associate with legends like James Brown and the Meters has given way to more drum machine, synth, and vocoder-heavy subgenres—boogie, electro, and all manner of microgenre hybrids. The emergent sounds of soul are now centered on the subgenres of the late 1970s and '80s, when soul and funk collided with more cheaply available drum machines, synths, hip-hop, and club music.

# NORTHERN SOUL

In the world of rare soul 45s, Northern ones consistently sell for the highest prices, with some auctions ending in five figures. Many of Carolina Soul's all-time top sellers are Northern records. So, we start our discussion here because it has traditionally driven the rare record world—so much so that all other emergent scenes tend to define themselves against it.

As mentioned above, "Northern" refers not to soul made, in say, Maine (shout-out to Night Fever from coastal Maine, though) but to records collected by, danced to, and obsessed over by soul fans in the North of England. Briefly put, the Northern soul canon consists of obscure, Tamla/Motown–sounding records. It represents the peppier, dance-oriented side of soul as opposed to the rougher, funkier stuff. When most think of the Northern sound, they think of speedy "stompers" ("speedos" want the "100 mph," as they used to say). But the Northern clubs also accommodate barely danceable "midpacers" like the Dynamics' "I'm a Lonely Man" (Dyna) and even much slower "beat ballads" like Joy Marshall's "Heartache Hurry On By" (Decca). The traditional Northern sound is the '60s radio soul in America, but with an emphasis on its lesser-known records.

The vocal stylings favored by '60s Northern heads can sound stiff and corny to modern Americans, who expect more funk and roughness in their soul music. But there are many great individual records in the Northern canon that require no initiation into the mod scene of England in the 1960s and '70s: no "Keep the Faith" patches, no memorized dance routines, and no memories of Wigan Casino necessary. For example, an up-tempo track like the Isley Brothers' obscure 45 "Why When Love Is Gone" (Tamla, 1967) is a barn burner in any genre. Robert Tanner's "Sweet Memories" (Megatone, 1970), so rare as to have been bootlegged multiple times in the UK, is a mid-tempo stunner. Tanner's stellar *New Sounds* (Turbo, 1970) LP, featuring an even more stripped-down, emotionally direct version of "Sweet Memories," is also a stone-cold classic.

Additionally, a more detailed look at regional variations within the Northern canon helps break up the oppressive sense of homogeneity one sometimes gets thinking about the genre. For example, horn sections from the Carolinas tend to swing rougher, verging toward what would become funk horns, as can be heard on the touching Appreciations' "It's Better to Cry" (Sport, 1967), and Moses Dillard's "Pretty as a Picture" (Mark V, 1967) and "I'll Pay the Price" (Mark V, 1966). The mega-rare DC Shrine label, on the other hand, tends to sound more like a variation on group Tamla sounds. Philly's Northern sound, as one would expect, features vocal styles that anticipate the "bow-tie" elegance Fred Wesley would later define as the Philly sound. The backing tracks are not funky in the way the Sound of Philadelphia was, but 45s like the Temptones' "Girl I Love You" (Arctic, 1966, featuring a young "D. Hohl," Daryl Hall of Hall & Oates, on vocals), Kenny Gamble & the Romeos' "Ain't It Baby" (Arctic, 1965), Frankie Beverly and the Butlers' "Because of My Heart" (Fairmount, 1967), and Honey and the Bees' "Together" (Arctic, 1969) anticipate the foreground-background dynamics of Philly's '70s soul records. And Baltimore, as represented by the Ru-Jac label's rare 45 "Nobody Beats My Love" (Sir Joe), features a much rougher, fast-and-loose approach to the arrangement of horns and lead and backing vocals.

The Northern soul movement's most enduring contribution to record culture was conceptual. Its collectors were fanatical in subdividing soul into genres and subgenres. Historically speaking, Northern soul introduced many of the soul collecting subgenres we use today, for example, Northern (naturally), sweet, and deep. The Northern scene, with its zeal for classification and rare records, prefigured (before the internet) the collecting scenes of other genres. This is important to remember, because some of the highest-priced, most-hyped Northern soul records now fall flat on younger ears. For those who didn't grow up within the Northern scene, it can be difficult to crack the code. For many younger Americans, it's hard to relate to white Englishmen's nostalgia for a moment in black American culture they experienced from afar. But it's also undeniable that this scene's zest for rare records has saved many gems from the literal and figurative dustbin.

And it must be remembered that in late 1960s and early '70s Britain, Northern was a way to carve out a working-class identity for Northerners separate from that of the often oppressive, cosmopolitan South. In this way the Northern movement, even though it worships American soul records by black artists, can also be considered a form of self-assertion by a (mostly) white Northern working-class scene. This spirit is evidenced in the two most well-known non-soul Northern covers, one by Mancunian post-punkers the Fall ("There's a Ghost in My House" [original by R. Dean Taylor]) and the other by Liverpudlian dance-poppers Soft Cell's "Tainted Love" (original by Gloria Jones).

## CROSSOVER

In the 1970s, crossover became a going concern in a Northern scene looking to change things up a bit in tempo and feel. Rod Dearlove's article "Crossover Soul," from his fanzine *Voices of the Shadow* (1990s), defines the general sonic parameters of crossover as "plusher and in many cases slower than an 'on-the-fours' Detroit pounder." A crossover tune like Lee "Shot" Williams's "It Ain't Me No More" (PM, 1972), for example, is downtempo and barely danceable, with a definable groove that inspires more of a strut than a straight-up stomp. Given the record's title, it's fitting that crossover often incorporates the piano line and general groove from Young-Holt Unlimited's "Soulful Strut" (Brunswick, 1968), as well as endless permutations of the Archie Bell and the Drells' guitar riff on "Tighten Up" (Atlantic, 1968). And it should be noted, as Matt Weingarden[2] has reminded us, that Tyrone Davis's late '60s 45s on Dakar were also foundational to the crossover sound. Friday, Saturday, & Sunday's "There

Must Be Something" (1971) demonstrates the way crossover occupies the mid-tempo, pairing recognizably '60s singing styles with a funkier, more swinging groove. Tony Drake's "Suddenly" (Brunswick, 1970), Margie Joseph's "One More Chance" (Stax, 1969), and Celeste Hardie's "You're Gone" (Reynolds Records, 1972) work in the same vein and demonstrate the way more laid-back horn lines accent most crossover tracks. Rarer bangers in the genre include United Sounds' "It's All Over (Baby)" (United) and Just Us's "We've Got a Good Thing Going" (Vincent, 1973), both of which sell for thousands of dollars when they (rarely) crop up online.

## '70S

When a soul 45 is described as "'70s" (obviously a retrospective designation!) as opposed to crossover, this means the sound is more orchestrally oriented with lush strings. Seventies tracks tend to aim for a more elegant, smoother vibe than crossover. A Brother's Guiding Light's "Getting Together" (Mercury, 1973) sets the template: a gentle, placid feel; measured, sophisticated vocal delivery; and an unbroken, easy head-bobbing rhythm that would soon morph directly into the mellowness of Philly soul. Other fine examples of '70s soul include the Van McCoy–produced David Ruffin hit "Walk Away from Love" (Motown, 1975); Daybreak's "Everything Man" with its early, lush, and almost schmaltzy strings from a pre-cosmic disco Patrick Adams; and perhaps *the* blueprint for the '70s groove, the Spinners' "It's a Shame" (V.I.P., 1970).

## MODERN

"Modern soul" means one thing to the Northern soul scene and another to the US. For the UK, modern was both a historical and aesthetic concept referring to newer (hence modern "newies nights") '70s records without a '60s sound: music that moved toward funk and disco. The UK's version of modern tends to include records we would call crossover and '70s, while we in the States tend to reserve "modern" for more '80s sounds, particularly in the vocals. Recently, Numero Group used the British sense of the term to put together their Spotify playlist "Pocket Full of Money: The Numero Guide to Modern Soul," which shows the general level of ambiguity surrounding these terms. But in current US usage, "modern soul" is usually used to mean '80s soul: Spade Brigade's "I'm Your Man" (Select Sound Studio, 1980), Split Decision Band's "Watchin' Out" (Network, 1978), and Bileo's "You Can Win" (M.T.U./Watts City, 1979) are three good examples. Modern soul sometimes features the introduction of "'80s" rhythm tracks—tighter, more bouncing and less swinging grooves. Synthetic bass lines often replace ones played by live instruments, but sometimes you'll hear drum machines and lead synth lines running in parallel with those of live instruments. The orchestral element of '70s soul may still be present, as in Tony Love's "We're Doing It Together" (Ham-Sen, 1980), but it's generally used in a more functional, less expressive way and features synthetic strings rather than actual players from an orchestra. The sound is more minimal and less lush. The vocal stylings tend to be flatter and less melodramatic than, say, most '60s Southern soul of the type you find on Stax. On "He's Scandalous" (Sue, 1983), for example, Kaiya goes in for cool detachment rather than a direct outpouring of hurt and heartache. And though it features a boogie backing, Popcorn's "A Song for You" (Shanell, 1983) demonstrates the modern soul vocal style in its mannered expression. It represents a sort of reduction and smoothing effect applied to the rawer sounds of earlier, gospel-inflected soul vocals. Modern vocals are catchy and expressive, but not necessarily expressions of private pain and joy, as listeners tend to rightly or wrongly assume older deep, sweet, and Southern soul tracks to be. They also tend to be catchier, with more backing harmonies, than the soul records of the past. Modern was the dominant radio sound of soul in the early to mid-'80s and so should be recognizable to even casual listeners.

The incredibly valuable Fayetteville, North Carolina, 45 "Reality" (1980, self-released) by Ice sometimes gets mislabeled as a boogie record, but to me, it's pure modern soul. "Reality" features all organically played instruments, a modified funky bass bounce, and a more stylized, smooth, polished, and cool vocal style. Henderson and Jones's "I'm Gonna Getcha" (Quality Blend, 1982) features a similar but more "grown 'n' sexy" vocal than Ice, along with a synth. Halo's "Let Me Do It" (Marshall, 1981) features the popping bass present on many modern soul tracks. Control's "Your Love" (Sounds Unlimited Productions, 1988), also a Fayetteville, North Carolina, record, is a late entry into the modern genre then dominated by new jack swing; it features a drum machine but is far too slow to be a danceable boogie track. Its beautiful vocal hides its passion under a cool and detached delivery. Its custom cover, something you don't see too often with 12" records (as opposed to LPs), is also quite wonderful. In black and white, it mixes the sublime with the ridiculous: It features a town car rolling through a city at night, underneath an outsized hat and sunglasses. The cover, like "Your Love" itself, captures modern soul's cool but faintly ridiculous vibe. Northern soul heads would call Magnum's "Tell Me Why" (Silver Bullet) a "two-stepper" (slow but still beat driven), while the average American collector would just call it a "slow jam" or modern soul—it has the common synth strings, and the giveaway vocal delivery of the genre. Coming from the Bahamas, 5th Degree's "You Got Me Hypnotized" (Degree) has an updated-for-the-'80s funky backing but is a sterling example of the modern soul vocal (despite the unfortunate flange studio effect put on its choruses). Cincinnati's Pure Essence's "Wake Up" (Mantra, 1976) also features some flange to de-intensify the funkier elements of their track, and in general the song anticipated the sound of the '80s in modern soul. Chain Reaction's "Search for Tomorrow" (Blue Wave, 1979) demonstrates the transition from the disco groove to the modern soul bounce, and Marshall,

Donovan, Broomfield's "Since I Found My Baby" (Augusta, 1978), another killer, does the same.

What about the mainstay subgenres of soul: funk, Southern soul, sweet soul, and deep soul? Well, in the 2000s, "funk" seemed to be undergoing a revitalization.

## FUNK

The Jazzman label put out a celebrated series of regional compilations: *Midwest Funk* (2003), *Texas Funk* (2002), *Carolina Funk* (2007 [compiled by Carolina Soul's own Jason Perlmutter]), and *California Funk* (2010). These were issued stateside by Egon's Now-Again label. The Stones Throw label put out *The Funky 16 Corners*, featuring fire from Carleen & the Groovers, Kashmere Stage Band, Rhythm Machine, and James Reese. These comps coincided with smaller-run reissues of single artists, which deepened the interest in funk as a going concern. Numero put out a compilation of "gospel funk" (*Good God! A Gospel Funk Hymnal*) in 2003. Rhino released *What It Is! Funky Soul and Rare Grooves 1967–1977* (2006), which brought together some of the best funky tracks in archives of the major labels Atlantic, Atco, and Warner Bros. This came replete with a cringy graphic of a black woman with an afro with a 45 adapter overlaid on top of it. Which is part of why perhaps straight funk is no longer the hot topic it once was: Funk became reduced to a stereotype less than an active genre, including liberal use of "afro" iconography of the most stereotyped, borderline racist variety. At the same time, the masculinist emphasis on "heaviness" and power in funk can seem overbearing to modern ears. It doesn't help that within the collectors' scene many funkers have a "tough guy" vibe that can be off-putting to younger collectors. For better or worse, people think of funk as more of a known quantity culturally and musically—casual listeners now feel they know enough to move on. As a result, in eBay listings, funk is still sold as a genre of its own, but also shows up as a modifier combined with a number of other genres: country funk, gospel funk, Northern funk, and so on. Individual funk tracks are undeniable (Communicators and Black Experience Band's "The Road" [Tri-Oak] from our home in Durham, for one!), and still fetch high prices, and the genre has its diehards, particularly in LA, but it doesn't seem to be attracting the same cultural cachet or heat it did in the first decade of the 2000s. It's telling that two of the most valuable funk 45s, Willie Wright's cover of Curtis Mayfield's "Right On for the Darkness" (Hotel) and Andrew Brown's "You Made Me Suffer" (Brave, 1973), are not up-tempo or heavy with funk breaks. Rather, these two tracks are mid-tempo meditative funk and blues funk, respectively. In other words, they swerve from the masculinist mainline. The funk records that compel me most these days are things like Deloris Ealy's "Deloris Is Back with Jerome and His Band" (Big Vick Hammond) because it adds a level to the expected funk breaks sound: Whether intentionally or not, the record overlays two separate vocals from Ealy, which phase in and out of sync with one another. You can listen to them as one shared vocal or two distinct performances, depending on your listening emphasis. This produces a dense listening experience, the audio analogue of studying a multiple-exposure photograph. But we shouldn't get ahead of ourselves, as we'll discuss Ealy's record in more depth in chapter 5.

## SOUTHERN SOUL

Southern soul as associated with Memphis soul (Stax/Volt, Hi Records, Jewel, Goldwax) and Muscle Shoals, Alabama, has suffered a bit among collectors, because of its success and overexposure in the popular imagination. For more casual fans, Otis Redding, Aretha Franklin, and Al Green *are* soul music and define and exhaust its possibilities. For this reason, Southern soul records are often collected and regarded as undeniably classic, at the same time they are taken for granted. Peter Guralnick's *Sweet Soul Music*[3] consolidated the canon for the mainstream and made an implicit argument throughout his book that the most well-known artists and labels are also the best. As with the rarer Tamla sides in the case of Motown 45s, in Southern soul collectors circles the more underappreciated records of Stax/Volt are the most exciting—for example, a 45 like Joni Wilson's "(Let Hurt Put You in the) Loser's Seat" b/w "Flame, Flame, Flame" (Volt, 1971). This 45 seems to be the only piece of music Wilson released, and collectors aren't even sure of her identity or background. It may be the rarest record on Volt, but people aren't sure—even Red "The Soul Detective" Kelly can't seem to locate her! And it's technically a Philly record, not "Southern," even though it's, of course, on a Memphis label. Both sides of the record—the mid-tempo "Loser's Seat" (itself a remake of George Clinton's pre P-Funk Parliament's "All Your Goodies Are Gone," Revilot, 1967) and the slow burner "Flame, Flame, Flame"—are stunning, equal to the most famous and popular soul songs.

## DEEP SOUL

Deep soul is sometimes used synonymously with "Southern soul," but it shouldn't be. The term "deep soul" was coined by Britain's Dave Godin, who was also responsible for originally coining the term "Northern soul." The "deep" modifier here refers not only to sonics or metaphysics, but to obscurity—these were British hipster downer soul tracks, non-pop "deep digs" and so more out of the way, less mainstream than the radio hits of the day. Somewhat confusingly, the term has also come to imply a mournful, "deep" aesthetic. Doris Duke's *I'm a Loser* (Canyon, 1970), one of Godin's favorite LPs, is paradigmatic. Godin's 1990s comps on Kent, *Dave Godin's Deep Soul Treasures*, are the obvious place for those interested in learning more about this British inflection of American traditions.

## SWEET SOUL

Sweet soul has seen a resurgence in collector interest in recent years and has a more descriptive (if not exhaustive) name than most. The records, after all, feature sweet and syrupy ballads. Sometimes called "low-rider" because of its association with LA car culture, and sometimes called "oldies" by its Angeleno fans, sweet soul's connection to nostalgia is undeniable. Google "oldies soul" or "low-rider soul" and you'll find record covers for comps and mixes with idealized pin-up girls, immaculately detailed classic cars, and snapshots from 1970s and '80s Chicano life in LA. For example, the YouTube video for the best Impressions 45 not made by the Impressions—Dayton, Ohio's Young Mods' "I Can't Hurt You Back" (Everblack, 1970)—features many emblematic user comments. These run the gamut from the nostalgic "Sunday night cruising in Old Baytown" and "cruzzin on a weekend down central ave.," to the poetic "playing this downlow and looking up at the stars," to the near anagrammatic "S.E.L.A. [South East Los Angeles]." A track like the Scorpion's "Keep on Trying" (SBP, featuring boogie artist Leroy "Ace" Miller) defines the sound: steady and stripped-down backbeat and heavy bass, falsettos, and a sad-hearted, downer lead vocal. While it features a funky horn intro and psych touches in its production, Soul Seekers' "Extrodinary [sic] Dream" (Soul Head) has a typical penetrating falsetto lead that is sustained throughout the track. North Carolina group Brief Encounter's "Where Will I Go?" (unreleased at the time), with its slowed-down elegance and precision vocals, suspends the listener on the thin line between hope and despair.

While LA diehards have long kept the flame burning, there's also been a resurgence of general soul collector interest in sweet records. Perhaps it's because as soul fans gray, they tend to go to the club less and listen to records at home more? In any case, the mellow sounds and highly emotive vocals are well suited to headphones and the rhythms of dishwashing or phone scrolling as much as they are for cruising the strip. In addition, the general inflation of prices of rare soul records by the internet auction effect must be a contributing factor. At the high end, the past five to ten years have seen a surge in prices: Now big sweet 45s will go for $2,000–$3,000 on eBay, which is a new development.

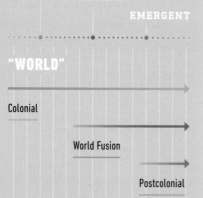

RESIDUAL

DOMINANT

EMERGENT

"WORLD"

Colonial

World Fusion

Postcolonial

## "WORLD"

Afrobeat · Bolero · Bollywood · Boogaloo · Bossa Nova · British Folk · Calypso · Compas · Conjunto · Cumbia · Dancehall · Descarga · Digi Dancehall · Digi Roots · Dub · Dub Poetry · Ethio Jazz · Field Recording · Flamenco · Highlife · Island · Junkanoo · Juju · Lovers Rock · Mambo · Mbaqanga · Mento · Merengue · MPB · Norteño · Nouvelle Chanson Qawwali · Raga · Ragga · Rai · Reggae · Rocksteady · Roots Salsa · Samba · Ska · Soca · Soukous · Spouge · Steel Drum · Tejano · Tex-Mex · Tropicalia · Zamrock · Zouk

I put quotation marks around the term "world" because it's such an inadequate name and concept. I use it, skeptically, only because a better concept has not yet emerged. On one hand, it seems too vague, as all records made on Earth are "world" records. On the other, it seems too specific—the result of a particular history of Western colonization and imperialism's division into the West and the rest—the countries of Europe and North America in the center, and a stereotyped "world" beyond. Until a new name comes along, we are stuck with "world" in all its imprecision and condescension—but don't forget that records made in Manhattan and St. John's Wood are "world" music, too.

# WORLD FUSION

The still dominant genres of "world" record collecting were set in the 1980s and early '90s—the era of Paul Simon's world pop LPs *Rhythm of the Saints* and *Graceland*, the Whole Foods–ready easy-listening world music compilations of Putumayo, the pan-cultural fusion of worldbeat, and Jon Hassell's internationalist dreams of a "fourth world" music that could blend high-tech with global folk traditions. This was the era of liberal incorporation of non-Western music into the West. Priding itself on having left behind the outright racism and exploitation of the colonial era, this genre projected an image of global inclusiveness. The world of musicians was one big happy family, and all the world's traditions could be hybridized into capacious forms. Artists featured on the records by Paul Simon and Peter Gabriel, like Ladysmith Black Mambazo, Youssou N'Dour, and Nusrat Fateh Ali Khan, often enjoyed a newfound familiarity in the West. In the public consciousness, this happy-go-lucky, one-world cosmopolitanism still dominates most folks' concept of what the "world" has to offer Western music fans.

This movement premised itself as a kinder, gentler relation of Western music to the rest of the world. It was based on inclusion, not exclusion, similarity rather than otherness—a sense that all global music traditions could fit together like pieces of a jigsaw puzzle. In many ways, this was a persuasive argument for the time. Early ethnomusicological field recordings were explicitly or implicitly tied up in imperialist projects. This included all manner of suspect framings for non-Western music that were bound up in primitivism, nostalgia, fetishism, and what the anthropologist Johannes Fabian called a "denial of coevalness,"[4] the representation of non-Western life as backward and behind Western modernity. Many popular representations of the music and culture of non-Western lands, on the other hand, traded in outright racist caricature and ignorant romanticization with little interest in the cultures they claimed to represent.

Yet something different is emerging. Newer labels like Sahel Sounds, Awesome Tapes from Africa, Sublime Frequencies, Mississippi Records, Yaala Yaala, and Ostinato have reframed world collecting, engaging in what a recent book calls "punk ethnography."[5] In the meantime, there's been a revival of interest in field recordings, anthologies, and reissues of a whole slew of archival material from the past—Smithsonian Folkways (Global Sound), Ocora, Lyrichord, Nonesuch, Rounder, UNESCO. Rather than pit these two tendencies against one another, they seem to share the same spirit, a desire to break with both the facile one-worldism of 1980s fusion and the outright racism of the residual past. The best thing about the new "punk" world labels is that they tend to focus on the music first. They want to share more recent experimental, popular, and confounding recordings that may have been lost on the ears of more aesthetically conservative ethnomusicologists from the past. At the same time, collectors are returning to field recordings with a different emphasis—to understand the music and its historical and political context. The best collectors now listen to both "punk" and traditional field recordings as music first, on its own terms, neither fetishizing it as wholly exotic nor reducing it to a cog in Western pop's gears. This is not to say a utopia in world music is in the offing—issues with royalties, flimsy liner notes, and misrepresentations persist from past eras. But collectors do seem more willing to take non-Western records on their own terms and treat them parsimoniously, with the same respect and passion they bring to Western ones. This is something that has scarcely been tried in the past. It is a hopeful sign that newer collectors, at least, seem willing to grapple with their own musical ethnocentrism in serious (not merely tokenizing and symbolic) ways. But until the producers of this music control the distribution of the music and fruits of their labor, "world" music won't truly be free from the distortions and exploitations of the West.

In the 1980s, Talking Heads, Brian Eno, Paul Simon, and Peter Gabriel made "intellectual pop" for academic types and jumped-up yuppies. While each have made fine music, all have had their reputations inflated as "intellectuals" who can talk in ways amenable to critics. Part of this prestige came with their appropriation of non-Western music. While not without controversy, successful "fusions" of styles were often adduced as signs of these artists' sophistication. While appropriation in and of itself is not a problem per se (all music works through reshaping: from this period, "Earthbeat" by the Slits and "Berketex Bribe" by Crass spring to mind), the reception of these figures was problematic. They were, and still are, viewed as auteurs in relation to the African and "world" raw materials of the lesser-known artists who they sampled, collaborated with, and (sometimes) ripped off. Eno and David Byrne encouraged the perception of themselves as privileged interpreters of non-Western music in their pretentious interviews of the time, which built up a set of commonplaces around their music as "heady." Meanwhile, they were benefiting from this music financially and artistically. As always, the problem of appropriation came primarily in the distribution of power and resources, not in the aesthetic process itself.

## POSTCOLONIAL

Thankfully, the 1980s era of first-world remediation of "world" music is weakening. The "one worldism" that allowed expropriation to go on in the name of world unity and liberal vision of cosmopolitan togetherness has been showing its age. In the '80s and '90s, the dominant image of the Westerner interested in "world" was an affluent, white cosmopolitan, projecting an air of low affect, listlessly sampling the world's cultural traditions like a gourmand at an "ethnic festival." Think Tim Robbins's ponytailed, orientalist world enthusiast in *High Fidelity*, or rich cosmopolitan musicians like David Byrne and Robert Palmer sampling and incorporating the local sounds of Island Records head Chris Blackwell's Compass Point Studios, in Nassau, Bahamas. Byrne has famously tried to atone for his sins in the *New York Times* op-ed titled "I Hate World Music"[6] (1999), in which he made by now familiar liberal critiques of myths of the other's "authenticity" (the world, after all, is a hybrid, polyphonic global space!) and the catchall nature of the category of "world," which he rightly says lumps together disparate music under a one-word category. These critiques are not wrong, but it's important to remember where this piece ends up. Byrne's critique of authenticity ends in an ideal vision of every musical genre getting an equal chance to "crack the American marketplace" so future bands like Colombia's Bloque can continue to "change [Byrne's] life."

Since Byrne wrote "I Hate World Music" in 1999, the internet has scrambled the global field of traditional, vernacular, and folk music. According to the self-presentation of newer, tonier internet-rooted labels, they are revolutionizing the once fuddy-duddy academic world of field recording and archival research. And they are doing this, they say, in order to liberate great music from around the world from the too-narrow confines of ethnography and its pretensions. Labels like Sublime Frequencies (for "world" music) and Fat Possum (for American vernacular "roots" music) have in the past claimed to be "liberating" the records from context. Instead of liner notes and archival research, you find self-consciously experimental or contrarian graphic designs and radically decontextualizing forms. The ideological vehicle for such "liberation" from staid tradition can be avant-gardist or primitivist: Sublime Frequencies' general strategy made an argument, sometimes implicit, that their radio comps harken back to Brion Gysin's cut-ups of "musical collage."[7] And for a long time, they took the same approach to their liner notes (the visual arts collage) with their anti-informational effects (e.g., liner notes and credits), like the decontextualized mix tapes of Mississippi Records, with their imitation of the aesthetic of xeroxed zines. Or, those putting the emphasis on the "primitivist" origins of American roots music, fetishizing delta blues 78s for the rawness and simplicity of early black music, like Fat Possum, used the rawness as a bludgeon against the supposedly curatorial, sanitizing effects of field recordings done by the Smithsonian for Folkways et al. Though they've cleaned up their act since, Fat Possum's *Not the Same Old Blues Crap* compilation series aimed to desanitize the tradition at the expense of making ridiculous the black artists on its roster. The covers for these comps included pictures of R. L. Burnside peeing, a bunch of blues musicians dressed in full military regalia awkwardly posed in front of a tank, and a photo of a dumpster with the words "I Love You Bitch" painted on it. To the for-profit "vernacular" music industry, the academic, ethnographic, and state-sponsored archivists represent what former Carolina Soul employee Ariane Ardalan Clarke calls a "mausoleum" for global music. But some of their extreme swings against the supposed "political correctness" of traditional folklore have resulted in tone-deaf acts of cruelty. If one is looking for an in-depth analysis of this set of issues, we recommend a look at the previously mentioned, fine *Punk Ethnography: Artists and Scholars Listen to Sublime Frequencies*, edited by Michael Veal and Tammy Kim.

There's no doubt that labels like Sublime Frequencies have increased mainstream interest in "world" and vernacular music. As recording artist and former Carolina Soul employee Jake Xerxes Fussell told me, the difference between the popular record-buying audience and buyers of traditional and vernacular music in the 1990s and today has dramatically changed: "Used to be I'd go into a CD store like Turtle's and this stuff would be in the most out-of-the-way, least cared for section of the shop. But now, if you are going into our store, or Other Music [RIP], this stuff has a new prominence, right up front." Fussell chalks a large portion of this up to the "Harry Smith effect," referring to Smith's *Anthology of American Folk Music*. I personally remember, as I'm sure some of our readers will, getting the CD reissue of this box set for Christmas 1997. The hype surrounding its release was immense and was marketed by mainstream media outlets as some sort of trad music key to all mythologies. Many claimed the set's initial release single-handedly jump-started the folk revival of the late 1950s and early 1960s, while Greil Marcus in *Invisible Republic* and other places touted its mystical properties in outlandishly mythopoetic terms. *The Nation* even hyperbolically called the box "gangsta folk," a phrase I'm still trying to figure out all these years later.

While there's no doubt the *Anthology* was a gateway for many (including myself) into traditional American music and the culture of 78 collecting, its marketing as the be-all and end-all representation of American traditional music, and as ground zero for the development for later folk and folk rock, did the field a disservice. First, no single record could perform such a function—with so many possible recordings to include, the omissions for this type of project will always far outnumber the selections. Dick Spottswood's *Folk Music in America* is arguably more comprehensive and interesting. Second, Harry Smith was a highly idiosyncratic individual: He made his own personal associations with folk music, through dabblings with the occult, Renaissance magick, and the like, rather than in the traditional folklorist fashion. And in this, he represents a sort of proto–Sublime Frequencies figure who spices up more institutionally supported, organized, rigorous collectors for bohemian types. (He found many of his records from Alan Lomax's Library of Congress lists of records and through his association with the Berkeley English Department.) In a sense, the Lomax-Smith relationship was a trial run for contemporary tensions between research and hipsterism described by Veal and Kim. And, as Fussell points out, Smith focused on Appalachian music and the Delta blues as the center of American traditional music. Even the set's outlier, the social music disc, is Cajun music and so arguably feeds into the set's centering of Southern-ness as representative of the true American tradition. This focus necessarily excluded whole regions and peoples (for example, indigenous music is nowhere to be found).

It's important to note that indie "world" and vernacular music compilations are a potential spur to more research—a stepping-stone, not a stopping place. They do not provide an understanding of the cultures from which they are drawn. At most they get out of the way and let the record speak for itself. The danger of taking such compilations as national representations is clear. It's important that listeners not treat decontextualizing compilations as able to speak for the conditions and culture of an entire nation. Don't be like the 2000s college radio DJs I knew who took Sublime Frequencies comps around to their "favorite" local Indian and Thai restaurants and asked to replace the restaurant's own musical choices with these CDs. Taken as partial and limited dispatches—in other words, as records first—such compilations are best considered as catalysts for further learning and contextualization.

Beyond issues of representation, the more vulgar question of fair payment seems vital. Both traditional field recorders and the newer labels have not always been on the spot in paying and crediting their artists. The traditional "folk process" of tune recycling and field recording without payment has set a precedent for artists to get ripped off. So again, it's more ambiguous than a battle between the good and bad guys. Both the labels and the academy have their particular grifts.

Even labels with ambiguous pasts, like Sublime Frequencies and Mississippi Records, have recently been putting out better-researched, better-contextualized releases, like Moushumi Bhowmik and Sukanta Majumdar's *The Travelling Archive—Folk Music from Bengal: Field Recordings from Bangladesh, India, and the Bengali Diaspora* (Sublime Frequencies) and Nathan Salsburg's *Root Hog or Die: 100 Songs, 100 Years—An Alan Lomax Centennial Tribute* (Mississippi Records). Whether these releases signal a full change in direction or not remains to be seen. Newer labels, like Sahel Sounds, which started in Portland as a sometime collaboration with Mississippi Records, seems to have learned from the mistakes of its predecessors. First, they fund musical and film projects from their artists, for example Mdou Moctar's Saharan remake of Prince's film *Purple Rain*. And while particularly their earlier releases didn't include liner notes, they always took a less self-important approach to presentation. What's more, they refreshingly made no recourse to mystifying talk of ritual, magic, or primitivism in association with the music. Their breakthrough release, the *Music from Saharan Cellphones* set, treats its music as contemporary—taken from the sim cards of "burner" phones, there is no "denial of coevalness" (Johannes Fabian) that's endemic on many other label's releases. Many of the works on *Music from Saharan Cellphones* feature synths, drum machines, and autotune, which are not used as a novelty so much as just plain instruments available to its performers. With Sahel Sounds, the familiar exoticization and authenticity narratives Byrne complained about are gone, but the label seems to have turned its back on cosmopolitan pretensions Byrne referenced in 1999. The point of Sahel Sounds releases is not to incorporate the music into the mainstream, but to let it speak both its difference and similarities to Western musics on its own terms. The great thing about a label like Sahel Sounds is that it treats the music with respect and care as something distinct and unique musically, and then gets out of the way. Releases like Mamman Sani Abdoulaye's *Unreleased Tapes 1981–1984* and Idassane Wallet Mohamed's *Issawat* keep the music foregrounded. The packaging prepares the way for a record to speak for itself, in all its aesthetic and conceptual power. In the world sector of the record business, there are still "remediations" involved between "us" and "them," possibilities for exploitation built into the profit motive—but the work of labels like Sahel Sounds offers hope that a truly level playing field between musics, rather than the sham capitalist "equality of opportunity," could one day emerge. Because the truth is that the world is filled with potentially libratory records. If the world of collecting is to amount to more than a neocolonial hoarding of the world's musical treasures, we must get in touch with the music itself in both its beauty and its critical functions.

This will require a willingness of folks to see through Vampire Weekend's preppy take on highlife, the disconnect between tUne-YaRdS' dabbling with "pan-global rhythmic loops" and DJ culture for songs about white guilt and extended liberal hand-wringing about her "white centrality," or Animal Collective's, and Gang Gang Dance's hipster neotribalisms of the mid-2000s. These are good signs, but we have further to go. Beyond such political considerations, people are also realizing that the music is two-dimensional as compared to the source material, the latter of which the internet lets you find easily. Thankfully the precious indie rock version of fusion, in which the world becomes your MFA project, feels more and more shopworn every day.

Before the internet, Western artists could more easily rip off less prominent ones without getting caught. The whole trick of a record like Paul Simon's *Graceland* or Lizzy Mercier Descloux's *Zulu Rock* was that they would strike only those unfamiliar with South African pop as a revelation. But now, it's much easier to connect a prominent Western record with the less prominent, non-Western works it is influenced by. Leaving the ethics of "remix culture" aside, this has had the salutary effect of exposing moments when Western musicians fail to live up to their sources. Now when Jim Jarmusch uses the incredible records of *Ethiopiques* stand-out Mulatu Astatke to soundtrack a maudlin Bill Murray "art" movie (*Broken Flowers*), the music does not make Jarmusch's film better but only leaves the viewer wishing it were as good as Astatke's music. When Dan Auerbach from Black Keys plays with Bombino, *he* sounds out of place. The record in general makes one want to hear Bombino's work without Americans. This is in stark contrast to the Paul Simon / Peter Gabriel / Talking Heads era of "world," when first-world pop stars were the guiding interpreters, the directors of the "world" music show. One day we won't need middlemen at all. But until then, we can take some comfort in the fact that modest steps in the right direction have been made.

## ISLANDS MUSIC: A SPECIAL CASE

Islands music, and Jamaican music in particular, is a special case within "world" record collecting. The US and UK have had a longer, more sustained, and more variegated relationship to Jamaican music than other nations. This has to do with geographical proximity, the history of colonialism, the willingness of major labels to invest in "reggae" as a global pop form, and the seemingly bottomless need for aging rockers to diversify their exhausted sounds. The sustained commercial interest in Jamaican music has meant that it broke out of the "ethnological" paradigm earlier than the music of other colonial nations. As a result, casual music fans have long had easy access to some Islands music, whether it be Bob Marley's music (if not original Jamaican pressings and the rarer 45s and 12" records), the Island Records catalog, or Trojan and Studio One box sets and compilations. Complemented by reissues from labels like Soul Jazz, Pressure Sounds, Blood and Fire, and Wackies, Jamaican music has a ubiquity that has made it more mainstream and less exotic to rarity-sensitive collectors. I've had people casually tell me things like "reggae is universally liked" and "a little dub will do," which points to a blasé overfamiliarity. The white reggae guy has even been lampooned by *Saturday Night Live* in its "Ras Trent" sketch, which depended on its audience's familiarity with the type. Anyone in music circles probably knows a Caucasian or two who thinks he's an honorary Jamaican and therefore authorized to pepper their everyday speak with "riddims" and "bredrin," or toast over dubs on their college radio show.

What's more, global exposure has led to a depoliticization of Islands music, particularly politicized genres like roots reggae. Before he became a brand used to sell products like cans of Marley Beverage Co.'s One Drop Mocha Moka (available now at Amazon's Whole Foods), Bob Marley wrote songs in support of Zimbabwe's national liberation from Rhodesia and in favor of a revolution of the oppressed. For him, as for many Islands artists, Babylon is not a vague signifier for anything the listener doesn't like; rather, it represents the twin imperial powers of the state and corporation. Though Marley's Rastafarian worship of Ethiopian leader Haile Selassie is undoubtedly politically problematic, it should not be dismissed as a cynical justification for smoking a lot of marijuana, as Keith Richards's biography recently claimed. Though there's a Sandals resort in Grenada now, it should not be forgotten that a brilliant roots 45 like Rex Harley's "Dread in a PRA" (Trex, 1979) speaks to the joy of the People's Revolutionary Army overthrow of the despotic Eric Gairy in 1979 and utopian socialist hopes for a more just Grenadian future—though this attempt would ultimately be frustrated by CIA infiltration, intense party in-fighting, and ultimately the Reagan-authorized US invasion into the tiny nation in 1983. The song, like Marley's work and much of roots music, needs to be listened to in this context. Its image in the West as weed-friendly, easygoing party music must be viewed as a marketing campaign for mass consumption outside of the Caribbean.

Another effect of Jamaican music's early incorporation into global pop music has been a lack of interest in thinking about its genres historically. Beneath what casually gets called reggae, there's of course ska and rocksteady (which technically predate it), roots, dub, lovers rock, dancehall, digi-dancehall, and so on. The ska of folks like Prince Buster, kick-started during celebrations of liberation from British rule (1962), was followed by its slower-tempo, less strutting cousin rocksteady between 1966 and 1968. This sound was best represented by Jackie Mittoo, the Techniques, and Phyllis Dillon's late but stunning genre summation

*One Life to Live* (1972): As one would expect, it sounds much closer to what we generally think of as "reggae" than ska. What we now think of as 1970s reggae is mostly roots, with tempos between the speed of ska and the drag of rocksteady, protestation of Rastafari, and the previously mentioned left politicization. Dub followed when producers like King Tubby, Lee "Scratch" Perry, Scientist, and Keith Hudson started messing with the speed and levels of preexisting reggae instrumentals for B-sides. Dancehall sped things up for, well, the dancehall and added more rap-influenced rhythms as the '80s wore on. And so on.

As a result of the music's exposure, collectors have to do more in the hunt for both distinction and unfamiliar records. This, in turn, has resulted in the salutary replacement of reggae with the more inclusive "Islands" genre designation. Records from "other" Caribbean nations, which may (e.g., Rex Harley) or may not interface with Jamaican styles, have gained interest in recent years. A record like "Together" (1984) from Tobagonian calypso artist Shadow is modern soul funk, with a synth that stabs and bends—it's built for the dance floor, but has little in common with dancehall. The Barbadian Blue Rhythm Combo's *Magumba* (Merry Disc) sells for hundreds of dollars. They've been marketed as a funk band in some corners (they cover "Shaft"), but a track like "Jesus" appeals more to contemporary collectors, with its chugging rocksteadyish guitar and politicized prayer. It's the sort of thing Ry Cooder would have covered on one of his '70s records. The calypso of the Jarvo Brothers' "Ziruma" has as much in common with American surf guitar as it does with the calypso of Lord Invader. Which is to say, in the thoroughly de-ethnographied field of Islands music, people are looking for music that chimes with other pop styles as much as sounds like an "exotic" other to those styles. This trend explains the continued fascination of radically different covers of American pop by non-American artists, whether it be Belizean Jesus Acosta and the Professionals' organ and horn-led take on the O'Jays' "Back Stabbers," Shinehead's brake-pumping transformation of Michael Jackson's "Billie Jean" into a mid-tempo stunner, or Trinidadian Michael Boothman and Charmaine Ford's retrofitting of Bobby Caldwell's "What You Won't Do for Love" for the dancefloor. This is an ambivalent development, as we've discussed above: It does away with the othering logic of colonialism (it's "just" funk or "all pop music") at the same time it threatens to introduce a new flattening approach to national cultures as indifferent sources of musical content for corporate-driven globalization.

Even within Jamaican sounds, collector interest has sprung up in new corners. Because it's so close to the United States, people can easily go deeper, traveling to Jamaica and buying domestically pressed vinyl and dubplates, often getting these records directly from artists, producers, and label owners. This does not guarantee better records, considering the fact that original Jamaican vinyl (like house records) was not always pressed well, and that the records were actually used a lot and so tend to be in worse condition than some other genres' vinyl.

Another option is to get deeper into particular subgenres like dub, popularized but misunderstood by casual fans and over-serious academics alike. To me, dub records do not all sound the same, nor do they seem like works of continental theory. On an LP like *Playing It Cool and Playing It Right* (1981), Keith Hudson has a dark, intense sound, the sort that makes music critics reach for the word "claustrophobic," whereas King Tubby's work with melodica master Augustus Pablo on classics like *Meets Rockers Uptown* (1976) has an airier, more spacious sound. King Tubby's protege, Scientist, on the other hand, shows a more automated approach to rhythm, leaving fewer traces of his live-tracked source material on *Scientist Rids the World of the Evil Curse of the Vampires* (Greensleeves, 1981) than his mentor. Lee Perry has been all over the sonic map in his dub career. And Phillip Fullwood's *Words in Dub* (1979) sounds nothing like Creation Rebel's *Starship Africa* (1980): the differences are there for those willing to listen.

## ROOTS AND BEYOND

Collectors also have been exploring more hybrid Jamaican roots sounds that were passed over or smoothed out of the mainline narrative of reggae on the way to global crossover appeal. The politically or religiously strident, jazzier, psychier, hand drum–heavy side of roots sound and Rastafari ideology that was perhaps a bit too musically "out" for mass crossover. Records from linked musicians like Dadawah, Count Ossie, and Cedric "Im" Brooks were mystical and Afrocentric, akin to "spiritual jazz." LPs like Dadawah's *Peace and Love: Wadadasow* (1974) and his Sons of Negus's *Freedom Sound* (1974), Count Ossie and the Mystic Revelation of Rastafari's *Grounation* (1973), and Cedric "Im" Brooks's *The Light of Saba* (1974) now represent a countertradition to rub against the grain of the more canonized roots records. Relatedly, some records made in the roots style after the genre's peak popularity in the '70s have become belatedly valuable now that the early dancehall, which supplanted roots, has also shifted from popular culture to collector culture. A 45 like Aksumites' "Ark of the Covenant," made on US label Kency in 1981, missed most listeners at the time of its release, and so now hits with a fresh power, sounding like a cross between obvious Black Ark / Black Art Lee Perry influences like the Wailers and the Congos (though it's a different song than the Congos' fine 1976 song of the same name).

# DANCEHALL

Dancehall has a reputation among collectors for being a hyper-masculinist genre, and it has been plagued by accusations of homophobia and misogyny. Blatantly gay-bashing songs like Buju Banton's hit "Boom Bye" (1992) have been an albatross around the genre's neck for some time. Social scientists Keon West and Noel M. Cowell even claimed in a 2014 article that dancehall fandom in Jamaica was a stronger indicator for "prejudice against lesbians and gay men" than education, religion, and socioeconomic status. Then again, the world's general power structure is hyper-masculinist, homophobic, and misogynistic—we say this not to make an example of something uniquely pathological about Jamaica vis-à-vis the "West," but only to point out that this notorious characterization of dancehall is both a genuine problem in music more generally and not all there is to dancehall records in particular. While this is a problem associated with some artists in the genre, it does not exhaust it, any more than the right-wing crusader Delores Tucker finished the discussion of rap when she called Tupac a misogynist. First-wave dancehall especially has been buried underneath these discussions. Michigan and Smiley's *Rub-a-Dub Style* (1979), just to name one, is a landmark record. And perhaps because of the political context in which dancehall emerged, many of its female artists' achievements have only come into focus in recent years. Sister Nancy's *One, Two* (Techniques, 1982), Sister Carol's *Liberation for Africa* (Serious Gold, 1983), and Shelly Thunder's *Small Horsewoman* (Witty, 1986) are essentials, as is Ranking Ann's dubbed-out *A Slice of English Toast* (Ariwa, 1982).

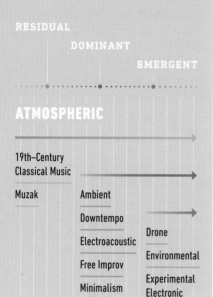

ATMOSPHERIC

| | | |
|---|---|---|
| 19th–Century Classical Music | → | |
| Muzak | Ambient | |
| | Downtempo | → |
| | Electroacoustic | Drone |
| | Free Improv | Environmental |
| | Minimalism | Experimental Electronic |
| | Modern Classical | Industrial |
| | *Musique Concrète* | *Kosmiche* |
| | | Library Music |
| | | Minimal Synth |
| | | Noise |
| | | Private Issue New Age (PINA) |

# ATMOSPHERIC

Ambient · Downtempo · Drone · Electroacoustic · Environmental · Experimental Electronic · Free Improv · Industrial · Library · *Kosmiche* · Minimalism · Minimal Synth · Modern Classical · *Musique Concrète* · Muzak · New Age · 19th-Century Classical · Noise · Private Issue New Age (PINA)

By atmospheric, I mean those records that work primarily with sound textures and create an imagined environment in the listener's mind. When atmospheric tracks feature traditional melodies or rhythms, they have been used sparingly and are often placed subliminally low in the mix. In other words, they are secondary to the open and immersive atmospherics these musics tend to create.

The dominant form of atmospheric music has largely been defined by one figure's records and self-referential criticism: Brian Eno. His music and writings consolidated the concept of ambient music, which is the dominant subgenre by which atmospheric music is understood today. His *Ambient* record series, his label imprint Obscure Records' releases of atmospheric music from the likes of Gavin Byers, Harold Budd, and Michael Nyman, and his collaborations with Harmonia, Cluster, David Bowie, Laraaji, and Jon Hassell form a large part of the corpus of ambient music. Eno gives his own definition of the genre in the liner notes to *Ambient 1*: "Ambient music must be able to accommodate many levels of listening attention without enforcing one in particular; it must be as ignorable as it is interesting."[8] This must be one of the most frequently quoted statements by a musican: so much so that it's been taken on by many as received wisdom. Eno's definition of ambient here is capacious enough to include the work of many twentieth-century composers, mostly "minimalists"—Erik Satie, Steve Reich, Philip Glass, Byers, and Nyman, as well as John Adams and many others. What's more, by positioning this music between nonentity (the "ignorable") and interest, he claims for it a status between Muzak and nineteenth-century classical music. As an ambivalent, compromise form, it can be taken seriously like classical without demanding absolute attention. On the other hand, it transcends Muzak by not being *just* ignorable. Eno's vision of a procedural, cybernetic, composerly music has dominated how we think of atmospheric music.

Muzak and nineteenth-century classical music are the residual genres of atmospheric records. While individual classical records go for outrageous prices (here's looking at you, Leonid Kogan!), only highly specialized collectors mess with them. And as for Muzak, there are no records to collect and, in any case, no market for their sound. While obvious antagonists in the high-low culture wars of days of yore, the two forms have bled into one another in a million ads, film and TV scores, and run-of-the-mill compilations to such a degree that popular interest in classical records has been completely blunted. This means, by the way, that there's room both for a true expert in the field to make some scores and for newbies to build a classical vinyl collection of staples for cheap.

What's emerging in atmospheric music is a broadening of horizons past Eno's definitions and practice. His records and writings remain essential to the foundations of atmospheric music, but they no longer center it. First, the work of German *kosmiche* and Berlin school artists—Harmonia, Kluster / Cluster, Neu!, Ash Ra Tempel, and Klaus Schulze, from whom Eno drew so much inspiration—has been rightly foregrounded in recent years. Second, non-Western countries, particularly Japan—both in gentle works like Hiroshi Yoshimura's and harsher DIY bedroom sounds on labels like DD—have their own long-running atmospheric music scenes. The Netherlands, Italy, and Scandinavia, too, have all staked out their own versions of ambient that sound distinct from Eno's canonical one.

## PRIVATE-ISSUE NEW AGE AND LIBRARY

In addition to the widening of geographic horizons, I also see a turn toward private-issue new age (PINA) and library records. On the one hand, people are getting into American and German new age traditions with therapeutic and / or spiritual approaches to new age quite different from Eno's detached, composer-as-theorist vibe. This music tends to be more low-fidelity and homemade than Eno's brand of ambient. And unlike Eno, many new age musicians took a more ambivalent approach to modern electronics. Whereas Eno touted the concept of the studio as an instrument, it's not uncommon to find new age musicians boasting that "NO SYNTHESIZERS were used in the making of this music" on their sleeve or J-card. (Thanks to new age music mensch Grant Bisher for this point.) Even the more high-tech-friendly new age folk are not content to let the machines run generative processes unaided—they want to direct their music with signs of their human agency—for healing and meditative effects.

On the other hand, library records have emerged as another alternative to the Eno school of ambient. If new age committed atmospheric music to specific spiritual purposes, library music channeled it to directly economic ones. Library records were recorded explicitly for use in commercials, by TV stations like the BBC, and for film scores. Musicians for hire on labels like KPM and Sonoton in Britain, for example, would knock out session after session of recordings, which would then later be licensed by production companies making TV commercials and shows, radio jingles, and (often low-budget and genre) movies. They were never sold in record stores, and if these recordings weren't used for a project, no one ever heard them. At best, they were filed away in music "libraries"; at worst, they were thrown in the dumpster. As a result, people have become keenly interested in collecting library music—despite the industrial nature of its production, many library records are fantastic. Unlike ambient, they do not seek to be almost ignorable. This is atmospheric music that, as fitting its economic origin, explicitly attempts to generate moods—of tension, relaxation, fear, and pleasure.

The first obvious thing about ambient and new age music is that they dispensed with one traditional justification for the aesthetic: the freedom of art from practical use, what Kant called its "purposiveness without purpose." Instead, its industrial origins in library music were if anything played up by Brian Eno's functional subtitling of *Ambient 1* "Music for Airports." The same goes for new age music, which was often made for use in particular settings like yoga retreats, relaxation workshops, conferences, self-help workshops, and cultish community meetings. What new age music and, to a lesser extent, ambient allow is an experience of power seemingly purified of politics. Whether it's the soft control of hypnotism played with by Young Scientist and Precipitation, the white magic of sonic healing promoted by Constance Demby, or the benign stereotyping of astrology, new age allows a feeling of power without responsibility for that power's effects in the real world. On the astral plane and in altered states of consciousness, one feels beyond earthly things.

Of course, the autonomy of art was always an oversimplification, a conceptual ideal rather than a material reality, but it was perhaps historically a real ideal—ambient and new age explicitly sought to perform specific affective effects on its audiences. The line between mystical revelation and crowd control/social engineering was blurred by music made for public settings, as a sort of second-order spiritualization of Muzak.

Passivity is at the heart of PINA's surprising resurgence. It projects an anti-individual, post-rational cosmic sound world. The individual is dissolved, and in its place comes a world without agents, without subjects or active verbs. The song titles are external descriptions of processes with human agency subtracted ("Freewheel to Freedom" [Carl Matthews]), passive states of being ("Brainless" [Young Scientist]), or pictorial descriptions of objects ("Crystal Waters" [Moolah] and "Merry Forest" [Ariel Kalma]). More than one excellent new age song is called "Space Walk"—the space walk being a paradigmatic experience of cosmic passivity. This free-floating sense of vastness, slow and directionless, represents both the appeal and the limitations of the genre. The appeal comes from the suspension of the need for decision and the need for development, in favor of an unfolding process. In general, PINA fosters in listeners what Keats called "negative capability": an indeterminate relation to decision, a holding in suspension of judgment and determinations. But if direction and agency are lost track of completely, the liberating cosmic vision of atmospheric music can turn into aimlessness.

The self-understanding of many new age artists as shamans is of course not new for popular music. Musicians have long dabbled with spirituality and the occult. The image of the musician as some sort of shaman enables a set of analogies to their own profession, an image of themselves as deeper than average, some sort of dark magus or mystic seer. It allows musicians to claim a supernatural power for their work, harking back to the supposed ritual origins of music in sacred ceremonies and festivals. Psychic TV's Thee Temple ov Psychick Youth, *kosmiche* artist Deuter's involvement with the Rajneeshees, and Father Yod's Source Family all spring to mind in this context. Less dramatically, careers in black popular music are often preceded and followed by gospel careers. Alice Coltrane's musical practices culminated in the founding of a Vedantic ashram. Richard and Linda Thompson converted to Sufism, Van Morrison dabbled in Scientology, and so on.

If musical practice in general and mysticism in particular have long been secret sharers, what makes the resurgence of new age (and "spiritual" jazz) unique and specific to our times? As mentioned above, until recently new age was a disreputable genre for "serious" collectors and hipsters alike because of its associations with hippies turned yuppies and its supposed sonic similarities to easy listening and Muzak. Music on late-period Windham Hill and labels like Narada, Lotus, and Higher Octave sound like bland background music no one wants foregrounded and come with distasteful orientalist trappings in both their marketing and music.

New Age's resurgence can be considered a breaking out from the cheesy and politically suspect turn it took in the 1980s. Until recently, yuppie new age obscured the more interesting records, tapes, and CDs out there, but now, these are easier to find and share on the internet. Private-issue new age, as opposed to yuppie new age, was marketed and distributed along underground trade routes. Instead of being routed to traditional record stores, many PINA tapes were sent to niche locations, along a circuit of health food stores, vegan restaurants, and crystal and tarot stores. In this, it's similar to spiritual jazz, which also was distributed through alternative networks—through black bookstores, black arts workshops, communes and ashrams, coffee shops, and cultural centers. As a result, receptive audiences of the time were kept niche. Consequently, reissues have a freshness that comes with delayed distribution. In comparison to the known quantity of Windham Hill that people remember, this stuff sounds like a revelation, often closer to familiar ambient, *kosmiche*, and "space" rock touchstones than George Winston. This, tied to the destigmatization effect we discussed earlier, is a large part of the contemporary new age renaissance.

But the delayed reissue effect and destigmatization effect are not the whole story. They have helped to push the price of originals up and have invigorated interest in the new age genre more generally. If the music didn't speak to us now and cause vital contemporary effects on our hearts and minds, no amount of hype could bring it back from the dead.

It could be that the time is again right for music that flows—for parallel musical processes and mimicry of nature through technological means—hence the titles of David Toop's books on ambient music, *Haunted Weather* and *Ocean of Sound*, the production of a gradual sort of spiritualization and revelry of technology, the mystical effects of landscape, weather, the stars. Though there are exceptional eruptions here and there, the music almost universally taboos violent shifts—it favors molasses-slow development or circular repeated process (its own glacial form of development and revelry in difference through repetition). It is not a representation of nature's full range of sounds, but rather a pastoral or utopian version of nature, skewing toward its gentler sonics as source material and in formal imitation of the natural, and stripped of sounds red in tooth or claw.

· · · · · · · · ● · · · · · · · · · · · ● · · · · · · · · · ● · · · · · · · ·

## ROCK & POP

| | | |
|---|---|---|
| Hard Rock | | |
| Mod | | |
| Rock & Roll | Alt Rock | |
| Surf | Classic Rock | |
| | Emo | AOR |
| | Folk Rock | Black Metal |
| | Garage | Death Metal |
| | Glam | Goth |
| | Grunge | Killed By Death Punk |
| | Hardcore | Krautrock |
| | Indie Rock | No Wave |
| | New Wave | Post-Punk |
| | Punk | Psych |
| | Rockabilly | Synth Punk |
| | | Thrash |
| | | Yacht Rock |

# ROCK AND POP

Alt Rock · AOR · Art Rock · Black Metal · Bubblegum · Cheesecake · Comedy · Death Metal · Doom Metal · Garage · Glam · Goth · Grindcore · Grunge · Emo · Exotica · Folk Rock · Freakbeat · Fuzz · Hair Metal · Hardcore · Hard Rock · Hot Rod · Indie Rock · KBD Punk · Krautrock · Lounge · Mod · New Wave · Novelty · No Wave · Power Pop · Post-Punk · Powerviolence · Prog · Psych · Radio Spots · Rockabilly · Shockabilly · Soft Rock · Soundtrack · Spoken Word · Stoner Metal · Streetpunk · Sunshine Pop · Surf · Swamp Rock · Synth Punk · Teen · Thrash · Yacht Rock (Easy Glide)

The dominant rock tradition stretches from the classic rock of the 1960s, to the hard rock and proto-metal of the '70s, to the punk and new wave of the late '70s and the early '80s, to the alternative rock of the '80s, to the indie rock of the '90s. From the Beatles to Pavement, guitar rock has held a pride of place in the critical imagination. In *Rolling Stone*, *Spin*, *The Village Voice*, and now even on *Pitchfork* and smaller music sites, rock still garners an inordinate amount of attention. As a result, its canonical genres and albums, the fodder for 1,001 best-of-decade and best-ever lists, are more generally established than the other genres we're discussing. The Beatles, Bob Dylan, the Rolling Stones, the Who, Neil Young, Led Zeppelin, David Bowie, the Ramones, the

Clash, R.E.M., U2, Metallica, Pavement, and Radiohead—these and the many records consonant with their style make up the by now slightly shopworn rock canon. Boomers and Gen Xers, even indie types with college radio, love guitar rock! (I am a rock fan myself, by the way, and still count Bob Dylan as my favorite artist.) And the known canon of rock classics, now encompassing parts of the punk, alternative, and indie rock genres, can be dependably sold online for high if not always outrageous prices.

The residual rock genres, as you might expect, are those at its origins—the blues- and R&B-derived (some would say stolen) 1950s and early 1960s music of acts like Little Richard, Buddy Holly, Gene Vincent, Elvis Presley, and Jerry Lee Lewis. Rockabilly and early rock and roll loom large in historical accounts of the genre but have only a highly mediated, abstract influence on the rock music being made today. Individual songs from the time can jump out at us as still vital—Buddy Holly's "Tell Me How" still has the power to startle us as the blueprint for the Velvet Underground's sound. And figures underappreciated in their time, like Bobby Fuller, sound fresher and more exciting to us than those who have been run into the ground on oldies radio. But for the most part, we use '50s rock as a fixed point against which to track historical and aesthetic changes in the genre.

Against this backdrop, collectors have been carving up the monoliths of rock into niche genres and boutique movements. At once an effort of reconceptualization and rebranding, this can maybe best be understood as a means to make rock relevant again in an era of easier access to all genres. Specified and mined down into microgenres like lo-fi, stoner, synth punk, shoegaze, dream pop, no wave, psych, goth, and garage, rock sheds its "rockist" associations as the default music of everyone's parents and grandparents. For many, collecting the oddball and weirdo swerves of the genre is now more invigorating than hunting down a low-numbered *White Album* or a "first state" Butcher cover of *Yesterday and Today*. This microgentrification of rock also gives plausible deniability to those with an Oedipal fear that they are simply reenacting the musical taste of their parents. It's rock with a different emphasis, and different core sounds and canonical records.

The overheated battle between "rockists" and "poptomists" in the early 2000s left no survivors. Critiques which identified "rockism" as ideology that treated rock music as more serious, formally inventive, and intellectually weighty than other genres were convincing. All you had to do was grow up with a hippie and/or boomer dad, read *Rolling Stone* or *Spin*, or even watch *MTV News* to know the critics had a point. On the other hand, those who celebrated "poptomism"—the elevation of top 40 hits to objects of serious, high critical attention—simply took over the methods and political assumptions of the rockists and applied them to pop. Either that or they blithely began to assume that the popular was popu*list*, as if a whole corporate music industry with huge marketing teams and a system of celebrity did not come between the "people" and their musical products. The result was something totally uncritical, a willingness to take corporate music at face value. In many ways, this debate restaged the debate within contemporary literary studies of the divide between high culture (modernist) and low culture (mass culture), but with rock, jazz, and token outliers from other genres (for example, Kraftwerk, Caetano Veloso, Public Enemy) standing for high culture (with its own academic apparatus) and top 40 pop standing in for low. Such critics were slow to realize distinctions between high and low culture are no longer relevant.

The only positive outcome of this otherwise absurd war of words was that it exposed the weakness of both positions: Plumping for either rock or contemporary pop seems a major category error. Anyone who listens to just classic rock vinyl and its immediate outshoots or just buys Pitchfork's "Best New Music" recommendations needs to expand their horizons.

True heads today have internalized the critiques of rockism and poptomism and moved beyond them. Collecting vinyl has proven to be an antidote to both popular media narratives; when you build your own collection from the ground up, you can more clearly see when people are bullshitting. In the case of the rock genre, some collectors have broken off from the "main" paths laid out in popular media. Today's record collectors show more indifferent respect than genuine love for the classic rock canon. This says nothing about the inherent qualities of classic rock artists, rather that, for newcomers, they come with a lot of generational and even Oedipal baggage. Fairly well-known contemporaries of the so-called rock gods are now more interesting to collectors than those "rock gods" themselves. For example, the Flamin' Groovies, the Byrds, Judee Sill, Free, and so on hold more appeal than boomer rock masters like the Rolling Stones, the Beatles, Joni Mitchell, and Led Zeppelin. The only semi-respectable approach to these old gods among heads now is a completist knowledge, a deep head knowledge way beyond the run-of-the-mill interest in Lennon-McCartney or *Blood on the Tracks*.

Another collecting trend has been to invest oneself (both financially and psychologically) in subgenres, swerves from the dominant rock modes. Below, we will detail a few of these: garage, KBD punk, D-beat, "art punk," extreme metal, *kosmiche*, and psych. This investment in "minor" rock musics is both logical and an overcorrection: No musical genre of the twentieth century has been more heavy-handedly gatekept by the mainstream media. Most have heard a lot more about the hugely popular rock genre in their daily lives than they have about other genres. For example, the continued investment in indie rock is baffling unless one sees it as the afterglow of rock's hegemony over the twentieth-century imagination. Because of rock's general overexposure, the paths less traveled in rock history appeal to many wishing to only slightly expand their tastes. When you start collecting rock records for yourself, you quickly recognize how much the established canon fails to cover.

Ideally, one would have time to absorb both the major and minor rock records and everything in between. If you did, you could put together an image of how major and minor relate to one another as a larger system. But the demands of the present moment mean that there is only so much you can hear from the ever-expanding archive of music. So as a sort of collector's triage, many rock collectors either fetishize obscurity for its own sake or stick with the major figures. Both are understandable temptations, if lamentable end-runs around the larger problem. The true breakthrough would perhaps be getting rid of major and minor thinking altogether, but we aren't there yet. There is too much to catch up with in the past that has only recently come to light, and we will be absorbing it for a long time. Reissue labels put obscurities back into the world, but these are really only the starting place for reconstructions of music history because the label with the rights to reissue something may not be the right one to contextualize it. And perspectives develop over time. People have been talking about *Revolver* for over fifty years, but some heads are still yet to hear its contemporary *Morgen*. Even well-known records like the 13th Floor Elevators' first two LPs are underrated in the sense that some people who like rock music haven't heard them, and they are not generally considered equal to or better than the Beatles. But arguments of contemporary popularity and influence are not necessarily decisive for arguments about relevance now. Now that the hold of the 1960s on the popular imagination has slackened, it has become totally reasonable to argue, say, against the Beatles in favor of the Elevators—or to think of them as musical equals.

## GARAGE ROCK

Garage rock has long offered a DIY vision that is more down-to-earth and accessible than other forms, and it's now highly collectible. Search for garage on Popsike and you'll find big price results for records from the Sonics, Fly-Bi-Nites, the Savages, the Rising Storm, and Moving Staircases. Any teenage band in their parents' garage can make a record, and it can sound as good as or better than those made in the big studios. As it favors low-fidelity, homemade sounds, and simple chords and conventions, the genre appeals to those who have tired of rock grandiosity. The essential idea of Lenny Kaye's *Nuggets* compilation was that what he calls "punk" was available to anyone, not just those living in New York or London. Primarily a 45 genre, garage's appeal is its immediacy. It was made by people "just like you" and didn't require a lot of means to do so—it seems closer to raw and weird vernacular expression than the polished pretense of *Sgt. Pepper's*. Garage allows the collector to sustain a vision of rock's "essence," uncorrupted by ornamentation, studio trickery, or puffed-up delusions of grandeur. But for the same reason, garage gets boring. It becomes its own cliché and gets monotonous. The reduction of rock to its rawest rudiments, part of its initial appeal, proved in the long run to have been an exhaustible formal approach. The same goes for many of the first wave of punk records, from which only a few recordings, like the first few Ramones LPs and the best individual Oi! tracks (Cockney Rejects' "Bad Man"), still sound vital.

# PUNK

I have no interest in defining what records are and aren't punk in 2020. But it seems clear that the most interesting punk and hardcore collectors are united in their sense that hyped first-wave punk of the Sex Pistols and the Clash is moribund. It functions in an analogous way as "old-school" rap does to trap and drill, broadside ballads do to modern singer-songwriters, and so on, as finished, more a monument than a living source of inspiration. Like garage, the sped-up '50s rock of early punk became tired quickly, even as its use as a fashion signifier became ubiquitous. The flight from this classic rock version of punk, now demystified as nothing more than rawer Gene Vincent or proto-radio new wave, has taken many paths. One path has been to dig deeper into the transgressive and homemade contents of early punk. The *Killed by Death* compilations of rare and obscure punk 45s have started a collectors' subgenre of their own. You'll now see a KBD tag on some of the more expensive punk auction titles. These compilations feature song after song about serial killers like the Hillside Strangler and Son of Sam, Nazis, aberrant sex, and suicide. Like random rap, the records were usually made outside of the scene's center, in this case everywhere but New York and London. These records participate in the same sort of scuzzy, young and snotty, anti-commercial, death-driven punk still apotheosized for some by Darby Crash and Dead Boys. For its fans, KBD still seems closer to the street and so "realer." Others have doubled down on the aggression and intensity of purer early hardcore and street punk, exploring the bludgeoning sound of Discharge and their D-beat offspring.

# AVANT-GARDE PUNK

Another swerve for those still interested in rock records has been to focus on more politically savvy bands, those who have attempted to keep faith with the avant-garde notion that vanguard aesthetics were vanguard politics. Much of DIY punk culture has lineages in the avant-garde and modernism of the first half of the twentieth century. Like the avant-gardes, punk and hardcore bands believed music could be a form of political practice. And like the avant-garde movements, the punk scene eschewed the compromising political middle for the extremities of freedom-oriented leftism and a violence-obsessed revanchism. Both depended on experiments in the new media of their times, and both produced manifestos that contextualized and furthered their artistic works. The second generation of punks particularly connected their DIY "messethetics" with communist and anarchist social interventions. For example, records like Crass's *Stations of the Cross* (Crass, 1979) and *Penis Envy* (Crass, 1981), Pop Group's *Y* (Radar, 1979), Lora Logic and Art & Language's theme song to Lizzie Borden's *Born in Flames,* subtitled "The Social Democrats' Song (with Art & Language, Rough Trade, 1980) from a film by Lizzie Borden," Au Pairs' *Playing with a*

*Different Sex* (Human, 1981), and the early 45s of Scritti Politti like "Is and Ought in the Western World" (St. Pancras, 1978) and "Hegemony" (Rough Trade, 1979) all thematized problems of exploitation, gender, class, and racial inequality. But they did it in a less direct, more "art-damaged" way than the earlier, angry first-wave of punk and hardcore groups. Despite its swerve from the hardcore sound, this was not music for yuppie liberals, either. The same can't be said for much American new wave like Blondie and Talking Heads, who left themselves wide open to criticism by their exclusion or trivialization of politics—for example, the camp pastiche of Talking Heads' "Life During Wartime" (Sire 7", 1979). Sections of Simon Reynolds's *Rip It Up and Start Again: Postpunk 1978–1984* (not concerned with his very British obsession with New Romantics like ABC) are an excellent guide to these late modernist experiments in political commitment through aesthetic experiment.

## ART PUNK

But the most enduring have been the bands who innovated most on a formal level, the bands who injected synthesizers and other nontraditional rock instruments, composerly experiments, and new rhythmic ideas into what is loosely called "art punk." Under this rubric, I include many records more conventionally called post-punk, minimal wave, EBM (electronic body music), industrial, and *NDW* (*Neue Deutsche Welle*). The records of such groups are abstract and their lyrics so encrypted that direct political references come few and far between. Yet this work can be considered a political achievement insofar as their records create whole alternate worlds of sound. Rather than focus on one injustice at a time, the best of these records represent a wholesale rejection of the world that produces injustice in general. They are standing reproaches to a world that cannot live up to their own intensity, neither in depth of expression nor conceptual creativity. In this category, some conspicuous examples include Cabaret Voltaire's *The Crackdown* (Virgin, 1983), Lora Logic's *Pedigree Charm* (Rough Trade, 1982), Devo's *Q: Are We Not Men? A: We Are Devo!* (Warner Bros., 1978), Pere Ubu's early 45s, the Raincoats' *The Raincoats* and *Odyshape* (Rough Trade, 1981), the first two Suicide LPs, This Heat's *Deceit* (Rough Trade, 1981), Throbbing Gristle's *20 Jazz Funk Greats* (Industrial, 1979), Coil's *Horse Rotorvator* (Force & Form, 1986), and the first few D.A.F. and Wire records. While some may be tempted to throw in no wave records here, that movement seemed too exclusive and tied to the coterie New York art world to qualify. Like Fluxus before it, no wave (with a few exceptions: Mars's "Helen Forsdale" is a banger) did not actually produce records that rejected the world as it is. Rather, they often reproduced the status quo of a small art scene for that same scene.

# EXTREME METAL

Though "extreme" metal fans love to bring up the genre's origins in early punk as a way to stake its validity as serious music, it's still a hard sell to many. Compared with the innovations on the "art punk" records listed above, much black and death metal sounds cartoonish. While some play up the working-class origins of, say, Florida death metal (like Slayer and Morbid Angel) in order to connect it with punk, this argument can only take us so far. Yes, some death metal was raw and heavy. And hey, who doesn't love a good blastbeat now and again? But even the best death metal becomes monotonous after a little while.

Black metal, however, is an even harder pill to swallow. Though its fans deny it, much of their fascination with the genre still comes from romanticizing its "dark" biographical elements—the church burnings, suicides, and murders in its recent Scandinavian past. The fact that black metal artists frequently dress up in corpse paint has done little to dispel the suspicion that black metal has become an outlet for middle-aged Caucasian edge lords. While the backing tracks of groups like Mayhem, Bathory, and Emperor can be emotionally resonant, the occult darkness many black metal vocalists strain for usually results in bathos rather than pathos. Black metal often lands squarely in Spinal Tap territory. Couple this with the genre's neofascist and white supremacist tendencies, and it often is just not worth the effort to sort the wheat from the chaff. While writer Kim Kelly and a minority of lefty musicians and fans are fighting the good fight to make extreme metal a more inclusive, less politically retrograde genre, this still seems to be an uphill battle. If all metal embodied the spirit of Napalm Death's cover for *Scum* (Earache, 1987), things would be much better. But as it is, if you have to google every record in a genre to make sure it isn't racist and fascist, there's something seriously wrong. Those still interested start by checking out https://www.metal-archives.com.

# PSYCH

If metal records offer the occasion to purge rage, psychedelic records promise the dispersal of such socially conditioned rage. Tracks like Psycheground Group's "Traffic" (Psychedelic and Underground Music, Lupus, 1971), Mad River's "Amphetamine Gazelle" (S/T, Capitol, 1968), and the entire 13th Floor Elevators catalog aim to relax the grip of the everyday. The same goes for spacy classics from Cold Sun; Morgen; the first line-up of Pink Floyd; Träd, Gräs & Stenar (and offshoots); the Chocolate Watchband; Daybreak; Bread, Love and Dreams; Relatively Clean Rivers; the C.A. Quintet; and many others. They aim to produce a Dionysian headspace in the listener, in which they can zone out and deprogram themselves of society's conditioning. Unlike new age, however, the best psych records are also intense, even aggressive at times. The point is not to lull listeners to sleep so much as to vitalize them into the realization that everyday existence is a façade—in other words, to rip the veil from the everyday and expose its horrors and absurdities as illusory. But psych records provide glimpses of transcendence that require their listener to complete and then manifest. One shouldn't let one's communion with the cosmic absolute turn into its reverse: condescension. This would be to take the universalist form and content of the music against its grain. The best psych records provide access to new zones of engagement with the world, and so shouldn't be used as a back-door means to assert one's dominance over the hoi polloi. This music provides access to otherwise blocked means of imagination and connection, not a way to spiritualize the status quo.

## KRAUTROCK

German experimental music represents a gateway for many classic rock fans to get into more outré sounds, whether they be psychedelic, electronic, or ambient. A single career like Manuel Göttsching's, for example, covers all three. Kraftwerk started out as the rock band Tone Float/Organization before engineering an electronic renaissance. Popol Vuh started as a Moog synthesizer research project. Suzanne Doucet's career bridges krautrock with new age, as does Deuter's and Brainticket's Joel Vandroogenbroeck. As opposed to the Anglo-American rock tradition, the appeal of the so-called *kosmiche* or *motorik* music is rooted in its hybrid musical sensibility. Its artists either take rock structures and surround them with non-rock synths or robotic beats (for example, Jaki Leibzeit's drumming for Can), or turn rock into something completely different (for example, the romantic soundtracks of Popol Vuh or the wholly electronic works of Kraftwerk and Ash Ra Tempel). The music stands on the verge of many genres—rock (Can), dance (Neu!, Kraftwerk), neo-classical (Cluster, Popol Vuh)—without ever fully committing to one. As a result of such flexibility, German experimental music has become a sort of skeleton key for collectors looking to dip into many genres. It is best considered a transitional genre, rather than a fixed achievement. It best functions as an archive of possibilities, future directions for music, rather than the endpoint of a discrete historical process: its strength was always its ability to push the limits of rock without breaking them. But it fell on later developments to complete this process, whether they be techno, new age, or ambient. In this, kraut and *kosmiche* resemble Italo, which similarly bridged the worlds of pop with a whole host of electronic musics.

As a German product, it seems to offer more philosophical rigor than Anglo-American psych rock, whether in its teenybopper or edgier, harder later developments. Not only is the music immediately compelling to many mainstream rock fans, but it also comes with an air of avant-intellectualism that British psych bands like Hawkwind do not. For example, Klaus Schulze's *Irrlicht* comes with a diagrammatic liner note insert that states at the top *"Musik ist Ästhetisierte Frequenz."* It then attempts to theoretically chart *Irrlicht's* union of two contrary strands of musical history, between consciously formed traditional music and more *unheimlich*, subterranean noise. The diagram starts with *"frequenz"* (sound at its most general) and ends in the *"bewusstsein"* (consciousness), presumably Schulze's, which segues into the *"produktion"* of his tape loop setup used to make the record. It's unimaginable that one would find such a theoretical self-analysis on US and UK psych records from the era. This accounts for its strong appeal for both more academic humanities types and druggier psych "heads."

HIP-HOP

Disco Rap

Old School

Turntablism

Boom Bap

Conscious

Crunk

Indie

Electro

New Jack
Swing

Gangsta

Random Rap

G-Funk

Jazz Rap

Miami Bass

# HIP-HOP

Backpack · Bass · Boom Bap · Bounce
· Chopped & Screwed · Conscious
· Disco · Drill · Dub · East Coast ·
Electro · G-Funk · Grime · Hip-House
· Horrorcore · Houston · Indie · Jazz
· Memphis · Random · Southern
· Trap · Trip-Hop · Turntablism
· West Coast

While hip-hop is the youngest genre under discussion in these chapters (born in the mid-1970s Bronx), it's had plenty of time to fracture into several subgenres. Under the weight of history, these subgenres have experienced different fates. Some feel fresh and generative while others seem more like moribund museum pieces. The rap you hear on contemporary radio draws on some subgenres heavily, while ignoring others.

The most critically and commercially popular records of the late 1980s and '90s have become the rap canon for record collectors. The era's subgenres—G-funk, gangsta, boom bap, indie, and to a lesser extent "Southern" rap—so dominate the tastes of collectors that many call the period they dominated the "golden age" (roughly 1987–1993) and "silver age" (roughly 1993–1997) of hip-hop. Any self-respecting rap fan can rattle off the epochal records from these eras—Eric B. and Rakim's *Follow the Leader* (UNI, 1988) and *Paid in Full* (4th & Broadway, 1987), Public Enemy's *It Takes a Nation of Millions to Hold Us Back* (Def Jam, 1988), Dr. Dre's *The Chronic* (Interscope, 1992), Snoop's *Doggystyle* (Death Row, 1993), Nas's *Illmatic* (Columbia, 1994), Wu-Tang Clan's *Enter the Wu-Tang (36 Chambers)*

(RCA, 1993), and so on. This was the moment when New Yorkers like Rakim, Nas, and the Notorious B.I.G. upped the lyrical complexity of the genre to a true art form, while producers like the Bomb Squad, Dr. Dre, Havoc, and RZA created backing tracks strong enough to stand alone as funky instrumentals or even electronic music. New York and California dominated the 1990s, only occasionally allowing incursions from elsewhere—Atlanta (Outkast), Memphis (Three 6 Mafia), Cleveland (Bone Thugs-n-Harmony), and coastal Virginia (Missy Elliott and Timbaland).

In this, hip-hop left behind the disco-sampling, nursery rhyme scheming, old-school styles of the hip-hop pioneers of the 1970s and '80s. In fact, the more rappers of the late 1980s and '90s namechecked these pioneers in their songs, the more they departed from the actual sonic blueprint set by the Grandmaster Flashes, Melle Melles, and Kool Moe Dees of the world. Disco rap, sometimes known as simply old school, represents the residual era of hip-hop records—while still collectible, no rapper today would think to return to its style in earnest. While disco rap has been sacralized as the root of all that came after it, most of it undeniably sounds corny, dated, and simplistic to modern ears.

Collectors diversifying their interests outside of these movements have looked to "random rap" and the regional hip-hop scenes outside of New York City and Los Angeles. As we'll detail below, random rap covers independently produced, low-budget 12" records, EPs, and LPs from the golden and silver eras that never broke through. Listening to random rap records, one gets a glimpse of what was happening outside of the major hip-hop labels of the 1990s—Def Jam, Tommy Boy, Priority, and Death Row. Stylistically, random rap troubles our sense of the late 1980s and '90s rap canon—it represents a grab bag of alternate directions for the genre. Some of these records were way ahead of their time, anticipating the trap and drill of today. Others sound like soundalike cousins of more established records, while still others are messy but fascinating experiments in sonic paths not taken.

In addition to seeking out random rap, collectors have also started to dig deep into the scenes surrounding cities like Houston, Memphis, and Atlanta. This is because, in addition to producing known classics and random obscurities, these cities also had vibrant tape, CD, and vinyl scenes circulating their music for strictly local consumption. This has resulted in collectors interested in hearing everything they can from these scenes, and it is responsible for the chronicle *Houston Rap Tapes*,[9] the rise to legend status of figures like DJ Screw, and the rediscovery of rappers like Memphis's Tommy Wright III.

## RANDOM RAP

Though we pay lip service to the innovators of old-school rap, little remains of their sonic blueprint on today's rap radio: Neither the disco and funk-breaks sampling nor the singsong, nursery rhyme flows ("basketball is my favorite sport...") of some of the early practitioners have endured. While it's true that today's global rap industry would not exist without its old-school records having blazed the trail, it's also true that rap is a form that constantly sheds old styles for new. Even one of the best songs of the old-school era, Treacherous Three's "The New Rap Language" (Enjoy 12", 1980) builds off of a nursery rhyme singsong lifted right out of *Mary Poppins*. Clearly, there's no going back to that, and the same goes for the best disco rap, like Manujothi's valuable "Shake Your Body" (Manujothi 45, 1980). The golden age of rap now dominates record collectors' consciousness, if not the contemporary rap charts. The golden age and the silver age that followed demonstrated a quantum leap of sophistication in both production and rhyming. Nevertheless, and in sharp contrast to today's trap and drill, the golden era was driven by a focus on sampling and lyricism.

Other terms to account for periods that came after old school, golden age, and silver age are much fuzzier: The concepts "bronze age" and "mumble rap" obscure more than they explain. This is partially because the music branched out in so many different directions after the so-called silver age ended circa the end of the twentieth century. Geographically, the Midwest, South, and Mid-Atlantic emerged as rivals of the coasts, and international rap scenes sprang up. Stylistically, backpack, indie, and experimental rap splintered off from more commercial forms.

Within the seams of these larger categories, record collectors have become interested in so-called random rap 12" records. Roughly coincident with the golden era, random rap's "randomness" is polyvalent. As in the phrase "that's so random," random can mean the opposite of mainstream/popular, geographically eccentric (not NYC or LA), or sonically "weird." Sometimes, it means all three. Random records did not come out on major labels like Def Jam or Columbia; rather, they were privately pressed by small-time outfits, sometimes in small enough numbers to be considered "vanity" presses never really meant to make money in the first place.

Random works as an aesthetic, geographic, and economic category all at once. While a good random rap 12" often sounds like a "lost" classic from the mainstream era, it's just as often an aesthetic response to that era's dominant standards. A random track like Sons of Sam's "Charisma" (Workshop 12", 1993) uses a treated sample of a Rakim line on 1987's "Let the Rhythm Hit 'Em" (MCA 12", 1990) for its chorus and title. With this, it turns Rakim's legendary flow into a discrete piece of a new song. In addition to being an easier-to-find sample source, chopping up another rap record has the aesthetic effect of turning Rakim into a sort of backup vocalist. Hip Hop Culture's "This Is How It Should Be Done" (*Waste Not Want Not* LP, Perfection, 1990) samples not a Public Enemy beat but just Flavor Flav's "Yeah, boy!" over Steve Miller Band's "Fly Like an Eagle" (*Fly Like an Eagle* LP, Capitol, 1976). One derivation of the "random" tag, then, comes from the spin it puts on the immediate rap past as a primary source of raw material, rather than the funk and jazz breaks associated with boom-bap. The sonic forms of the golden era often become random rap's content. And economically, many of these 12" records and LPs were pressed in limited numbers and sold out of the back of cars, only to give to friends and family and maybe a few radio stations. It's no surprise that as a result of this they are scarce; they did not have big labels doing A&R for them. Which means that, yes, geographically they tended to come from places that had yet to establish themselves on the national, mainstream rap scene of their time: Delaware; Newark, New Jersey; Winston-Salem, North Carolina; even now-known quantities like Houston, Atlanta, and Memphis. At a time when New York City and Los Angeles were the only places to get signed by major labels, random artists in more peripheral locales were doing for themselves and pressing their own records.

So, to be "random," a track must be sonically, economically, and/or geographically eccentric to its own dominant time, or some combination of the three. To complicate matters, the term, like any tag that has become appealing to collectors, has been applied to records that are in no way "random." Anytime a subgenre becomes a hot commodity, in fact, you will see this happen in sales listings: Less-than-scrupulous dealers will throw a tag like "random" on a record it doesn't belong on, fishing for credulous buyers.

Random rap represents neither the source for a parallel history nor a debased mistake better left forgotten. Random is best considered in conversation with the known world of rap highlights, the Wu-Tangs, Rakims, Nases, Biggies, and so on. Random may mean many things, but one thing it doesn't mean is disconnected: It was always plugged into the common culture of rap. The gruff- voiced, Mad-Lionesque Deansta, for example, sends "big up to Method Man, Wu-Tang Clans [sic]" on his druggy, time-bending, dancehall-flavored random 12" "Put Your Hands in the Air" (IZM 12", 1994). Deansta and Wu-Tang were part of the same New York scene, so the first's "randomness" comes down as much to accidents of distribution as anything else. Even with more mainstream figures, sales do not map onto aesthetic value. Behind every Notorious B.I.G., there's a Kool G Rap, behind every Nas there's an AZ and OC, and so on. Crossover success comes down to contingencies of timing, distribution, and networking: The major label system and mass popularity are just as random as anything else. So, we shouldn't let our retrospective sense of what broke into the mainstream cloud our vision of the total field of rap. Tracks like Da Madd Klique's "Come wit It" (Black House Entertainment 12", 1997), Hip City Swingers' "I'm the Man" (B-Brothers Platinum 12", 1992), and Lo-Twon's "Wicked Leaf" (*Wicked Leaf* LP, Player City, 1995) have earned random rap's place at the table. Even a cursory perusal of the fine vinyl reissue label Dope Folks' re-presses should convince any skeptics.

As you might expect, random recordings tend to be more lo-fi than the major label rap of the era, even the grimier contemporary stuff from those on majors like RZA of Wu-Tang and Havoc of Mobb Deep. There was less money for fancy studios, producers, and mixers. While 1990s lo-fi indie rock musicians like Guided by Voices, Sebadoh, and Smog are described as auteurs for music recorded on four-tracks, random rappers using a lo-fi sound have never received the same glowing treatment. In retrospect, the production similarities between lo-fi and random rap are better understood as a manifestation of a formula of Karl Marx: They made their own music, but not under the conditions of their choosing. They were neither geniuses creating with an absolutely free hand nor victims of less-than-ideal studios and janky tape machines.

The vernacular used on random records often differed from what you'd hear on more mainstream recordings of the time. For example, Houston rap records and tapes have a lot of Houston-specific lingo on them. Of course, part of this can be chalked up to geography, but it bears remembering that vernacular in music is part of a stylized presentation and not a documentary reflection of how people *really* talk. Which is to say, rap is representation and not "Black America's CNN" if that is to mean a naturalistic presentation of facts, a direct reflection of empirical truth. While the slang of Houston reflects the street, it also reflects the usage heard on other records. The linguistic regional variations heard on random records are exciting and fascinating, but the immediacy of these records can seduce some to think of their use of language in sociological rather than aesthetic terms.

RESIDUAL

DOMINANT

EMERGENT

**DANCE**

Oldies

Disco

Proto-Disco
(Funk & Soul)

Boogie

Electronic Body
Music (EBM)

House

Italo Disco

Techno

# DANCE

Acid House · Balearic · Baltimore Club
· Bass · Boogie · Breakbeat · Chicago
House · Cosmic Disco · Deep House
· Detroit Techno · Disco · Drum and
Bass · EBM · Electro · Euro Disco ·
Euro House · Freestyle · Footwork
· Gabber · Ghettotech · Happy
Hardcore · Hardcore · Hi NRG ·
House · Italo · Jungle · Mutant Disco
· New Beat · Psy Trance · Synth Pop ·
Techno · UK Garage

Dance music collecting is more tied to music making than any other genre. Unlike many of the other genres, buyers of dance records often *use* them for the purpose of live DJs sets, mixes, and as samples for new records. Due to this fact, dance records must pass the test of public opinion in a way that others do not—DJs must be alert to what moves crowds. Perhaps because the currency of dance records is constantly subject to such tests, trends and fads in collecting turn over faster in dance music than perhaps any other genre. This means there's often a disconnect between what's currently being played in the club and what's hot on the collecting scene. Right now, record collectors and broader music fans are decades behind what's going on in the clubs.

The synthesizer represents the major dividing line in dance collecting. In the 2000s, dance collectors reinvested in disco—in Salsoul Records, Larry Levan, David Mancuso, Tom Moulton—and in proto-disco as crystallized in the smooth Philly soul-funk of Harold Melvin and the Blue Notes' "Bad Luck." Tim

Lawrence's brilliant book *Love Saves the Day*[10] (2003) retold the story of 1970s American dance music for Gen Xers and nascent millennials. For the most part, this was music played "organically" by bands and orchestras. While Levan and company used the turntable to stretch out mixes and beat-match 12" records, the music itself tended not to feature synthesizers, which were then the expensive plaything of prog groups like Emerson, Lake & Palmer. At the same time, supposedly weirder disco records, many of which shared affinities with non-dance genres like punk, began being classed as "mutant disco" or "disco not disco." And around the same time, people started rediscovering the synth-heavy "cosmic disco" of producer Patrick Adams and his work with groups like Cloud One, Universal Robot Band, and Sine. People also started dabbling in synth-happy Italian disco, known as Italo for short. But electronic dance music still felt somewhat remote from the mainstream of hipster collecting.

Soon, though, record collectors fell for the synth-heavy underground dance music of the 1980s and early '90s—above all boogie, house, and techno. These genres, as with every foundational American musical movement, started as black countercultural music. As a result, even white hipsters were slow to start taking them seriously and invest their time and money in collecting records in these genres and subgenres. I am old enough to remember the late 1990s and early 2000s, when you could pass for a clued-in college radio DJ without knowing a thing about disco, boogie, Italo, house, or techno.

But all that's changed now, for better and worse—there's a popular white techno artist who performs under the name the Black Madonna. Black-led synth dance genres are becoming more collectible and are finally being recognized as "important" by (some) mainstream music writers and (some) hipster types, even the ones still clinging to the indie rock glory days. These days, goofily beautiful Italo synths and dour minimal synth dance records are now more popular than orchestral disco. Dance DJs and collectors draw their inspiration more from Detroit, Chicago, and Berlin in the 1980s and '90s than they do New York City in the 1970s. The once-futuristic dance music of the 1980s and '90s now has people dreaming of their own futures. Chicago house and Detroit techno of course were no secret to the mostly black audiences who attended clubs like the Warehouse/Music Box and the Music Institute and were die-hard fans the first time around. But for those not at these clubs when house and techno centered youth culture, the music has hit with a delayed impact. Time will tell if revival and reevaluation will come for the many niche dance subgenres that came out of the raves and clubs of 1990s—gabber, happy hardcore, New Beat, drum and bass, UK garage, and the like. There are already signs that hipsters are dipping their feet in such waters, with the Boiler Room in New York City recently featuring a gabber set alongside its more standard fare.

As you might expect, the R&B, soul, and teen dance music of the 1960s and earlier falls into strictly residual territory for dance collectors today. If a DJ is playing these records, they are doing so in a deliberately retro fashion—for a select audience of aficionados of "oldies" records or as a lingua franca for wedding guests. Songs like the Isley Brothers' "Twist and Shout" and Wilson

Pickett's "Mustang Sally" ceased being relevant to dance audiences decades ago and have now moved into solidly respectable classic territory.

## BOOGIE, BOOGIE FUNK, AND MODERN SOUL

Boogie is what happened to disco after that term was discredited in the public imagination circa 1979. It can be viewed as an updating of disco dance records for the 1980s. With more synths and drum machines, it is distinguished from modern soul by its danceability and its modification of disco grooves and beats. Modern soul and boogie both took inspiration from Michael Jackson. Because his songs are so well known, it might be helpful to think about it this way: "Don't Stop 'Til You Get Enough" is a boogie record, while the slower "Man in the Mirror" is modern soul. A record like L.S. Movement Band's "Move Everything You Got" (LA/Veg 45, 1981) is pure boogie funk, with simple mechanical hand claps, a repeating synth swell, and a drastic step-down rhythm that would make contemporary boogie practitioner Dâm-Funk proud. Modern soul and boogie can of course combine in a single song, for example Curtis Hairston's "I Want You (All Tonight)" (Pretty Pearl 12", 1983), which bears that modern '80s sound in its vocal production and piano adornments but is pure boogie in its rhythm—all treated bass groove, drum pad effects, and synth solos. Zapp's "More Bounce to the Ounce" (WB 12", 1980) and Dayton's "We Can't Miss" (*Hot Funk* LP, Liberty, 1982) are boogie funk, though rap fans may retrospectively categorize them as G-funk. In fact, boogie records—often but not always the ones featuring vocoder—were a foundational influence on electro boogie rap like World Class Wreckin' Cru, which via Dr. Dre led directly into the G-funk rap era. For example, depending what mix you're hearing, in "California Love" alone you'll encounter boogie samples of Kleeer's "Intimate Connection" (*Intimate Connection* LP, Atlantic, 1984), Ronnie Hudson's "West Coast Poplock" (Street People 12", 1982), and Zapp's "Dance Floor" (*Zapp II* LP, WB, 1982). The revival of the boogie sound in the 2000s is sometimes called "sweater funk," after dance parties thrown in San Francisco, itself inspired by LA's Funkmosophere boogie sets. Reissues from labels like Andrew Morgan's Peoples Potential Unlimited, City of Dreams in the US, and Barely Breaking Even in the UK, along with a host of other labels, have helped keep the boogie fires burning in the hearts of collectors.

## DISCO AND ITALO

A large portion of white boomers hated disco. The racist and homophobic scorn for the music on display at the Disco Demolition Night in the old Comiskey Park in 1979 has become a well-known symbol for white rockist resistance to dance music. Even many of the best punk, hardcore, and metal bands of the early 1980s shared this resentment of disco. As a result, by 1982, "disco" had become discredited in popular culture as mass-produced junk. But this did not mean the death of the disco aesthetic; the actual dance scene and musical forms lived on in altered form under the catchall name "club" music in America and "boogie" in Europe. In any case, since then, a critical reversal has taken place. In Lawrence's *Love Saves the Day*, the utopian potentials of both disco music and disco lifestyle are stressed. Lawrence finds in disco an open and loving scene, interested in the search for transcendent communal aesthetic experiences. At the same time, in the late 1990s and early 2000s, younger record collectors of my generation were going back to disco without the preconceptions of either boomers or hardcore punks. I remember playing Flakes' "Sugar Frosted Lover" on my radio show around this time and having my father call me afterward in surprise that he could "like a disco song so much." Clearly, times were changing. Reissue labels like Disco Strut and a rebooted ZE Records were becoming popular, and the "left-field" or "mutant" disco tag was born to make rock-oriented hipsters feel cool in liking dance music. The awkward compound phrase "dance punk" was in the air. Italo instrumentals, the ones that sounded more professional, closer to Kraftwerk, house, and electro funk, were hot again—Doctor's Cat's "Feel The Drive" (Il Discotto 12", 1983), Charlie's "Spacer Woman" (Mr. Disc Organization 12", 1983), Pluton and Humanoids's "World Invaders" (V.S. 12", 1981), and the like. In 2004, Dutch DJ I-F started the internet radio station Cybernetic Broadcasting System (CBS). In addition to their Italo-heavy shows, they published top 100 lists running down their recent obscure Italo 12" discoveries. Though I-F rightly points out that CBS played a lot more than just Italo, the lists, along with I-F's *Mixed Up in the Hague* compilations, were a huge impetus for the Italo revival.

Now, at a time when dance and electronic are staples of college radio playlists and online radio streams, it's easy to forget how recently it was that things changed. Fifteen years ago, underground and indie rock were still king. Of course, there were folks who loved dance from day one, but the integration of dance and electronic into college radio, for example, which the label DFA capitalized on, happened late in the history of popular music. In the early 2000s, dance became hot for non-dancing collectors. Reissues of Arthur Russell, DFA's artists' outright aping of dance classics, alongside Cologne-label Kompakt's and Berlin's Basic Channel's "minimal techno" vibe, made it okay for neophyte radio kids to listen to stuff other than indie rock. Suddenly, Giorgio Moroder was a hero again.

This movement included a rage for Italo instrumentals. But in Italy in the '80s, the "Italo" tracks that tended to be popular were the ones with lyrics and vocals dripping with sleazy pop schmaltz, like Ryan Paris's hit "Dolce Vita" (Discomagic 12", 1983), or the embarrassing disco rap of Pino D'Angiò's "Ma Quale Idea" (Rifi 7", 1980). The popular Italo of its time was corny and oversexed, but endearingly so. This was not the stuff that American hipsters in the late 1990s and early 2000s were picking up on. "Mutant," "left-field," and above all "space" became modifiers attached to Italo in the 2000s in order to make it safe for American hipsters weaning themselves off MTV's *120 Minutes* and *Spin* magazine.

Italo's origins were as much a product of vinyl scarcity as artistic inspiration. American disco records were hard to come by in the Italy of the late 1970s. So, with access to the real thing blocked, some enterprising Italian musicians took a stab at making their own dance tracks. Italo popularized synths in disco. For example, in a track like Doctor's Cat's "Feel the Drive," warm electronics, washes, and solos are played against more regimented arpeggiated lines. Italo is electronics with a human face: There's nothing clinical about it. Rather than fighting over its authenticity, it's better to see Italo as a representation of a playful response to cybernetics and modern technology. The female vocals, the warm electronics, and the more *motorik* rhythms of the track relate as separate systems, complementary but not fused. The best Italo tracks combine such warm human elements with mechanically looping synth rhythms. For example, this can be said on Mr. Flagio's "Take a Chance on Me" (Squish 12", 1983), in which a vocoder and a human voice duet. Italo represents a world in which the machine can be used as a means to human enjoyment, or at least the invention and prolongation of desire. Italo's introduction of synthesizers into the center of disco was incredibly playful. Rather than following the self-seriousness of speed, violence, and heartlessness that "the machine" offered to the Italian futurists, the synthesizer and vocoder seem to offer the possibility of high tech with a sense of humor. In the home of Marinetti and the proto-fascist Futurists of Italy's modernist era, this must have come as quite a relief!

## HOUSE AND TECHNO

The resurgence of Italo and "mutant" disco in the late 1990s and early 2000s paved the way for the current resurgence of interest in house and techno. Both Chicago house and Detroit techno of the 1980s drew inspiration from Europe, itself an early adopter of synth culture. The Chicago house scene took rhythmic cues from German stuff like Kraftwerk's "Numbers" and Manuel Göttsching's *E2-E4* (Inteam GmbH, 1984), and the Detroit techno scene soon followed. At the same time, house and techno DJs were paying close attention to Italo 12" records like Kano's "Holly Dolly" (Emergency, 1980), Doctor's Cat's "Feel the Drive" (Il Discotto, 1983), A Number of Names' "Sharevari" (Capriccio, 1981), Klein & MBO's "Dirty Talk" (Zanza, 1982), Alexander Robotnick's "Problèmes D'Amour" (Fuzz Dance, 1983), Simonetti/Pignatelli/Morante's "Tenebre" (Cinevox, 1982), 'Lectric Workers' "Robot Is Systematic" (Discomagic, 1982), Capricorn's "I Need Love" (Delirium, 1982), and others. For example, an Italo record like D.F. and Pam's "On The Beat" (World, 1983)—which blends a funk/soul vocal with a borderline cheesy synth, pad drums, and a mechanistic guitar line—in retrospect sounds very close to a house track.

Derrick May, one of the architects of Detroit techno, claims to have been the first to bring Italo records from Chicago to Detroit. As its name suggests, techno was a more transhumanist enterprise than Italo or house, and often aimed at a cybernetic fusion of musician with musical technology. The cover of Cybotron's *Enter* LP

(Fantasy, 1983) represents this cyborg ideal. It shows a realistically rendered runner merging with an abstract computer green screen. The panel "digitizes" the runner's image into choppy cyber patterns. A record like Juan Atkins's Model 500's "Testing 1-2" (Metroplex 12", 1986), with its chopped and panned vocal samples and pummeling synth line, sits uneasily between the dancefloor and a more headphone-friendly headspace. Compared to Italo, the sound of techno is a sleeker, more integrated one, in which everything human and natural sounding becomes processed, even the human singing voice. In general, Chicago house and Detroit techno are less ornamental and more minimal even than Italo. Rhythm Is Rhythm's "Strings of Life" (Transmat 12", 1987) aside, the orchestral flourishes that one associates with '70s dance music have been subtracted out of the mix. The result is a leaner, more streamlined sound—and one that has made it easier to emulate by new musicians.

As dance record maven Zack Richardson told me, part of the appeal of house and techno now seems to rest in the historical oblivion of the genres' first, classic Chicago and Detroit iterations. As a result, these scenes, highly localized to specific cities and historical periods, can be collected by completists. Those scenes are not producing any more records, and their fetishization by late-coming collectors can be a way to hold on to what Richardson calls "early blackness." For house collectors, there is a delimited set of records from Chicago labels like Trax and D.J. International necessary to own and master. The same goes for techno, including Transmat, Metroplex, Underground Resistance, Berlin's Tresor, and a few others. For contemporary house and techno music makers, the blueprint has been completed by these records, labels, and scenes. And as a result of the music's minimal sonic and machine origins, house and techno's musical blueprints can be followed fairly easily by newcomers, without a prohibitive amount of technical and musical training. Thus, newer house and techno artists sometimes open themselves up to claims they are reproducing the all-too-familiar Elvis effect with their work—white artists using a bigger platform to simulate an innovative black music of the past.

But it's also easy to understand why the music has been reignited, by both new interpretations of the old stuff and new uses by new DJs. Recently hot labels like L.I.E.S., Russian Torrent, and L.A. Club Resource have popularized the sounds and added some darkness around the edges, though they seem to have lost a little steam (and clout) recently. Theo Parrish's Sound Signature, Omar-S's FXHE, and a host of others are still maintaining and putting out vibrant dance music.

But as Carolina Soul employee (and fine DJ) Katie O'Neil has pointed out, the dance music record scene has "gotten so niche, sometimes it becomes hard to tell what's 'important' and what's not." A brief scan of Resident Advisor's Top 1,000 DJ charts or a listen to NTS will show the international scope of contemporary dance music, and the proliferation of records, with microgenres and small labels popping up daily. If you're club-shy but interested in dance music, you can check out Boiler Room's live DJ sets. But even though Boiler Room is doing something new every day, it does not and cannot pretend to cover the entirety of the dance music scene.

JAZZ

Big Band

Dixieland

Vocal

Bop

Funk Jazz

Fusion

Hard Bop

Modal

Post-Bop

Third Stream

West Coast

Free

Spiritual

# JAZZ

Acid · Big Band · Bop · Dixieland ·
Ethio · Free · Funk · Fusion · Hard
Bop · Modal · Post-Bop · Soul ·
Spiritual · Third Stream · West Coast

Jazz is integral enough to the American
mythos that a number of familiar sayings
have attached themselves to it. Maybe
the two most famous are Gerald Early's
tendentious claim that the Constitution,
jazz, and baseball are the most beautiful
things US culture ever created, and
so will be the "only three things that
America will be remembered for 2,000
years from now." The second more
simply states that "jazz is America's
classical music." The second statement
is best understood as "proof" of Early's
first one—jazz is a quintessentially
American form that does in music what
the American Revolution did in politics:
confirm America's chosen status as the
next step forward in human freedom.

As with most clichés, there's a little
truth and a lot of distortion in these
sayings. They obscure more than they
explain. Jazz has had many historical
moments, during which both its
sociological role and its aesthetic form
have changed. There is no one "jazz"
to speak of—no red thread of unbroken
Americanness that runs through Jelly
Roll Morton to Matana Roberts and
everything in between. While there
are many continuities between jazz's
subgenres and historical periods,
there are also so many divergencies in
practice, sound, and intent contained in
the history of jazz that the name cannot
cover them. Certainly a descriptor like

American classical music won't cut it. Furthermore, to treat jazz like an unbroken expression of the American spirit also erases its fundamental blackness and so turns it into a bland expression of a fictional universal American ethos.

When most think of jazz records today, they think of the golden age of the Blue Note and Prestige labels of the 1950s and '60s, as well as Impulse!, Atlantic, Riverside, and New Jazz. Artists on these labels defined what we think of as modern jazz—Miles Davis, John Coltrane, Lee Morgan, Bud Powell, Art Blakey, Dexter Gordon, Hank Mobley, Charles Mingus, and so on. Following in the wake of both the chaotic bebop of Charlie Parker and the more measured compositional genius of Duke Ellington, the records and artists on these labels invented the mainstream. To this day, these are the records people pay the most money for, often coveting specific copies with specific etchings in the dead wax and deep grooves in the vinyl behind the label. These records dominate any high-end record auction you'll see on eBay, including Carolina Soul's own. From the modal cool of *Kind of Blue* to the proto-spiritual freak-outs of *Ascension*, you will find the foundational patterns for all jazz records which followed them in this era.

While of course incorporating many of its traditions, the Blue Note and Prestige era outmoded the Big Band, Dixieland, and vocal jazz that preceded it. While figures like Gene Krupa, Sidney Bechet, Charlie Christian, and Billie Holiday are rightly collected as legends, the genres they are associated with seem only distantly relevant to the world today. Their music was often put out on 78s and 10" records that remain highly collectible, but you will find few fundamentalist devotees of the jazz styles they worked in. In many ways, they are now prized for their antiquity. In this, the 10" sleeves designed for these styles by David Stone Martin for labels like Norgran, Clef, Mercury, Verve, and Progressive are like the music itself—partially beautiful because and not despite the fact that they seem so distant from us in time.

The emergent subgenres for jazz collectors today are free and spiritual jazz. These genres had their heyday in the 1970s and represent a divvying up of the dominant Blue Note/Prestige/Impulse! tradition described above. Free jazz artists took the wild, atonal improvisational tendencies latent in the tradition and intensified them. On the other hand, spiritual jazz musicians took the more meditative, gentler side of the tradition and foregrounded it. Both movements, although with different emphases, took black nationalism and black consciousness into the center of their music making. For example, artists like Horace Tapscott and Haki R. Madhubuti explicitly politicized their practice, while artists like Alice Coltrane and Pharoah Sanders explicitly spiritualized theirs—but they all shared a devotion to reinterpreting the meaning of black life in America and the world at large. Because plenty of ink has been spilled about free jazz already, our focus below will be spiritual jazz. Readers looking for more discussion of free jazz can skip ahead to our final chapter's discussion of Cecil Taylor's *Unit Structures*.

# SPIRITUAL JAZZ

"Spiritual" jazz is a classic example of an internet collectors' genre, as you rarely if ever would have heard the term used in the 1970s when its records were being made. The first of Gerald Short's *Spiritual Jazz: Esoteric, Modal, and Deep Jazz* compilations on Jazzman came out in 2008, but the term was used more sporadically before that. On the other hand, it's nowhere to be found in Valerie Wilmer's groundbreaking book *As Serious as Your Life: The Story of the New Jazz*[11] (1977), even though many of the artists covered in its pages are now considered "spiritual" jazz musicians in some shape or form. The phrase is somewhat of a catchall and often includes what used to be called modal, soul, free, and funky jazz. Most people agree it started with "jazz messiah" John Coltrane's late-period experiments with the avant-garde (his newfound interest in Albert Ayler, his collaboration with Pharoah Sanders, and so on) heard on the improvisations of *Ascension* (Impulse!, 1966), and the live and posthumous records that followed his death in 1967. The idea of jazz as "spirit music" was sometimes promulgated by the artists themselves, as implicit in Albert Ayler's messianic claim that "Trane was the Father, Pharoah was the Son, I am the Holy Ghost."

But not only is spiritual jazz a somewhat vague aesthetic marker, it also belies the fact that the music carried over an intensified political liberation from the 1960s. Following the tenor of LPs like Archie Shepp's *Attica Blues* and, to a lesser extent, Max Roach and Abbey Lincoln's *We Insist!*, "spiritual" jazz can't be understood without an understanding of the revolutionary desire for black self-determination in the early 1970s. Following in the footsteps of Sun Ra's Saturn label, the key labels of the movement—Strata (Detroit, 1969), Strata-East (New York, 1971), Black Jazz (Los Angeles, 1971), Tribe (Detroit, 1972), and Black Fire (Washington, DC, 1975)—were founded by black musicians tired of exploitation by the major jazz labels of the time. Smaller labels in Philly (Dogtown and Vagabond King) and Washington, DC (Lloyd McNeill's ASHA and Baobab, Andrew White's Andrew's Music) also made significant contributions to the subgenre. And a few free and spiritual labels were started by white jazzbos with disposable income—both ESP-Disk' and Indian Navigation were started by white lawyers, while Nimbus was run by professional gambler Tom Albach. Self-determination or patronage seem to have been the two avenues for spiritual jazz at this time. The Art Ensemble of Chicago were exceptional for taking a third route—they moved to France and put out albums on the European labels BYG and Actuel.

The next question this subgenre's name raises: Was previous jazz "unspiritual"? The equation between noncommercial music with spiritual purity and depth is not as automatic as the name implies. Anyone who's hung around contemporary noise scenes knows that avant-garde anti-commercialism alone does not ensure aesthetic quality. Plus, is spiritual jazz still spiritual now that the records are highly collectible? Not only does the name obscure the political and social impulses of the music, associating it with rarefied, metaphysical matters, it also deemphasizes the music's continuities with that which preceded it. As it is, like "cosmic," and Afrofuturism, the term "spiritual" has crept from a particular usage to a more diffuse, general one.

Many key spiritual artists got their start as participants in new forms of communal experience: Chicago's Association for the Advancement of Creative Musicians (AACM) fostered the likes of the Art Ensemble of Chicago, Phil Cohran, and Anthony Braxton; in Los Angeles, Horace Tapscott's Pan-Afrikan People's Movement was half band, half educational center and had its home base in Watts's Union of God's Musicians and Artists Ascension (UGMAA). After John Coltrane died, Alice Coltrane changed her name to Swamini Turiyasangitananda, started the Sai Anantam Ashram in Santa Monica, and made music primarily for her followers. These are only some of the more prominent examples of small collectives attempting to control the making, meaning, and distribution of their music. In many ways, "spiritual" jazz is actually the musical offshoot of the political Black Arts Movement, though the authors get most of the attention (never mind that Amiri Baraka and Haki R. Madhubuti, to name just two BAM authors, also made jazz LPs, with Baraka also running his own Jihad jazz label in the late '60s).

Recent interest in Alice Coltrane demonstrates a welcome shift in jazz collectors' taste. While the old-school market for RVG-etched Blue Notes and Prestiges, Impulses!, and Riversides continues to thrive, the interest in "spiritual" signals a generational and aesthetic shift away from its dominance. Even ten years ago, if you were to bring up Alice Coltrane to many "serious" jazz connoisseurs, you would get the side-eye and a lecture on the superiority of John Coltrane's music to his wife's. As disheartening as this sexist Yoko Ono–ing of Alice Coltrane was, it also represented the degree to which many jazz fans, until recently, still privileged sheer technical virtuosity over feel and imagination. Much of Alice Coltrane's music featured atypical instrumentation even for "out" jazz, both synthesizers and non-Western instruments (sitar, zither, and djembe). What's more, LPs like *World Galaxy* and tapes like *Turiya Sings* sometimes approach new age. As noted above, much of Alice Coltrane's later music was explicitly made for a select number of ashram members—older jazz fans didn't necessarily even have the internet savvy to track such limited releases down, so they were underheard. In general, Alice Coltrane's sound is more free-floating and textural than straight-ahead jazz, and so represents spiritual's departure from the harder hitting atonality of late '60s free jazz associated with artists like Albert Ayler, Cecil Taylor, and Milford Graves. This softness was sometimes mistaken for weakness in the serious jazzbo days of heady, free atonality. For a long time, what's now known as spiritual jazz went misunderstood by both old-school traditionalists and hardline free experimenters. It's taken a while for collectors to catch up, but they finally have.

Spiritual now appeals to collectors who can't necessarily connect with the golden age of the '50s and '60s bop and post-bop but have tired of or are intimidated by the unrelenting outer reaches explored by free jazz. We live in times seriously in need of chill—you have to be in the right headspace to listen to free jazz innovators, and sometimes it can seem like the music intensifies the heavy dissonance readily available in everyday life. By contrast, a track like Brute Force's "Doubt" (*S/T* LP, Embryo, 1970), in addition to anticipating the *Twin Peaks* theme, holds terror in abeyance and occupies a middle ground between eerie and easy listening. The title track of Idris Ackamoor and the Pyramids' *Birth/Speed/Merging* (Pyramid LP, 1976)—featuring what in the day would have been called "Afrocentric" instrumentation—generates a similar confrontation between disparate polyrhythms and calming flute. In general, this is what "spiritual jazz" seems to do best: contain the intensity of sublime terror in a shell of beauty. Rather than express the boilerplate love of a Hallmark card, it expresses the active struggle of love in a world cordoned by political and cosmic terrors: "They Play to make music Fire, They Play to make the soul Burst out of the Body" as the liner notes to *Birth/Speed/Merging* state. If this is spiritual practice, it is an active bodily one that treats soul as a living "bursting" force, not a passive one. Even the so-called chillest of Alice Coltrane's music is still dynamic and searching. If we are to hold on to the "spiritual" jazz tag, it should be in this power-laden sense that carried over from "free," and not the more passive connotations "spiritual" sometimes has. There's nothing passive about the forward drive of a track like Julius Hemphill's "Dogon A.D." (*Dogon A.D.* LP, Mbari, 1972), with its insistent cello, pounding drums, and fiery sax. And a song like Cecil McBee's "Agnez (with Respect to Roy Haynes)" (*Music from the Source* LP, ENJA, 1978) stages the relation between passive and active forms of "spiritual jazz" in almost schematic form—the opening features a lovely swirling of chimes, accompanied by melodic, undoctored piano and flute. Only McBee's bowed bass gives a hint that you are not listening to a contemporary classical piece of the time, and that something radically different is in the offing. This introduction represents the "meditative" side of spiritual jazz, but at the 3:45 mark, the song breaks wide open—someone counts off to four and the band goes off. The track speeds up and gets noisier, dominated by saxophonist Chico Freeman's sheets of sound, McBee's driving bass lines, and a heavily hit conga. This is spiritual jazz in the second, active sense, of a band finding expression of a spirit through the energetic process of improvisation. The joy in a song like Dollar Brand's "Jabulani–Easter Joy" (*African Space Program* LP, ENJA, 1974) forcefully separates the musical components of a religious march's unity and brings out the jubilant voice of each instrument. It exposes the way spiritual unity is made, not born.

Even a more placid track like Khan Jamal's "The Known Unknown" (*Infinity* LP, Jam'Brio, 1984), dominated as it is by Jamal's xylophone, sharpens the perceptions rather than performing a narcotic effect. Marion Brown, who once collaborated with ambient pioneer Harold Budd, produced jazz bordering on new age in theme and form—but his songs also feature dynamic interactions between distinct musical levels. Brother Ahh's *Sound Awareness* (Strata-East LP, 1972) deals largely in spacy atmospheres but, as the title suggests, calls for active co-creation of its sound world by the listener. The Black Artist's Group's "Something to Play On" (*In Paris, Aries* LP, BAG, 1973) creates a cacophony of rhythm out of pieces of metal and found percussion—it, like the best of the free jazz, is more spirited, even aggressively so, than the "spiritual" tag might suggest.

What's more, the music on Strata-East, Black Jazz, and Tribe ranges widely from funky, straight-ahead composition to textural, free-floating atmospherics that approach the sound of ambient and new age. For this reason, "spiritual" should be viewed as a shared general approach to the tradition of jazz, and a shared desire to build new forms of black community outside of the mega-institutions of the church, state, and corporation. In the case of Strata-East, Max Roach's drum collective M'Boom's *Re:Percussion* LP (1973) features eight percussionists, and explores African rhythms and instruments: It has little to do with the generally swinging, throwback soul jazz sound of the Descendants of Mike and Phoebe's *A Spirit Speaks* LP (Strata-East, 1974). A group like the Ensemble Al-Salaam splits the difference between funkiness and texture on tracks like "Peace" (*The Sojourner* LP, Strata-East, 1974). The track features Leroy Seals's Fender bass played melodically and produced in a way similar to Jaco Pastorius's tones, and features a soaring soprano sax from Fred Kwaku Crawley and intermittent free vocals from Beatrice Parker.

Though reviewer Thom Jurek has claimed the Tribe collective practiced a "kitchen-sink approach"[12] to musical genre, the parameters of the Detroit label's sound are clear. Generally heavier and more cleanly produced than Strata-East, records like Harold McKinney's *Voices and Rhythms of the Creative Profile* (1974) and Marcus Belgrave's *Gemini II* (1974) prominently feature Minimoog synthesizers. In general, artists in the Tribe cadre go for a spacier, more layered sound and more studio effects. This contrasts with the relatively straight-ahead engineering of Strata-East. Even beneath the straightforward groove of Doug Hammond and David Durrah's black self-reliance anthem "Wake Up Brothers" (*Reflections in the Sea of Nurnen*, 1975), a song that wouldn't sound out of place on Strata-East, you can hear Durrah's subtly mixed, distorted synth vibing away. You wouldn't hear such production undertones if the record were on Strata-East.

While jazz of the 1950s and '60s has been assimilated to the high cultural tradition as "America's classical music," the records covered by the category of "spiritual jazz" still resist such burial in prestige. While the term "black classical" was never a good fit for jazz in general (it denies the specificity of jazz's aesthetic by conflating it with that of the European masters), the jazz of the 1970s and '80s we now call "spiritual" is neither particularly American nor classical. With its origins in black nationalism, it in some ways can be considered a counter-American genre, or at minimum a genre that asks America to finally live up to its stated ideals of "liberty and justice for all." And as with all music made by Americans, many of its historical starting points and aesthetic influences came from outside the US's borders. And as for the classical part—that music has become so irrelevant to contemporary life that it only benefits from a comparison with jazz. Of all subgenres, spiritual jazz least needs prestige by association with European high culture—the music still speaks for itself.

## "ROOTS"

| RESIDUAL | DOMINANT | EMERGENT |
|---|---|---|
| Bluegrass | | |
| Contemporary Country | Alt Country | |
| Sermons | Black Gospel | |
| White Gospel | Classic Country | "American Primitive" Guitar |
| | Downhome Blues | Cajun |
| | Electric Blues | Country Blues |
| | Jump Blues | Country Boppers |
| | Singer-Songwriter | Downer Folk |
| | | Field Recording |
| | | Funky/Soulful Gospel |
| | | Loner Folk |
| | | Old Time |
| | | Outsider |

# "ROOTS"

Alt Country · "American Primitive" Guitar · Black Gospel · Bluegrass · Cajun · C&W · C&W Bopper · Classic Country · Contemporary Country · Country Blues · Country Boppers · Downer Folk · Downhome Blues · Electric Blues · Fiddle · Field Recording · Funky/Soulful Gospel · Jump Blues · Loner Folk · Old Time · Outlaw Country · Outsider · Sacred Steel Gospel · Sermons · Solo Guitar · SSW (Singer-Songwriter) · Trad Gospel · Western Swing · Xian Folk · Zydeco

By "roots," I mean American music with its sources in vernacular folkways rather than in modern popular culture. Under this heading, we include the genres gospel, blues, and folk and the many subgenres developed within them. But before we start, it's important to note that roots is almost as imperfect a descriptor as "world." In popular practice, "roots" has been used to decide what music counts as truly American and what does not. For example, it has been used to marginalize and exclude the music of the indigenous people of North America. The roots canon tends to minimize the polyglot, global wellsprings of American vernacular music, whether as a product of colonial exploration (Spanish, Dutch, British, French), the African slave trade, relations with our Mexican and Canadian neighbors, or a host of homegrown invented traditions passed off as authentic American folk culture. I will not be able to do justice to the breadth and depth of the sources of roots music. Because the recorded archive of older, nonwhite "Americana" is spotty, the deeper roots of roots music are either impossible to collect or uninteresting to many record collectors. Additionally, few popular music histories (as opposed to many excellent academic ones) have put these records in their proper historical context.

But before we move on to specific discussions about folk, blues, and gospel subgenres, I recommend an intial dive into the parts of the Smithsonian Folkways, Arhoolie, and Dust-to-Digital catalogs that highlight nonwhite, non-"Americana" roots music. Also, check out Light in the Attic's fantastic *Native North America* box set (2016), a crucial survey of under-the-radar twentieth-century music by what LITA calls "diverse North American Aboriginal community." I write this before we deal with the more familiar and popular record collector usage and definition of "roots" to note that prominent record collector trends do not cover all that's out there or what's left to explore.

## GOSPEL

The average choral gospel record you find in a thrift store will probably leave you cold. Most such records feature all-white choirs singing old standards in a homogenous style that varies little from record to record. Gospel of this sort has very few, if any, hardcore collectors. For a long time people have assumed this sort of record was all gospel had to offer. Steering clear of outright religiosity, most record collectors assumed the genre to be stylistically one-dimensional. Yes, they would tokenize a religious singer here and there, such as the amazing Sister Rosetta Tharpe, but until recently gospel records haven't been given the attention that other genres have.

Because unappealing records make up the majority of the gospel vinyl out there, one could perhaps be forgiven for thinking the whole genre was suspect. But the fact remains that most records in any genre are going to be bad—with gospel, you just need to be able to read the signs. To do this, one needs to leave behind the boomer counterculture's approach to spirituals and gospel. For many children of the 1960s and '70s, gospel music was anathema. The counterculture generally considered the Christianity of their parents to be oppressive, placing too much emphasis on discipline and social control, and not enough on the actual practices of love, caring, and togetherness. Among this generation, there was perhaps a grudging respect for gospel as the starting point of many soul singers—Sam Cooke (son of a Church of Christ minister) and the Soul Stirrers, Aretha Franklin (daughter of an itinerant preacher), the Pentecostal Little Richard, and so on. But this was often as far as it went: Hippies had little interest in going deep into the genre, black or white. Buddhism, Hinduism, new age, cults, atheism, and indifference all held more appeal to a newly politicized youth, something many carried into the yuppie era and beyond. And the few that were open to gospel records distanced themselves from its actual message while praising the "soul" of the music in blanket terms.

Because of these preceding attitudes, the current revival of interest in gospel records depends on a few things. First, the boomer generation giving way to younger collectors, who were not necessarily more religious but were less allergic to the rhetoric and tropes of gospel's Christianity. The further away in time these records are from us, the easier it is to destigmatize their contents. They have fewer bad contextual associations for collectors than they once did, allowing the listener to hear them on their own terms more easily than before. A similar process has occurred with other genres, whether it be house or new age. In gospel's case, however, the destigmatization process has been particularly drastic—the music has been stripped of its political connotations, while aesthetically, its best records always sounded good. By way of comparison, modern soul's biggest collectors are mostly those too young to have heard it on top 40 radio the first time around. Whereas modern soul's resurgence depends on the lifting of taste taboos, gospel's rise depends on the lifting of an unwritten taboo on spiritual contents.

Second, the temporal focus of gospel collectors has broadened. The boomer generation of critics treated the 1950s as ground zero for their limited appreciation of gospel. They centered discussion on the 1950s for a few reasons. First, it was the decade of their own childhood, so it was most familiar to them. Second, the 1950s were the moment when many boomers' most cherished soul musicians were cutting their teeth in gospel choirs and in sacred song. A period of transition, in the 1950s, figures like Sam Cooke were recording songs bridging gospel and soul, paving the way for their better-loved, more popular secular careers. To find interesting gospel records, newer collectors had to decenter the 1950s. Some went back in time to pre–World War II spirituals on 78s, while others went forward in their collecting, developing an interest in nontraditional detours of traditional gospel into boogie, modern, funky, and even free jazz shapes in the 1960s, '70s, and '80s.

If the 1950s gospel of the Soul Stirrers, the Dixie Hummingbirds, and early Staple Singers is still the quintessential gospel sound for many, collector attention has for a large part turned to gospel bands that followed in its wake. Writing their own songs, these small bands were as much influenced by commercial radio as they were by Sunday services. For example, the Clark Sisters rewrote the "Pepsi Has a Lot to Give" jingle as "Jesus Has a Lot to Give" (*Jesus Has a Lot to Give* LP, Bilesse, 1973), Shirley Able turned Marvin and Tammi's "You're All I Need to Survive" into "God's All I Need" (*His Life's Testimony* LP, Joy Partnership LTD., 1981), and many riffed Al Green's secular "Love and Happiness" onto sacred ground. If the birth of R&B and soul can be understood as a secularization of gospel music, then post-1950s gospel can be considered the resacralization of soul and funk. Of course, this two-way exchange between sacred and profane has been a constant throughout American music's history. However, in post-1950s gospel, the balance of sonic invention has been reversed, swinging toward secular forms and away from traditional backing—at least on the records. Bands in the post-1950s era took Charles Wesley's old saw about not wanting the devil to have all the best tunes seriously.

What might be most surprising to newcomers to gospel collecting, then, is the diversity of styles available. Gospel vinyl ranges from the placid new age, slow funk of the Singing Tornadoes' "Walking on the Sea of Galilee" (*In That Great Gettin' Up Morning* LP, Expression, 1984) to the scarifying private avant-gardism of the Biblical Jacksons Family's "Hell (The Lake of Fire)" (*Jesus Is Coming Again—Soon...Unexpectedly!!*). The Singing Tornadoes track, an instrumental, glides along over a field recording of ocean waters, mellow resonant vibraphone, rhythms played with the gentlest of touches, and a soft electric guitar providing commentary. As befitting its title, it puts the emphasis on mystery, miracle, and love, and it produces an oceanic feeling of calm in the listener. Like Shirley Murdock's "The Beauty of It All," it's decidedly New Testament, while the Biblical Jacksons Family track spews fire and brimstone straight out of the book of Jeremiah. It starts with a spoken dedication to everyone the Biblical Jacksons believe are going to hell and just gets more aggressive from there: Male and female screaming from the pit begging for forgiveness, screeching admonitions on how to avoid hell, and random bursts of guitar riffs govern the improvised, chaotic proceedings. This track, like Dorothy Norwood's "Time Is Winding Up" (*Jesus Is the Answer* LP, Atlanta International, 1982), represents the other side of the nouveau gospel tradition—a righteous, almost arrogant pleasure taken in the imminence of the apocalypse. These tend to come in more hard-charging musical forms, whether the free jazz caterwauling, as in the Biblical Jacksons' case, or Norwood's passive-aggressive disco funk. Between the two tendencies rests Cleveland's Corinthian Singers' "Why (It's a Shame)" (Bounty 45, 1983), which can be divided into two parts—a bouncy, compelling, loving instrumental and a cruel critique of drug addiction in its lyrics. In post-1950s gospel, all popular styles are tried on for praise, from funky sacred steel (Chester Lewis's "Wade in the Water," Eternal Gold) to the modern soul of Soul Liberation's "Who Are You" (*Who Are You* LP, Rainbow Sound, 1982). But if this is starting to sound like Christian rock's tendency to belatedly co-opt and ruin once vital popular styles, don't worry—these records are the equal or better of the secular material they rework. What's more, they were made contemporaneously with the pop records they reference. Nor is gospel music limited to America, as Mike McGonigal's three compilations of Jamaican gospel on his Social Music label, among many other international examples, demonstrate.

A label like Tennessee's Champ Records shows both how beautiful and how funky post-trad gospel records can get (its sublabel Skyland skews whiter). Champ was started by engineer Jim Stanton (who also produced United Sounds and the Black Exotics in West Columbia, South Carolina). Columbus, Ohio's Evangelist Maria Scott's vocal on "I've Got a God That Is Real" (*I've Got a God That Is Real* LP, Champ, 1982) rivals any Stax track—including those of the Staple Singers, whose guitar sound it references. This music puts the listener in the subject position of belief and helps them to understand from the inside out the peace that passeth understanding that comes with worship.

## FUNKY AND SOULFUL GOSPEL

In this vein, independent labels like HSE, Gospel Roots, and Su-Ann gave Champ a run for their money. From Raleigh, James Sanders's *A Witness for God* (HSE, 1980) finds a compromise form between heavy funk and sweet soul on tracks like "It's Gonna Be Hard, but We're Gonna Make It" and "Come on Up to My Glory." Post-trad gospel like this achieved a representation of the tension in Christianity between the spiritual softness of universal love, on one hand, and the harder-edged critique of sin and the world's "fallenness," on the other. These records dance between the Christ of abiding love (as represented in John and the gospels more generally) and Christ with sword in hand (as found in Revelation). In Sanders's hands, such a formula tilts toward sweetness, with the "roughness" of the struggling world and its churning funk conjured up just to be redeemed by the overall sonics of sweet comfort in the vocals. A record like the Staples Jr. Singers' *When Do We Get Paid* LP (Brenda, 1975) makes a similar sonic compromise between the ploughshare and the sword, reserving the roughness for the rhythm section and the sweetness for the vocals. Few records, however, resolve such a stark contradiction as seamlessly as Sanders and the Staples Jr. Singers (as the previously mentioned extremes of Biblical Jacksons Family and Singing Tornadoes shows).

Chicago faith huckster T. L. Barrett's two LPs, *Like a Ship (without a Sail)* (Mt. Zion Gospel Productions, 1971) and *Do Not Pass Me By* (Gospel Roots, 1976), have become hipster hits. This status can be traced to both a fine reissue by Light in the Attic and to Kanye West's sample of "Father I Spread My Hands" for the only halfway decent song on *Life of Pablo*. Having mined the ARC Choir for the "Jesus Walks" sample, West has gone back to the well of post-trad gospel (in addition to Numero comps, Aphex Twin, Daft Punk, and just ever so slightly more obscure sources) more frequently as people tired of his use of sped-up soul samples. Just Blaze's sample of Andrew Brown's stunning "Lord, Lord" (1974) for Drake's "Lord Knows" (2011) participates in the same gospel turn in recent sampling—the need for newer, more obscure content as old forms become exhausted. This turn, obviously, is partial, as only super-wealthy artists like West and Drake can afford to clear expensive samples.

Beneath small-label releases and gospel records on not wholly "gospel" labels like Style Wooten's Designer (Memphis), there are also truly private gospel releases. These were self-released records with vanity label names, names without real labels behind them, or no label listed at all. There are thousands of private gospel 45s and LPs out there—these include groups like the Sensational Interns, Sensational Trumpets, Sensational Highlights, the Quadralaires, the Visionaires, and the Zionaires. It's worth pointing out, then, that there will always be more good records to reissue; labels couldn't make a profit on all of them, even if there were enough vinyl pressing plants to print them all (which there aren't). So, the reissue glut we're seeing now is produced by the tastes and record-sourcing abilities of people in the financial position to reissue music, not because the world is running out of good, undiscovered, or under-known records. After all, we live in a world in which the Straughter Brothers' *I Love Gospel Music* LP (Holy Cross), and so many classic songs like "Jesus Is My All In All," still haven't been reissued! (The same goes for scarce tapes and CDs in many genres, by the way, so get out your '90s maxi-singles from whatever closet you've stashed them in!)

## DISCO, BOOGIE, AND MODERN SOUL GOSPEL

Disco, boogie, and modern soul gospel records are a particularly compelling set of records, considering the dance club and pulpit are usually considered to be opposite numbers. Along with the previously mentioned Soul Liberation, the Spirit of Love's "The Power of Your Love" (Birthright, 1978) shows that the two are compatible. In fact, the song can be read as an immanent critique of secular dance music, as it inhabits the sound of a late 1970s disco banger while the lyrics begin with a statement on the limits of "just disco partying." The infamous modern Joubert Singers track "Stand on the Word" (Next Plateau, 1985)—whether or not it had anything to do with famed DJ Larry Levan—was an underground club hit in New York, its anodyne lyrical content never getting in the way of the groove. The Hunter Singers' "Beatitudes" (from the *Precious Moments* LP) lurches along on a slow and heavy groove, with synth-like guitar effects that offset its gentle vocal soul riffing on the Sermon on the Mount.

All this being said about 1970s and '80s gospel, another effect of the weakening of the boomer proscription on gospel has been the opening up of older R&B, rock, and rockabilly for collector consumption. Modern collectors have taken a particular interest in slightly more out-of-the-way material, out of the Specialty Records mainstream of the time. This material ranges from white Pentecostal Brother Claude Ely's sides in the 1950s and '60s on major label King (known for R&B) to more obscure records like Lucille Jordon Trio's private *Rough, Tough in Jesus' Name* (Jordon) and Brother William and the Saints' *Hold Your Head Up High* (Su-Ann). Both harken back to the rougher, energetic side of '50s rock, with Jordon channeling Chuck Berry as much as Sister Rosetta Tharpe, while Brother Williams takes a Buddy Holly–esque tack on the garage rock with gospel harmonies of "Sweet Lord of Lords." In sum, gospel records are no longer the sole provenance of true believers. Their current vogue, one suspects, is both musical and ideological in nature. Musically, gospel presents an archive of unexhausted variations on the already collectible sounds of soul, funk, boogie; ideologically, the spirituality expressed in the records is no longer tainted by association with its oppressive origins in the conservative church practices of yesteryear.

## BLUES

Despite the best efforts of debunkers like Elijah Wald, who in *Escaping the Delta* deconstructs the mythos surrounding Robert Johnson and the "country blues" more generally, no American record genre continues to be more steeped in historical fantasy than the blues. With Robert Johnson, for example, even the surface noises of particular 78 transfers have become engrained in our sense of his music. Some blues collectors have attached so much import to the particulars of the records themselves that they've left behind all thoughts of the world that produced them. Because the records are all that remain, and they still have the power to build imaginary worlds for us, it's easy to attach all sorts of mythopoesis to them. The records come to stand in for our concepts and mental pictures of the Mississippi Delta, with its hoary clichés about black rural poverty and hard living, mixed with fantasies about deals with the devil at the crossroads and so on. Around the grain of particular recording techniques of individual performances, whole worlds of fantasy have sprung up.

Memphis of course has a "storied" musical history in line with the above, from W. C. Handy's 1912 blues-inaugurating smash hit "Memphis Blues" on through Sun, Stax, and Ardent Studios right down to the 1980s and '90s influential rap and garage rock scenes. Memphis is as much a creation of records as of brick-and-mortar—people who go to Beale Street or Graceland might be disappointed with what they find there. No real place can compete with the musical Memphis. This is the context from which the High Water Recording Company label emerged. It was a Memphis blues label featuring only Memphis artists. Started in 1979 and most active in the early 1980s, High Water was founded by a musicologist, Dr. David Evans, with the support of his employer, Memphis State University. This seems on the face of things to be an inversion of the country blues mythos—a label supported by a National Endowment for the Arts grant and run by a white ethnomusicologist seems a million miles away from "Hellhound on My Trail" territory. Now perhaps best known for its R. L. Burnside and Junior Kimbrough sides, the label started as a 45-only outfit. Each of its sleeves bore a black-and-white photo of the featured artist, along with band and track names, with the High Water logo positioned next to a unique catalog number. The logo features a generic "bluesman" playing an acoustic guitar on the roof of a house mostly submerged in "high" floodwaters. Located on the Mississippi River, Memphis is no stranger to floods; the logo probably also refers to Charley Patton's foundational blues 78 "High Water Everywhere," which commemorated the Great Mississippi Flood of 1927. The label, despite its academic origins, in its graphic design set out to produce a series that branded Southern space in its iconography. This Evans did with an eye to future collectability—stamping each issued record with a serial catalog number on its sleeve and maintaining a uniform but still homespun typography and layout.

The 45s themselves project a compromise sonic "space" for modern blues. They are electric blues, but still "downhome" (Evans's word). Recorded in John Fry's Ardent studios, where Big Star produced their meticulous *#1 Record* and *Radio City*, Jesse Mae Hemphill's "Jessie's Boogie," for example, almost sounds like it could have been taken from a Lomax field recording (as does the flip "Standing in My Doorway Crying"). But the microphones recording Hemphill's voice are clearly more sensitive than ones of old, and there's sonic separation between her electric riff and tambourine, on one hand, and her vocal, on the other. What results is a sort of presentation of country blues song form in a subtly new production container. The effect, as with the other High Water 45s, is both a demystification of the Southern gothification of the country blues and a way of keeping continuity with that genre's general songcraft and performance traditions. The production—positioned between the past's country blues and the more aggressively generic electric blues pilloried in *Ghost World* with the fictional band Blues Hammer—carves out a modern space for the blues. This sound represented the Memphis of the late 1970s and early '80s, neither the nostalgic past nor its travesty in the worst of the electric blues. The production of the "downhome" electric blues sound as heard on High Water suggests a compromise between city and country, mobility and rootedness. This portable roots sound, made accessible for a wider public, would later be capitalized on labels like Fat Possum, whose exoticizing marketing of High Water artists like Burnside and Kimbrough represented craven attempts at crossover (for example, Kid Rock on an R. L. Burnside LP). In liberating itself from the corny mystique thrown on the South of the country blues, the High Water aesthetic was then ironically left open to a new wave of white exploitation.

## OUTSIDER, PRIVATE, LONER

The outsider tag comes to records from the visual art world, Irwin Chusid having borrowed the term for his book *Songs in the Key of Z* and the compilations of the same name. "Outsider" is familiarly used to designate art brut creations made outside the established channels of galleries, museums, patrons, dealers, and academic art history departments.

In both the art and musical world, the term "outsider" has a double valence. This is because it started as a sociological term, rather than an aesthetic one: to call a work of art "outsider," you are implying the artist, too, is an outsider (art brut, with its emphasis on rawness, is no better) and situate the formal work first and foremost using the identity and situation of its artist. Therefore, the oppositionality of "outsider" art is built into the concept—no matter that outsider art and music widely ranges in style, theme, and intent (let alone social situation). Outsider art assumes naïve intent on the part of the artist.

When carried into the realm of music, the discourse of "outsider" and "loner" music becomes even more murky. Yet they are problematic terms for real musical phenomena, championing outsider status. Some records do deserve the tags "outsider" and/or "loner" because they were made outside the major label system, often privately pressed, and feature genuinely "far-out" labels, packaging, and music.

But the term at its worst, while perhaps a catchy line on a one-sheet, participates in the fetishization of identity—often mental illness, as in the case of Daniel Johnston, Wesley Willis, Wild Man Fischer, Moondog—and a further marginalization through exoticization. Outsider now, like "freak" in the 1960s, functions as a sort of condescending compliment, hovering between genuine appreciation for the work of the outsider and an inevitable exacerbation of whatever marginality the artist already has as a human being. Daniel Johnston's "Monkey in a Zoo" (*Songs of Pain* tape, 1980), covered later by Vic Chesnutt, allegorized this issue better than many of his "champions." The reception of the outsider/*Songs in the Key of Z* fetish of the 1990s and early 2000s, with its focus on the naïveté of the artist and their songs, in retrospect itself looks incredibly naïve. It was as if the only frame by which to understand true difference from these musicians was an exoticizing one, which emphasized either the music's strangeness or pathos as accidental—not the willed product of a musician. Rather, the outsider/loner framework ended up finding only *unintentional* genius or biographical objects of pity. But not formally, as music, or as something that could possibly be equally powerful or better than "real" art.

In this context, the words "champion" and "discoverer," smacking as they do of a white liberal savior complex, have unfortunately persisted in discussions of contemporary records from "outsider" black musicians, like Lonnie Holley and Abner Jay. It seems that the music industry and fans are still bouncing uneasily between exoticism and pity. The outsider movement at times can come uncomfortably close to what social scientists call "predatory inclusion," in which "outsiders" to the financial power structure are brought into it but on disadvantageous terms. Bad record deals, shady and unseemly marketing, and outright exploitation still occur in the modern "outsider" record game. Aesthetically, a solution to this problem is to treat the music on its own terms formally first, not biographically. The solution to the economic problem seems simple: People need to pay artists fairly.

What the term "outsider" does more blatantly, the terms "loner folk" and "American primitive" do slightly more subtly. Both "loner folk" and "American primitive" put an emphasis on the social marginality of performers. "Loner folk" refers to private press, obscure also-rans of the 1960s and '70s, perhaps most familiar through reissues on labels like Drag City (e.g., Bill Fay's *Time of the Last Persecution*, Gary Higgins's *Red Hash*), Shadoks (e.g., JW Farquhar's *The Formal Female*), and Numero (e.g., Sixth Station's *Deep Night*). The term "loner," like the term "outsider," seeks to draw attention to the exceptionality of artists working within a quite popular, well-known genre. One suspects that the word "loner" within the phrase "loner folk" serves to sex up a field associated with traditionalism, the black-and-white distant past, and finger-in-ear singing, namely folklore. "Loner" is often associated with heavy use of psychedelic drugs, failed or obscure records, and bouts of mental illness. The tapes are always "lost," the artists always "unheralded." But beneath the marketing gimmickry, some true masterpieces and really interesting figures exist. While many obscure records deserve to stay that way, it is not the case that all the records that deserve to be known already are. Even if they had been, our understanding of them and their relation to the past/field is still relatively immature. It should be noted that there has been terminology creep, as these terms have been extended to artists who are perhaps not so well-known now but were at one moment—like David Ackles, Pearls before Swine, or even artists as big in their own time as Tim Hardin or Fred Neil.

To find some lesser-known and "outsider" or "loner" artists, you often don't need to look further than the accompanists for more well-known artists. For example, from Bob Dylan's "side" players and collaborators, you can get to records like Ron Elliott's *The Candlestickmaker*, Happy & Artie Traum's *Double-Back*, Karen Dalton's *In My Own Time*, Bruce Langhorne's *The Hired Hand*, Pete Drake's *Forever*, Steve Douglas's *Rainbow Suite*, Jim Dickinson's *Dixie Fried*, and on and on. Or you can go from the Band to its producer John Simon's *John Simon's Album* (1970), and so on. In the analog past, cross-referencing these players took more time, and finding all their records was nearly impossible. Now you can buy all of them or stream most of them for free. Scratching the surface of one seminal artist's back catalog is now made incredibly easy by Discogs. Dig one level deeper than this, and you'll find connections to all sorts of interesting records.

The same goes for every "star" in the folk-rock singer-songwriter vein. In the Laurel Canyon scene alone, you look beyond Joni Mitchell's LPs on Asylum to find Judee Sill's *Judee Sill* and *Heart Food*. Look into the Byrds or Gram Parsons, and you will find even better records like Gene Clark's *White Light* and Terry Melcher's *Terry Melcher*. Go exploring through Neil Young's Discogs entries, and you'll find Jack Nitzsche's breathtaking if nihilistic *Three-Piece Suite*, the music of Doug Kershaw, and a host of others. In Greenwich Village, get into Fred Neil and you'll soon find out about his partner Vince Martin, whose "Snow Shadows" is one of the finest songs ever written. The same goes for any genre: look into Earth, Wind, and Fire and you'll find the Pharoahs, look into the Ohio Players and you'll find Robert Ward, and so on. Again, it's not as if every minor figure is better than any major one—the musical careers of Dylan cronies David Blue and Bob Neuwirth attest to that. But the field of the past's records is much deeper than legacy music media's canon building regimes ever let on, and new archives require new interpretations.

At its most valid, "loner" means something aesthetically—downer vibes, recorded in warm low fidelity, and played with just enough technical proficiency to get across inventive musical and lyrical ideas without routinizing them into formula. So not merely weird, not "freak folk" or "acid folk"—lifestyle markers masquerading as musical genres—but something that rises to challenge the known folk and singer-songwriter conventions, pushing beyond them. A book like Patrick Lundborg's *The Acid Archives: Underground Sounds 1965–1982* includes many records we would now classify as "loner" or "outsider," but also includes straightforward folk and hard rock, psychedelic cash-ins by Chubby Checker, and straight-up garage records from the Sonics and the Savages. It's clearly a pre-internet list, just like the famous Nurse with Wound list and Puszone's hardcore record lists in *Thrasher*. This being said, what counts as loner to some may not to others, and vice versa: The boundaries are real but open, meaningful but not ironclad. For some, only truly private press records count. For others, the canon is broad enough to include the sort of major label "failures," also-rans, and lesser-known artists mentioned above. The work of Bert Jansch and Jackson C. Frank certainly fits the bill in the second category but is not always considered part of the genre due to the relative polish of their recordings and their lack of total obscurity. The power of "outsider" or "psych folk" seems to be its ability to channel new forms of disillusionment, beyond the bored white suburban middle-class cliché into something more.

But used unthinkingly, "loner" and "outsider" sometimes become a code for disaffected whiteness; folk from black musicians of the period—like Jerry Moore's *Life Is a Constant Journey Home,* and works of Terry Callier like *Occasional Rain*—often goes uncounted.

Its appeal seems rooted in the twilight of the 1960s for collectors without any direct experience of the era. My parents were children of the 1960s, but my younger collector friends are one step further removed. The era is no longer drenched in the nostalgia it was in the 1980s, for example, when boomers' self-regard for their past was at its height. As a result, the music's being valued less as a representation of an era that never was and more as a concrete body of music with a series of interrelations, a system. The romance of the era's "idealism," taken as a homogenous whole, has been replaced with an engagement with specific labels, scenes, and artists, and their interrelations, as a network. The specific political struggles of the 1960s have been left behind, but an interest in the more obscure records of the time remains.

The best loner and outsider folk records evoke a homemade, private 1960s, one of deep personal experience: something more authentic beneath the blanket coverage of the mass media's official "memories" of the era. The strangeness of a true loner record, one that doesn't fit with stereotyped representations of a time, therefore appeals as if a disclosure of a secret private history. The idiosyncratic, personal expression of experience on a record like F. J. McMahon's *The Spirit of the Golden Juice* (Accent, 1969) lets people imagine a new way into social movements of the past. In a time when mass collective action on the scale of the 1960s seems blocked, what still strongly appeals is its musical imagination, the filtering of public events through the language of private mythology. For example, even in the record's song about the draft ("Five Years Kansas Blues"), McMahon approaches the issue from the particular personal perspective of a single draftee.

The love songs take quotidian details of loves and friendships for the starting point for inner exploration. Loner and outsider, then, means a reduction of known contents to a single eccentric's point of view. They tend to find metaphysical profundity in the singer's own everyday experiences. Individual records in the genre at their best capture the homespun side of a period's more general zeitgeist in a way that is still acceptable to dream and imagine within our present. This is both the appeal and danger of an experiential delay for a musical genre like outsider—it can preserve in its most seductive form an ideology or way of life that's no longer relevant to today's times, but as music still feels alive for the listener. This also seems to be the appeal of new age tapes and the resurgence of interest in astrology, yoga, tarot, crystals, and cults for today's scenesters.

ENCOURAGE THE PEOPLE ... ROBIN KENYATTA

RUFUS HARLEY

ROBIN JUMP REV

WORKIN ON A GROOVE THING / POLACK

GIPSY MAN

THE HOLIDAY / THE FIRST VERVE SESSIONS

PD 5525

CHICK COREA AND RETURN TO FOREVER / LIGHT AS A FE

PHILIP UPCHURCH / DARKNESS, DARKNESS / BLUE

FRANK LOWE / FRESH

AIN'T DOING TOO B-A-D, BAD

NEXUS

GENE HARRIS

GENE HARRIS

GENE HARRIS

IN A SPECIAL

FUNK REACTION / LONNIE SMITH

LOSA!

KING BL

RL XS AND BL

# CHAPTER 4

# The Politics of Record Collecting

Both insiders and outsiders agree that record collectors are an eccentric breed. But they interpret this eccentricity in different ways—while collectors tend to view themselves as endearing loners, outsiders are apt to see aimless losers. Like everyone else, record collectors tend to romanticize what they do, and so often represent themselves as modern-day renegades saving musical treasures from the neglect of an indifferent world. There's no doubt many record collectors are genuine outsiders—I've heard of enough fish tanks filled with 45s and goats weaving between LP stacks to be convinced of their strange lifestyles. But is every eccentric record collector an unheralded genius? Comedian (and record collector) Gregg Turkington (Neil Hamburger, *On Cinema at the Cinema*) certainly doesn't think so. In fact, in a truly dystopic description of record fair culture, he takes the opposite view: "There's no women there–just these sad, sad people with real issues and real problems. I don't know, they're kind of more interested in the artifacts and objects than the art itself. It's kind of missing the whole point there."[1] But neither this position nor the romanticized one account for the whole truth. Contradictory tendencies are at work in modern record collecting. Record collecting is not one thing; it is a field of competing forces, some retrogressive and some progressive, some reactionary and some radical. It's neither heaven nor hell, but a mix of the two.

What's needed to sort between these tendencies is a sense of the *politics* of record collecting. By politics, I don't mean party politics but rather, the way power is distributed and practiced. In the case of record collecting, an analysis of power asks questions like: Who is encouraged to collect and who is discouraged? Who has authority in the record world and why? How do the power structures of the world shape the use and interpretation of artists, records, and even whole genres of music? Only by considering politics in this sense can we understand where record collecting has been and where it's going.

Before I get into my analysis of the competing forces and cultures of record collecting, let's deal with the most prominent ideological premise of record collecting. This is that record collecting is apolitical, and that music provides an escape from politics into a world of pure imagination. To me, this view is wishful thinking—itself of a political kind. First, to say something is apolitical is a conservative political statement—you are taking a position that argues that others should take politics out of a subject. Second, music of course provides listeners with an escape, but that need to escape has political origins. There's no such thing as pure imagination. Even the feelings of release and escape a record provides are feelings of escaping a political dispensation. Record collecting and listening do not form a magic circle that keeps the real world out; rather, it's better to conceive of the world of records as part of the real world. Different groups within this world reproduce its "apolitics," while others take it in democratic or elitist directions. But as long as records remain social artifacts and take on meaning only as they're shared in communities, there's no such thing as an apolitical form of record collecting. And insofar as all music is made out of a social impulse and the desire to share with publics real and imagined, it can never be considered politically neutral. To ignore this dimension of the records themselves leads to a weakened understanding of them, even on aesthetic grounds.

This pervasive belief that records are free from politics has been fostered and amplified by the modern internet and social media. As we've discussed, the internet has greatly increased the quantity of records that we can buy and sell, but narrowed the channels of discussion. The internet presents the world of records as an impersonal emporium—you buy records from sites and they show up at your door. You don't need to talk to anyone. It makes collecting and listening a lonely, isolated, and essentially self-oriented activity. As such, it can be easy to imagine that the relation you have to a record is the only one that exists—that the record was made just for your personal enjoyment and not as part of a larger social process. It becomes easy to imagine you are the only one who cares, because people don't share music as much as they did in the past. The whole experience of purchasing and listening is mediated by the internet, which has subtracted out face-to-face discussion and social relations. An antisocial series of consumer transactions—buy, sell, I like, I don't, etc. now stands in the place of community. Simple and reductive, the convincing, arguing, thinking, and relating facets of music fandom have weakened. A complicated social process now gets condensed into a relation between the consumer and their consumer good, which they judge flatly "good" or "bad." This may be fine for most consumer goods, like vacuums and keyboards—they either work well or poorly—but records are complex cultural works and so need qualitative analysis to be done justice.

As such, the internet has become a machine to paper over the function of race, class, and gender in record life. But these things can only be obscured, not erased. The fact that the most powerful and respected record collectors are disproportionately white cannot be denied. Nor can the fact that a majority of the most valuable records were made by black people or crucially inspired by them. It's also obvious that rich people can and do build great record collections more easily than everybody else. Finally, it's common knowledge that most record collectors are men. None of these facts are particularly controversial. But when it comes time to talk about them in practice, old-guard collectors are much less willing to admit the extent to which they structure the world of collecting. Newer collectors are much more likely to grapple with these realities, even if they're still unsure how to go about changing them.

This chapter will break down the politics of online record culture—both the status quo it represents and the countermovements bubbling up among coming generations of collectors. While race, class, and gender are as intertwined in the record world as everywhere else, I'll be devoting separate sections to all three below. I do this because while interrelated, each category has its own power and particular provenance. Structures of race, class, and gender in the record world interlock but are not identical. I'll start with race, move to class, and finish the chapter with gender.

**RACE** The demographic of collectors is much less racially diverse than what is represented by the records they collect. Though a large proportion of rock records are made by white musicians, rock music would not exist in its current form without strong influence of black R&B and blues artists. An overwhelming number of the most expensively traded jazz records were made by black artists. The Chicago house and Detroit techno scenes were made up of black artists making records for a predominantly black audience. Rap, "world," and even stereotypically "white" genres like old-time, country, and folk were built on the contributions of nonwhite artists. Yet when it comes to the people who consider themselves record connoisseurs, it's my impression that not enough of them are nonwhite. As a result, white people own—literally, in the form of collected records—a disproportionate amount of a recorded musical heritage made mostly by nonwhite musicians.

Now this is not to say that different genres' collectors do not have strong nonwhite collecting numbers (e.g., Islands and rap), or that non-Western countries might not offer useful counter-models to the West's. It's really to say nothing more than this: The cultural capital in the form of records tends to flow toward those with money and away from those without it.

White appreciation of records made by nonwhite artists is not itself a problem. The alternative, a world in which white people only listen to "white" records, would be nothing less than an expression of white supremacy. What's less assuring, however, is that white ownership of and interest in black records does not correlate to a white interest in the politics of black life. One can, and many do, cultivate a high level of taste for the music produced by black and brown people without championing true racial equality. The long history of racial fetishism, exoticism, and tokenism in the US, for example, shows us that fascination with the cultural products of nonwhites can be compatible with political and economic expressions of white supremacy. The classic historical example is white minstrelsy. Today, for example, an abiding love for rap music is no guarantor of a love for black people.

Not all acts of inclusion include everyone equally. Recent books on the concept of "predatory inclusion" by Tressie McMillan Cottom (on education)[2] and Keeanga-Yamahtta Taylor (on real estate)[3] have shown the way black people since the end of World War II have been unequally incorporated into American institutions. They are "included," but at a higher financial and social cost than whites. In the case of American record collecting, black records dominate the canon of most genres and they tend to be the highest priced and most influential. In this way, black culture is included in the mainstream of record collecting. It could probably be said that it centers the thoughts and imaginations of most record collectors, but the people profiting most from these records and who therefore have the most authority to define their history and meaning are not black.

The fact is that those with the most extensive record collections are often treated as de facto experts on the music they own. This has resulted in a situation where a majority white ownership's taste and judgment of music made by nonwhites has become hegemonic. Insofar as this represents a wresting of control of the history and memory of nonwhite music from nonwhite folks themselves, this is an obvious problem. The authority to speak on, say, the history and meaning of the Florida funk scene shouldn't automatically devolve to the person who manages to find and buy the most records made by that scene. Or, now that techno music is again resurgent, white artists shouldn't feel they can gentrify the genre, erase its roots in the black Midwest of the 1980s, or claim "reverse racism" when called on it. In our economic system, ownership of course flows toward the financially advantaged and away from the working classes and marginalized, but the right to speak and define the meaning of records should not flow with it—not least when the originators of the music itself come from the marginalized and working classes in the first place.

What's more, now that the internet has deterritorialized records, the biggest collector of records from, say, Mississippi in the 1960s might live in Vienna or Krakow. But even if they possess total mastery of the *sound* of these records, they will have to do a lifetime's research to understand the historical and cultural context that produced that sound. It's an unfortunate by-product of the digital age that because the internet uproots records from their home context and decontextualizes them as pieces of "pure" music, collectors are not expected or encouraged to do this. The focus is almost exclusively on the artifacts themselves.

Now, as I said, the problem is not white interest in nonwhite music per se. It is the domination of the story and meaning of nonwhite records by a majority white body of collectors. Newer collectors, more educated about the realities of racial disparity, are working to collect records more thoughtfully and equitably. While these newer collectors still often come from a place of white privilege, they tend to acknowledge that privilege rather than hiding it or pretending it doesn't exist. This grounding allows genuine collaboration between musicians and collectors of different racial backgrounds. Younger collectors also tend to realize that ownership of records does not mean ownership of the music and culture expressed on these records. The democratizing slogan of the disability movement (and now every other major civil rights movement of our time)— *nothing about us without us*—has purchase here, too. A real change in the racial consciousness of record collectors seems to be on the horizon.

But consciousness-raising alone cannot halt the racial gatekeeping and the resegregation of vinyl altogether. As long as records continue to dramatically rise in price, and the racialized wage gap persists, vinyl will continue to be redistributed accordingly—away from the people who made the records. Mutual aid and respect, collaboration, and honesty are the first steps to addressing pervasive racial disparities and inequities in collecting.

In the best circumstances, imagination can bridge differences and produce empathy and shared understanding across racial divides. Records, of course, can be a very strong means to bind and unite people from different walks of life. But this is not their only use. We in the record community need to remind ourselves that imagined acts of empathy and connection through music are no substitute for true racial and economic fairness. The latter come from truly egalitarian sharing of wealth and power, something that's yet to be made standard in the record economy.

## CLASS

Within the world of record collecting, social media has become primarily a tool to signal one's class status as a collector. Instagram and Facebook have made it easy to turn one's acts of consumption into expressions of personality. Because these sites favor the visual over text, simple images of records have replaced more qualitative discussions of these records. On record Instagram, expensive records are assumed to have inherent value and are displayed as "treasures," "gems," and "grails." Rather than a space to share new and unheard musical discoveries, record Instagram often feels like a place where everybody displays images of the "known classics" to prove their belonging in elite circles of collecting. So the online record community is no stranger to what Thorstein Veblen long-ago termed "conspicuous consumption"—the purchase of items for the purpose of display and prestige seeking. In fact, by replacing discussion and debate with raw images, social media has made such conspicuous consumption much easier than before. There's nothing wrong with displaying records you are excited about. The problem, though, comes when such display becomes the dominant form of social expression of record life. When analysis, discussion, and sharing between friends gets mediated through a system of up-and-down votes online, it starts to seem like record collectors have nothing new to say about the vinyl they spend so much of their time and money pursuing.

This blank and empty relation to records comes about when one thinks of oneself primarily as a *consumer* of records. When you take this view, your identity can only be expressed through the playing and displaying of your vinyl commodities. If you *are* the records you own, you must display these to others in order to prove you exist, and that you count in the world of collecting. Presenting oneself as a consumer of records depends on the assumption that others can deduce the personality of the record collector from the records they own. In the process, the hard work of thinking and feeling in relation to complex musical works is replaced by a serial display of pictures of already famous record covers and labels. But a series of pictures of records says nothing about the way their owner uses them or what they think about them. In other words, nothing about their personality or being, ethical or otherwise, is expressed. Republican senator Marco Rubio's favorite record is, surprisingly, Tupac's *All Eyez on Me*,[4] but you'd be hard-pressed to connect that simple fact to his politics. The mere fact that someone enjoys certain records says nothing about how they interact with those records or how those records have shaped their identity.

If such self-presentation through one's record collection is so patently superficial, you may be asking, why is it so popular among collectors? First, it's fun to share pictures of records! But also it may be partially rooted in class anxiety. The occasional display of records you love is one thing, but continual self-definition through displaying the records you own seems to be encouraged by our class-conscious, hypercompetitive society. This means collectors, like everyone else, tend to measure themselves and their collections against everyone else's. Much of the display of vinyl commodities that takes place online and in real life can be explained by this fact—people are in essence selling themselves to other collectors, competing against others to be valued in the record world's eyes.

Sometimes this competition comes in the form of belonging—"I have this, too"—and sometimes in the form of distancing—"I have this and you don't." The first form is often expressed with hashtags—#vinyligclub, #vinylcommunity, #vinyljunkie, and so on—which express one's belonging on the sheer basis of preferring vinyl to the other formats. In this way, even pics of common records signal one's belonging to the club. The second form, which we've already discussed elsewhere, comes in the display of rare records. Here the point is to distinguish yourself by sparking interest and perhaps even envy in your friends and followers. If the first type of display shows you belong in the record game, the second establishes that you are doing something special within it.

The connection between records and status seeking is never more clearly expressed than in the genre of Instagram post that pairs a picture of a rare LP (usually but not always a jazz record, preferably an old Blue Note) with a fancy wine, whiskey, or luxury food item. With a studied casualness, such posts are inevitably captioned something like "just relaxing with a full-bodied Malbec and Hank Mobley's *No Room for Squares* #straightnochaser." Here, it's not uncommon to see hashtags like #analogonly next to ones like #jazzandwine or #singlemaltwhiskey. In this genre of leisure class vinyl post, as with so many acts of display, records are equated with other "high-end" lifestyle signifiers. So not only are records used to sell oneself as a serious, prestigious collector; they are also used to self-market one's connoisseurship more broadly to the world at large.

But the competitive display of one's record prowess also can take a more down-to-earth form, under the sign of hashtags like #dustyfingers and #digginginthecrates. Posts in this genre boast not of one's superior spending power or taste but rather one's ability to find valuable records in the physical (as opposed to the digital) world. As the dirt and dust in these hashtags (and in the pictures they accompany) attest, these posts celebrate one's prowess at doing the hard, manual labor of "digging." They are a way to distinguish oneself from internet-only record collectors, who get their records strictly from eBay and Discogs. These posts, often taken "in the wild" in basements, small shops, and other "digging spots," seek to prove the poster's bona fides as a real digger, not just an internet shopper. Often, these posts come drenched in machismo—tender pictures of dirty hands as proof of a poster's masculinity. While connoisseurs' posts imply the potency of their wealth, diggers' posts imply the power of their minds and bodies. Both, however, are engaging in competitive shadow plays of a bygone era. The fact is that the internet has knocked the legs out of both old-school "tough guy" digging and refined vinyl connoisseurship. When you can buy (or at least download) almost every record you want online, all the puffed-up display around record collecting is exposed for what it perhaps always was—a form of competitive shopping for men. With both these forms delegitimized by changes in the vinyl economy, it's time to put the focus back on listening, thinking, and feeling with the records themselves. Here, I again put my hope in younger record collectors. They seem to share record links on social media for reasons beyond self-positioning in games of cultural capital, such as the simple fact that a record moves them, intrigues them, or makes them curious about the historical moment that produced it. The best of the young collectors share music online in the spirit of the communal record pools like David Mancuso's New York Record Pool, and not the record fairs Gregg Turkington so scathingly describes in the introduction to this chapter. If record culture is to remain a zone for active listening and discovery of new sounds, collectors will need to stop asserting their status through displays of known "classics" and the received wisdom that comes with them. But insofar as I've touched here on masculinity in record collecting, I'm anticipating the next and final section of this chapter on the function of gender in the record world.

## GENDER

The field of record collecting is overwhelmingly male. Of Carolina Soul's 16,000+ Instagram followers, only 21 percent identify as female. The known "names" of record collecting—Tefteller, Moerer, and Manship—are all men. Turkington's description of the record fair—"there's no women there"—while hyperbolic, points to an absolutely real problem. If love for music is universal across all gender lines, as I believe it is, it seems to be a political phenomenon (and not a biological "fact") that women are so woefully underrepresented in the world of record collecting. If biological determinism (just-so stories like "guys like to dig and hunt" dressed up as hard science) won't explain this grave gender imbalance, what will?

We've already hinted at one explanation in the section above—masculine competition. The toxic masculinity that drives this sort of behavior puts off many lovers of music, male and female, but particularly women and nonbinary folks. Men being socialized to compete—in business, sports, war, and sex—bring their nonegalitarian socialization into record collecting. As a result, all those who don't view collecting as a blood sport essentially have to decide if finding great records is worth the hassle. Every one of our female co-workers and/or record collecting female friends can reel off a list of times they've been sexually harassed, intimidated, or talked down to by male collectors with an aggressive, competitive attitude. If you are a woman working behind the counter at a record store, a man may tell you he's seen dogs there before but never a "female"; or he may only speak to you about female artists in order to flirt, or ask you what record he should buy for his wife, or just generally condescend to you as if you have no knowledge of or experience with records. Even though you obviously *work in a record store.*

Google "guy with vinyl records" and you'll find pictures of a lot of identikit record nerds looking through records. Google "woman with vinyl records," however, and you'll see something quite different. The first image, as of 2019, is of a woman licking an LP; the second a woman in a short miniskirt and a half-unbuttoned flannel shirt next to a pile of records. Almost every image on the first page of search results is highly sexualized in some way, featuring photo shoots of made-up women in various states of undress modeling alongside records. In these pictures, records and women alike are used as props—whereas many of the pictures of "guy with vinyl" show them playing the expert with real records, most of the pictures of women are highly theatricalized and read as staged. Record Instagram is filled with accounts dedicated to women posing erotically with albums or reproducing racy album covers. It's not uncommon to see DJ sets and record fairs marketed with cheesecake-style photography. In posts like these, the hashtag #vinylporn takes on a nearly literal meaning. This is not to say that the hashtag #vinylporn demeans through its association with sexuality, but because it has nothing to do with the music itself, women are more likely to be equated with records as objects of desire than to be represented as fellow collectors. In this context, the "porn" could be a picture of anything "sexy" or luxurious. What's worse, many posters for record stores and dance parties still use such softcore iconography as a "draw" for their stores and events, just as many funk and soul events unwisely use retro pictures of black life to lend their parties some sort of ambient racial credibility.

The message is clear—every herby white guy is a collector, while women are just accessories. The double fetishism that sometimes comes with blackness and "black" records also comes into play in such sexualized images of women with records—the reification of living culture into pieces of plastic goes hand in hand with the objectification of women in music. And while Safiya Umoja Noble convincingly made the case in *Algorithms of Oppression* that search engines reproduce old biases and foster new ones, this can't be chalked up to Google's problem alone. A culture that until recently thought it was okay to call a genre of records "titty-shakers" (we call it "mod instrumental") and still supports an active market for softcore "cheesecake records" from the 1950s and '60s still has a lot of work to do on the gender equality front. Men have politically and numerically dominated record collecting since its inception and have over time built a culture that is at best indifferent, but often outright hostile, to women. It's no wonder that more women and nonbinary folks feel excluded or included as less-than tokens or sexualized accessories.

As music critic Mike McGonigal recently reminded us in a Facebook thread, record "digging" has become a macho way for men to masculinize record *shopping*, an activity that has been historically coded as feminine. This attitude, too, with its casual sexism, of course also inhibits women from becoming more active in the record game. If shopping projects a banal, leisured image of a stroll from shop to shop, digging projects an active world of strenuous physical labor. The image of the digger is inherently masculine, and as a result, there's much casual machismo on record collector Instagram. People display their "digs" (often hashtagged #DITC or #digginginthecrates) in the same way game hunters take pictures of their kills. Hashtags like #waxwars play up the competitive, martial aspect of collecting, as if the ease with which you can find records online hasn't rendered all this posturing as obsolete as it is laughable. There's a desperate sense of people trying to project their coolness into the ether through their consumption, with countless videos of people digging through what usually look like fair to middling stacks of vinyl. Any average record store becomes aggrandized in elevated diction as "the field" or "the stacks," just like any home recording studio for a SoundCloud rapper gets played up as "the lab." Male collectors often post prices under pictures of their finds—and of course they always are scoring #greatfinds from the dollar bins. If an outsider were to take these posts at face value, they would be forgiven for thinking record collecting was a violent contact sport of some sort.

When women are not being fetishized as sexual accessories for #vinylporn posts, they are being tokenized as outliers and oddities. While record collecting is taken as a perfectly normal, natural hobby for a boy or man, it can never be taken as such in a woman. Women or nonbinary collectors who don't participate in the sexualization of their relation to records get treated as eccentrics, weirdos who are "making a statement" or "just trying to make themselves stand out." They are doing something slightly aberrant or strange—not just pursuing a love of music as is assumed of their male counterparts. Most of my female collector friends do it more quietly and less ostentatiously than their male counterparts. They aren't constantly posting pictures of records or bragging about their finds on Twitter and in Facebook groups. I suspect this is partially to avoid exceptional treatment, in which they are treated more as a novelty or oddity than a peer. Talked over, condescended to, or sexualized, it can be generally unpleasant to be a woman in a sea of male record nerds. Not to mention the fact that women are assumed to only be interested in "girly" records—Joni Mitchell's *Blue* is a great record, but I'm sure women in vinyl could do without ever talking about it with a male record collector ever again.

When women are not being sexualized or tokenized, they are sometimes used as foils for a male collector to burnish his own status as a vinyl expert— hence the figure of the collector's wife. This genre of representation of women in collecting often takes the form of the long-suffering wife of the record collector. The blog *My Husband's Stupid Record Collection* caused a minor furor in collector circles a couple of years ago—it features reviews and selfies featuring records in the author's husband's collection. While it was divisive with its defenders and critics, to our mind Judy Berman pegged it, writing that the blog ultimately "perpetuates the more general, '70s-Woody-Allen-worthy idea that heterosexual relationships revolve around men educating women."[5] In the grand scheme of things, the blog seems harmless—it doesn't set back gender equality in any serious way, and there are bigger battles to be fought. But it does reflect a patriarchal dynamic between men and women often encountered in collecting, in which women are positioned as vinyl helpmeets, not quite autonomous music fans themselves. These are the sort of meek and supportive women you sometimes see forced to wait while their husband or boyfriend digs through the stacks of a record store. The quirky faux-naïveté projected in the blog and by many partners of male record collectors I met can perhaps best be understood as a way of coping with a husband who doesn't treat you as their intellectual equal. But it is also a far cry from a full-throated feminism of the sort necessary to shake up the boys' club of record collecting.

Finally, there are structural barriers, as well as attitudinal ones, holding women back from reaching the highest levels of the record world. Consider, for example, that when it comes to going on house calls to buy records, men can obviously navigate going to a stranger's house with much more freedom and safety than a woman or nonbinary person. In this, the threat of gendered violence no doubt has a prohibitive effect on many women who might otherwise get more seriously into buying vinyl. The same goes, unfortunately, for many brick-and-mortars—they are not as welcoming to a non-male clientele. Men in such spaces are much more likely to challenge the record knowledge and general authority of women. Consciously and unconsciously, the competence that is assumed of any random man selling or buying records is not afforded to women.

I realize the claims in this chapter can probably be taken in one of two ways. For some, the slightest mention of politics in record collecting is "too PC," an impolite and unnecessary insertion of a divisive subject matter into a hobby we use to "escape" politics. To these people, I say simply, wake up. Your desire to escape politics through a hobby is itself a political statement, one that usually comes from a place of immense privilege—the inability or unwillingness to tolerate political readings of "hobbies." After years of working in the vinyl industry, it is clear to me that people's politics show up in the records they collect, the way they think and talk about music, and the way they use their records. Putting your head in the sand when problems come up is the surest way to perpetuate them.

Or you might read this chapter and think, "Of course." Of course white male record collectors, taken as a class, can be "problematic." For you, I'd suggest that it never hurts to remind yourself that theory and practice are two different things. How many of us have betrayed our beliefs in practice? If you find yourself agreeing with much of what's above in this chapter, think about whether you are consistently practicing your stated commitments. Antiracism, antipatriarchy, and economic egalitarianism are easier to claim than to manifest in everyday life.

Much of what we've discussed is structural and systemic, not changeable by random acts of kindness by isolated individuals. The personal is political, but politics is not only personal—ethics and politics are related but not at all the same. There are differences of scale between the two. All one can do is critique the system and be attuned to what one can do as an individual and member of various record communities.

HE'S COMING ROY AYERS UBIQUITY
BOB MARLEY & THE WAILERS UPRISING
NATIONA
MES THE SUN - NINA SIMONE
LEROY HUTSON/LOVE OH LOVE
ROY AYERS/LET'S DO IT
ETTA JAMES • COME A LITTLE CLOSER
WHERE I'M COMING FROM • STEVIE WONDER
S - 21.126
HOT BUTTERED SOUL - ISAAC HAYES
ISAAC HAYES TO BE CONTINUED
CURTIS MAYFIELD/SUPER FLY
ISAAC HAYES · IN THE BEGINNING
ORIZON SP 736
C FUNK ■ JIMMY McGRIFF
D ARTISTS WAR
UNITED ARTISTS RECORDS, INC., LOS ANGELES, CALIF
"DO YOU SEE WHAT I SEE?" THE BAR-KAYS
JE BLAND • DREAMER
Electronic Magnetism – Solomon Burke

# CHAPTER 5

## Experiencing Records

We feel our way through the world. Some neurologists believe there are twenty-one discrete faculties of perception. But because music is abstract—we can't see or touch it—it doesn't use all of the senses equally. Rather, it works on our fundamental inner perceptions, the sense of things not seen. And records, because they allow for the most intense, directed form of experiencing music, have the most potential to reshape our perceptions at the root. The right records can revolutionize not only *what* we think and feel, but *how* we think and feel.

In this chapter, we discuss four building blocks that records manipulate to alter our perceptions—time, voice, space, and dynamics. I picked these because they're equally central to both life and listening. It would be impossible to navigate fully the world without a feeling for life's tempos, voices, atmospheres, and patterns of change. And it's just as difficult to listen to music without a grasp of these zones of experience.

But our senses are made, not born. Real life pulls them in one direction, records in another. More and more, the two even contradict each other. On the one hand, our day-to-day life is increasingly shaped by corporations and states pushing behavioral norms on us. The powers that be present certain tempos and atmospheres, certain conceptions of identity and change, as normal, natural, and inevitable. This they do in order to make us more pliant consumers and more governable citizens. On the other hand, records (the good ones at least) work to unravel and transcend the norms society habitually pounds into us. They can make us less predictable, more joyous, and freer people. Listening to records can make over our senses of time, voice, space, and dynamics, and in doing so work to transform our being. In other words, while the world disciplines our senses, the best records educate them. Records are tools for the unworking of social control—a means to experiment with our most elementary ways of experiencing the world. They disclose new ways of living blocked by today's dominant political and economic system. What the "system" presents as fate, records reopen to the imagination and questioning.

But how best to unlock the transformative potential of records? While every listener and collector can and should find their own ways into this experience, there's also no substitute for a sound method. Without one, it's pretty easy to get lost in the vinyl wilds, groping in the dark for a path forward. So below, I'll elaborate a listening method that I hope will help you get the most out of your day-to-day record listening.

To experience a record fully, I believe you first need to understand the perceptual conventions it reshapes. Let's start by briefly summarizing the standard forms of time, voice, space, and dynamics that prevail in the world today. These are the ways of perceiving thrust on us as givens in daily life. First, consider time. As employees, consumers, citizens, and users, we're expected to shift gears continually from one speed of life to the next. Second, think about voice. Online and in "real" life, the search for a voice has mutated into so many acts of self-branding. More complex experiences of self-making have given way to theatricalized self-marketing on and off of social media. Third, think about sonic space—the sound atmospheres that surround us. As we move from private to public space and back again, we're increasingly asked to accept the generic sound environments that accompany gentrification and "development." And fourth, when it comes to dynamics, we must consider our expectations about what can and cannot be changed in the world. Here, we've been led to believe we no longer have the power to reimagine and transform our world. Corporations and governments are at liberty to "disrupt" and "innovate," while we are left to bow and scrape before them as loyal followers.

Thankfully, records provide escape routes from these contemporary norms. For each of the four norms I've selected, we'll explore three modes of alternative experience that records have the power to open up. For time, we'll examine the ways records can slow us down, set us cruising, or speed up our inner sense of time. In doing so, these records model coherent and exciting paces for life outside the norm. For voice, we'll look at records that use the human voice to expand our sense of what's expressible—singular, double, and collective uses of singing to transcend the economically rational, self-interested brand of selfhood we're each expected to sell to one another. For space, we'll break down records

| EXPERIENTIAL ZONE | NORM | ALTERNATIVE 1 | ALTERNATIVE 2 | ALTERNATIVE 3 |
|---|---|---|---|---|
| Time | Fragmented | Braking | Mid-tempo | Accelerating |
| Voice | Branded | Singular | Doubled | Collective |
| Space | Generic | Alienating | Defamil-iarizing | Immersive |
| Dynamics | Balance/stasis | Breaking down | Recycling | Transforming |

that carve out an atmosphere for local, augmented, and virtual worlds of sound, beyond the canned atmospherics we now encounter everywhere in public and digital space. Finally, for dynamics, we'll examine musical systems that break down, recycle, and radically transform from moment to moment, empowering the listener to feel the world as still pregnant with the possibility for change despite history's late date.

For each zone of experience, we'll use three examples that model alternative ways of thinking and feeling outside of the norm. After this, we'll run down the ways different genres use a given technique to produce different effects from the main example. Without an understanding of genre, it's easy to lump together all records that share a certain stylistic characteristic, such as a slow tempo or an ambient atmosphere. But as we'll see, the same musical features can work to different ends depending on genre. For example, the draggy tempo of the Cure's "Faith" (*Faith*, Elektra, 1981) has much different effects on us than Joe Brown and the Soul Elderados' soul-psych ballad "Vibration" (F.F.A. Records, 1974), despite the fact that they share a tempo. And as in this Cure/Joe Brown example, I've chosen to use both rare and familiar LPs, 45s, and 12" records for discussion. In this way, I hope to expose you to new ways of hearing familiar records and have you see the connection more obscure ones have to the larger world of records.

I recommend this general method for experiencing records. We recommend it as a way to connect multiple layers of your record-listening experience. It begins with the individual, visceral reaction to a single record and ends in consideration of the dreams implicit in whole genres. It works in the present to uncover possibilities for the future. It attempts to do justice to the breathtaking variety of feelings and dreams that records drawn out of the vinyl deeps can produce. I hope this method will enable you to link your private experiences as an isolated record listener to some of humanity's most enduring and powerful visions for a better world. Up first, time.

## EXPERIENTIAL ZONE 1: TIME

The modern experience of time is fragmentary—on any given day, we're expected to shift from private time to public time and then back again. We navigate social media platforms, wade in and out of the twenty-four-hour cable news cycle, track stock tickers and betting lines, play video games, spend time with friends and loved ones. We work, then crash, and repeat the process the next day. Maybe we worry over the accelerating pace of climate change; maybe we nervously eye the Bulletin of Atomic Scientists' Doomsday Clock as it creeps a bit closer to Midnight; maybe we fret over the instantaneous killing force of today's drones and nuclear missiles, terrorist attacks, or the heat death of the universe. Maybe we have face-to-face conversations or take time out for walks, runs, and drives. Wherever we are and whatever we're doing, we're immersed in a jumble of incommensurate time worlds. Each of these has its own tempo, and each is incompatible with the next. No one coherent rhythm of life prevails over any other.

To keep up we must be always on, constantly adjusting our inner tempo to one system after another's particular pace. And each time we switch from one tempo to another, it drains us a bit. Such temporal gear shifting is exhausting, chaotic, and disempowering. It tends to leave us in a perpetual state of limbo, alternately anxious or distracted, but never stable enough to feel expansive emotions like catharsis or euphoria. Constantly recalibrating our sense of pace, we usually feel just mild irritation or boredom. At best, we feel constantly behind—at worst, victimized by a battery of corporate and government clocks, each out of sync with one another and each indifferent to our own senses of time. Perpetually put back on our heels, it's hard not to feel out of rhythm, out of step, and out of joint.

This is where records come in—they model coherent, freeing rhythms for life. They organize time in ways that point the way out of our current temporal jumble. Good records train us in paces of life that go beyond today's hodgepodge of mismatched rhythms. Shirley Murdock's "The Beauty of It All" (*The Beauty of It All*, v/a compilation, Sound Trak, 198x) pumps the brakes to help us seek the divine in the everyday, Logg's "I Know You Will" (Salsoul 12", 1981) turns clock time's beat around in order to set us cruising, and Günter Schickert's "Puls"

(*Überfällig*, Sky, 1979) pulses with overdriven feeling of purpose. In a world of too many clocks, records like these help us keep our own time.

## TIME ALTERNATIVE 1: BRAKING

An obscure gospel record, Shirley Murdock's "The Beauty of It All" asks us to slow down so we can see the world anew. "The Beauty of It All" was released in the early 1980s on a private Toledo, Ohio, gospel label, Sound Trak. It came out years before Murdock's duet with Zapp's Roger Troutman on "Computer Love" (Warner Bros, 1985) and before her solo R&B hit "As We Lay" (Elektra, 1986). Even for gospel collectors, it's not a particularly well-known track, but it should be. Maybe better than any other record, it embodies the potential to be found in records that brake our sense of tempo. Despite their differences in other respects, all genres that slow the rhythms of our perceptions ask us, as "The Beauty of It All" does, to take the time needed to reinterpret the world around us.

From the beginning, "The Beauty of It All" demands that the listener slacken their inner pace: We are immediately drawn in by the sound of waves gently washing ashore. Before we know it, the song has sucked us in—we slow down to meet the rhythm of the waves. After a few seconds more, a flute and languorous drumbeat enter the scene. Murdock then joins these with a meditative, gentle vocal. A Rhodes piano soon follows, layering a stream of sound beneath the proceedings. The track begins to flow like water, submerging you in its time-taking pace. The lyrics ask us to break through appearances in order to find the deeper meaning of God's creation. Amid the chaos of everyday life, the song suggests, we fail to grasp the divine mysteries around us. We take them for granted, misunderstand them, or just plain stop looking for them. For Murdock, the tempos of secular life produce a sort of false consciousness. As a result, God's love and beauty are universal and eternal, but hidden from us. To perceive them, we need to put the brakes on modernity's deluge of competing rhythms and focus. In order to help us perceive the evidence of things not seen, "The Beauty of It All" suspends the listener in a warm and enveloping tempo.

But the record's no sermon: It doesn't just preach the need for second sight. Rather, "The Beauty of It All" produces a longing in us to slow down and see the world how Murdock and company do. It calms and soothes, physically putting us in rhythm with the turning of the tides both literal and theological. In this way, the record produces belief without resorting to dogma. It seduces rather than harangues. The genius of the best slow, dreamier gospel songs like "The Beauty of It All" comes in this power to show rather than tell. They manage to incarnate on record the feeling of belief. Such ambient gospel songs interrupt the jumbled time codes of contemporary life in order to clear space for a spiritual relation to elemental things. From the Singing Tornadoes' atmospheric gospel masterpiece "Walking on the Sea of Galilee" (*In That Great Gettin' Up Morning*, Expression Records, 1984) to Bob Dylan's last great Christian song, "Every Grain of Sand" (*Shot of Love*, Columbia, 1981), in sacred music, we find time run at half speed so the listener can track the traces of the divine. Regardless of genre, songs that brake time ask us to stop wasting our attention on surfaces and start penetrating the surfaces of modern life. But each genre also harbors different, sometimes contradictory dreams of what would emerge if we truly slowed everything down. We'll examine a few of these competing visions below.

The ballads, sea shanties, and dirges of the British folk revival of the 1960s and '70s slow our inner sense of time to forge communal spirit. Born of a counterculture suspicious of organized religion, the UK folk revival's braking tempos train listeners to imagine better ways for life to be lived in common. Songs like Anne Briggs's "Willie O'Winsbury" and Nic Jones's "Annan Water," and LPs like the Watersons' *Frost and Fire* and Shirley and Dolly Collins's *Anthems in Eden*, make use of ritual folk forms that predate industrialism. They explore an early modern–era (1500–1800) slowness not in order to put us in touch with God's majesty, but to help us imagine new organic forms of community. They immerse us in a pastoral sense of time, one that predates even mechanical clocks and the standardization of time. Even when UK folk artists added electric guitars and jazzy touches into the mix, they still aimed to keep time with vibrations from the woods, sea, and manor. To name just a few lovely examples: Steeleye Span's "Prince Charlie Stuart" (*Please to See the King*, Big Tree, 1971), Fairport Convention's "Who Knows Where the Time Goes?" (*Unhalfbricking*, Island, 1969), and Pentangle's "Lord Franklin" (*Cruel Sister*, Transatlantic, 1970) all reach back to bucolic time and ask listeners to do the same. Their tempos are a vehicle for us to reconnect with old ways explicitly presented as superior to those of our plastic present. In other words, the slowness of the British Isles folk revival kindles a desire for an artisanal life lived within the time of the forest. It presents us with a chance to reignite the communal rituals of the past. Of course the folk revival's pastoral idylls were always rooted in myth as much as in historical fact—but this does nothing to dampen the appeal of the genre's trips backward in time. These records help us press pause on a modern sense of time that keeps us separated, and generate a pace of life we could all share. This flowery utopian tradition endures explicitly in the works of artists like Richard Youngs, Alastair Galbraith, and Trembling Bells, and in a more subterranean form on pastoral records like Virginia Astley's stunning *From Gardens Where We Feel Secure* (Happy Valley, 1983).

American singer-songwriters of the same era found fewer assurances in pastoral time. When they engaged in medieval fantasy, they did so in the past tense, as on Tim Buckley's "Once I Was" (*Goodbye & Hello*, Elektra, 1967) or through a series of conditional propositions, as in Tim Hardin's "If I Were a Carpenter" (*Tim Hardin 2*, Verve Forecast, 1967). In other words, they treat pastoral time as a costume from the past to be donned and cast off at will. Rather than elaborating full-on dreams of medieval revival, American folkies tended to use slow tempos for self-searching, existential explorations.

In North American hands, Tolkien's tagline "Not all those who wander are lost" became less a statement than a question. Because Britons had a history they could trace back to the Roman Empire, it was naturally easier for British musicians to imagine they could actually recapture an early modern sense of time. Oxford and Cambridge are medieval institutions, *The Canterbury Tales* was written a century before Christopher Columbus was born, and some of the Child Ballads can be traced back to the thirteenth century. But UK folkies' American counterparts didn't have the history needed for a complete retreat into a mythic deep past.

Yet American singer-songwriters of the 1960s and '70s shared with the British a need to escape the fracturing speeds of modern life. Their ballads were less about lords and ladies and hills and dales, and more about inner states of limbo and waiting. Tim Buckley's "Song to the Siren" (*Starsailor*, Straight, 1970) and Tim Hardin's "If I Knew" (outtake from *Tim Hardin 2*, Verve Forecast, 1967), for example, take on the churning tempo of a boat rocking on an empty sea. For them, slow motion is no guarantee of purpose—one person's soul journey can become another's rudderless drift. Leonard Cohen's entire body of work was built negotiating this state and the deep feeling of indeterminacy it can produce. Braked time for (North) American singer-songwriters tends to be a vehicle for doubt more than anything else. Even Judee Sill's theologically assured "Lopin' Along thru the Cosmos" (*Judee Sill*, Elektra, 1971) figures slowing down as risk. "Lopin'" maunders without a set goal, depicting a pilgrim's progress without a map or guide. The only sure thing such songs register is a need to escape the "straight" world's time. But every American folk odyssey threatens shipwreck: Only time will tell. More recent records in this tradition—such as Kath Bloom and Loren Connors's *Sing the Children Over* (Ambiguous Records, 1982), Vic Chesnutt's *West of Rome* (Texas Hotel, 1992), Jana Hunter's *Blank Unstaring Heirs of Doom* (Gnomonsong, 2005), and Grouper's *The Man Who Died in His Boat* (Kranky, 2013)—are even darker, preserving a slow, questing pace while expecting less to come from it.

The sweet soul of the 1960s and early '70s, too, deals in glacial paces. But it is a city form which expresses no great longing for a return to the deep time found in heathers and glens. Nor does it explore the navel-gazing inner time that obsessed American folkies. Rather, it throttles our sense of time in order to dwell on every detail of modern romance. And this it does with melodramatic intensity. Like most sweet soul records, "Sunday" Williams's "Where Did He Come From" (Chess 45, 1969) brackets out the entire world to focus on the particulars of a single romantic relationship. Williams's phrasing invests a conventional boy-meets-girl story with world-important significance: Everything else pales in comparison. For sweet soul records, amatory feeling, loving and delicate, requires a simmering pace. For a listener lingering in the time of love, the rest of the world's time becomes unimportant.

Unlike "Where Did He Come From," the recently unearthed "Deep Shadows" by Little Ann Bridgeforth (an unissued Kent recording, 1966) has no happy ending. But it too slows time down to focus the listener on every nuance of pain and pleasure that love (or lack thereof) can bring. For sweet soul, as for its subgenre cousin deep soul, sensibility matters more than the narrative. For those looking to dig deeper into sweet and deep, start with obscure "oldie" jams like Brief Encounter's "Where Will I Go" (unreleased Seventy Seven side, 1970s) and the Highlighters' "Have a Little Faith" (Lulu 45, 1970s) and follow where they lead you.

Sweet soul above all other genres seeks to make time for love in a world that pretends to have more important things to do. But as soul moved into the 1970s, slowness began to be used for less-gut-wrenching, more polished effects. A song like the Floaters' "Float On" (*Floaters*, ABC, 1977) lives up to its title, creating a world of detached cool for the listener far from the immediate aching of sweet soul. Seventies duets like Roberta Flack and Donny Hathaway's "Be Real Black for Me" (*Roberta Flack and Donny Hathaway*, Atlantic, 1972) and Marvin Gaye and Diana Ross's "Just Say, Just Say" (*Diana & Marvin*, Motown, 1973) split the difference between raw pain and cool detachment, refining the directness of slow sweet soul ballad for success in the smooth '70s. Even into the '80s, the soul ballad form persisted in the radio-friendly "quiet storm" genre in the work of artists like Anita Baker, Sade, and Luther Vandross, and even in disguised form on crossover hits like Kate Bush's "This Woman's Work" (*The Sensual World*, EMI, 1989).

Like sweet soul, country ballads, too, use slowness to live on the pulses of romantic time. Gram Parsons and Emmylou Harris's "Hearts on Fire" (*Grievous Angel*, Reprise, 1974), for example, uses Al Perkins's pedal steel to lock the listener into its tale of love and loss. With or without pedal steel (an instrument that generally slows our sense of time), ballads like the Delmore Brothers' "I'll Be There" (King 78, 1951), Willie Nelson's "Blue Eyes Cryin' in the Rain" (*Red Headed Stranger*, Columbia, 1975), and John Anderson's "Wild and Blue" (*Wild and Blue*, WB, 1982) do the same, producing similar dreamy effects. These songs, too, slow our perceptual tempo to bend everyday life to the inner logic of love.

In sharp contrast, goth records use slowness to transcend the time of human relationships. This has sometimes led to the genre being written off as nihilistic. And it's true goth records slow time to render the time of the dead, as on Joy Division's "The Eternal" (*Closer*, Factory, 1980), or to touch the millennia-spanning time of primordial gods and monsters, as on Bauhaus's "Hollow Hills" (*Mask*, Beggars Banquet, 1981). But this isn't nihilistic. Rather, goth slowness is a means for human identification with eon-spanning inhuman forces. It seeks to cultivate a stoic otherworldliness in the listener, not an appetite for destruction. This desire for permanence manifests in both the goth obsession with statuary, and with authors like Arthur Machen, H. P. Lovecraft, and J. G. Ballard, whose stories and novels situate short human lives within the cosmic vastness of time. The icy slow motion of Joy Division's "The Eternal" expresses an abject vision, but not a hopeless one. Joy Division seeks a negative transcendence—an overcoming of human need—in favor of a more austere worldview more in touch with unchanging things. Bauhaus's creeping track "Hollow Hills," too, shuns the bright and sunny things of the sensual world. But if "The Eternal" uses slowness to develop an icy indifference to the painful insignificance of human time, "Hollow Hills" uses it to imagine an occult counter-time, a realm in which real terror and mystery are still accessible. Both Joy Division and Bauhaus find in slowness a means to resist modernity's powers of disenchantment. Doom metal, the sludgy, heavy offspring of Black Sabbath's first five LPs, could be said to be doing something very similar. And the slowcore genre, at least in the hands of its best 1990s practitioners Low and Bedhead, also finds in dragging tempos a means to raise garden variety suburban blues to the level of metaphysical melancholy. In this, slowcore shares goth's desperate search to find either a way out of suffering or, barring that, the power to accept it.

Psych, spiritual jazz, new age, and ambient records tend to build more obviously affirmative worlds out of slowness. They share singer-songwriters' focus on the expansion of inner experience but have little time for introspective dithering. Rather, they use mesmeric, hypnotic sounds to produce altered states in the listener. This they do to help us open ourselves to a cosmic, joyous sense of time. Psych pathbreakers 13th Floor Elevators created woozy, disorientating hymns out of Tommy Hall's electric jug runs, Roky Erickson's expressive phrasing, and Stacy Sutherland's echoing guitar lines. Songs like "Dust" (*Easter Everywhere*, International Artists, 1967) and "May the Circle Remain Unbroken" (*Bull of the Woods*, International Artists, 1969) are cosmic prayers. They bend the listener's perception of time in order to produce oceanic feelings of connection between all parts of the vast universe. The lyrics of "Dust" unite seemingly disparate categories of experience under the banner of love and pleasure— starting from a speck of dust, they leave us in space time. Slowness for 13th Floor Elevators and bands like them represents the true language of being, continually buried under the detritus of daily life's many incompatible tempos.

Like "Dust," Brazilian obscure psych outfit Satwa's "Valsa dos Cogumelos" (*Satwa*, Rozenblit, 1973) takes the listener on a lysergic-tinged voyage through time. Like a slow-moving hurricane, the song swirls with vertiginous energy. Led by a hypnotic acoustic guitar line from Lula Côrtes, the song waltzes the listener toward a peaceful state of union with a benevolent universe. But such meditative effects are not limited to psych records. Instrumental standards like Fleetwood Mac's "Albatross" (Blue Horizon 45, 1968) and Santo and Johnny's "Sleep Walk" (*Santo and Johnny*, Canadian American, 1959), not to mention Santo and Johnny's slept-on "Sea Dream" (*Disco d'Oro*, Pausa, 1975), all produce similarly otherworldly senses of slow time. And dreampop like Julee Cruise's *Floating into the Night* (Warner Brothers, 1989), which set the tone for David Lynch's *Twin Peaks*, uses slowness to forge a compromise between goth's sense of cosmic horror and folk's pastoral visions of natural calm. Psych and its inheritor dreampop, too, use slowness to imagine linkages between all things great and small to be found in the universe.

Spiritual jazz seeks mystical truth through experiments in deceleration. But as jazz is an inherently improvisational form, it puts the emphasis on process rather than preconceived ideals of perfection. Rather, slowness in spiritual jazz becomes the precondition for musicians to find truth together, in the actual moment of recording. Tracks like Phil Cohran's "White Nile" (*African Skies*, Captcha, 2010), Pharoah Sanders's "Harvest Time" (*Pharoah*, India Navigation, 1977), and Khan Jamal's "The Known Unknown" (*Infinity*, Con'brio, 1984) feature bands coming together to produce gently accreting streams of time. In the listener, they produce floating, peaceful states of consciousness. Alice Coltrane's "Turiya" (*Huntington Ashram Monastery*, Impulse!, 1969), built around glissandos from Coltrane's harp, produces mesmeric effects. It suspends the listener in a cloud of lush textures, as each instrumentalist begins pursuing their own slow tempos, improvising until they find a shared sense of time. Like Satwa's "Valsa dos Cogumelos," "Turiya" doesn't develop in the traditional sense so much as it experiments with endless variations on a theme. It doesn't progress so much as slowly concentrate power around the fixed point of Coltrane's harp.

Finally, new age more than any other genre trades in slow tempos. Unlike records in other genres, however, new age albums were often explicitly made to reduce listener stress and relax the body. In other words, slowness in new age often has an explicit therapeutic function. It's not for nothing that Grammy-winning new age pioneer Steven Halpern has published music therapy books with titles like *Sound Health* and albums for incredibly specific therapeutic purposes, like 1994's *Overcoming Substance Abuse*. Constance Demby, whose "Darkness of Space" (*Sunborne*, Gandarva, 1980) is a new age classic, to this day runs sound healing workshops she claims provide attendees with "a therapeutic bath on a cellular level." Whatever the medical validity of new age's more outlandish promises, it's undeniable that the genre can produce profound states of relaxation in body and mind. For example, Pythagoron's twenty-one-minute "TR1" deploys a calming synth thrum to deliver subliminal pulses of serenity. Kevin Braheny's "Lullaby for the Hearts of Space" (*Lullaby*, 1980 [not on label]) is built around the sounds of deceleration and begins with a spacy synth ripped straight from a 1960s sci-fi TV serial. The song works to center the listener, to bring them a feeling of control, which develops over time. It bends the linear pattern of traditional song structure into a gentle, circular pattern in which its beginning and end are interchangeable.

Composerly works not classed as new age, nevertheless, sometimes use slow, repetitive figures to produce healing effects in the listener. Records usually found in the classical section of the record store, like Hiroshi Yoshimura's *Music for Nine Post Cards* (Sound Process, 1982), Robert Ashley's *Automatic Writing* (Lovely Music, 1979), and Eliane Radigue's *Biogenesis* (not on label, 1974), regenerate and bring peace to us in ways that feel distinctively new age. Either through extended use of drones or via lush daubs of textured sound, they too guide the listener toward the few remaining still points to be found in this turning world.

# TIME ALTERNATIVE 2: MID-TEMPO

If slow records produce meditative states, fast records do the reverse. Acceleratory music, as we'll see in the next section, drags us along with it kicking and screaming, leaving time to react but not reflect. But what about the many records that fall between slow and speedy? While it might be tempting to dismiss mid-tempo music as a bland compromise form, this would be selling it short. After all, a huge number of musical works are neither fast nor slow—and can be found in every genre of popular recording, from garage to G-funk, old-time fiddle to house and techno. Mid-tempo vinyl wouldn't be as ubiquitous as it is if it didn't offer something perceptually unique.

In fact, the mid-tempo's intermediate status makes it powerful. Situated between the speeds of contemplation and sensation, mid-tempo helps the listener bridge thought with feeling. By uniting mind and body, it asks for us to test our dreams in action. It can do so because it moves in the rhythmic range of everyday life, which encompasses the normal heartbeat, the average walking pace, and most popular dances. Mid-tempo records require active engagement, whether this be physical (singing and dancing) or psychic (visions and plans). Because they ask for our participation, mid-tempo records can be classed as what folklorist Harry Smith dubbed "social music"—they're made to be shared. Unlike our private joys and pains, which begin and end in isolation, the hopes and fears carried by mid-tempo records are public in nature. Even the most obscure record—the most "private" of privately pressed 45s or the one-of-a-kind Voyager Golden Record (sent into outer space in 1977 to communicate with extraterrestrials)—was made for an imagined public. And of all records, the mid-tempo ones are most conducive to the creation of what George Lipsitz calls a "plurality of new social relationships"[1]—whether these relationships are forged on the dancefloor or among the record store stacks. Mid-tempo records were made both to share inspiration and to inspire sharing.

When caught up by mid-tempo records that cruise, "choogle," groove, glide, or strut, we relate to the world with desire and interest. In this state, what we see both with our eyes and in front of our mind's eye abounds with meaning and potential. By freeing up our desire to move, love, and assess; to entertain friends and strangers; and to plan new projects, they encourage action. By pleasing and teasing us, they inject stakes back into our often inert and dull social existence. They body forth a present and future that matter, to which we cannot be indifferent. They ask for a poetic sense of life to replace our workaday one. For both bedroom wallflowers and dancefloor freaks, the best mid-tempo extinguishes feelings of detachment and stasis. And in their manipulations of listener joy and pain, these records demand a passionate grappling with the present and future. When a mid-tempo work no longer inspires this passion in listeners, it can be consigned to the scrap heap. But because rhythms often age better than melodies, the great mid-tempo grooves and glides still reach out to us from the past all the time.

They have the power to do this insofar as they can make our feelings of tension pleasurable. Mid-tempo records work on us in two major ways. The heavier, more groove-oriented genres that use mid-tempo—like funk, Afrobeat, hard rock, and EBM—tend to build up tension without releasing it. On the other hand, poppier genres using mid-tempo—like easy glide, high life, modern soul, and "classic" rock—tend to build up pressure in order to release it. But as we'll see below, these are just general patterns—all genres use mid-tempo to provoke both heavy pleasures and soft torments in listeners. If much of the world at large asks us to pursue ultimately nihilistic ends—profit and prestige—mid-tempo records produce the belief that comes with love, passion, and the imagination to break the bonds of the merely factual.

No mid-tempo genre depends on this interplay between listener pleasure and pain more than boogie, and few artists negotiated the relation between the two as expertly as producer, mixer, and Paradise Garage DJ Larry Levan. Boogie, as you'll recall from earlier in this book, is what disco turned into after 1979's rockist backlash. As disco's currency for the general public waned, boogie musicians replaced live orchestras with synthesizers and drum machines while remaining faithful to disco's danceable four-on-the-floor rhythms. As with disco artists before them and house and techno ones after, successful boogie musicians worked to both bind and free their listeners. Larry Levan was a master of both mid-tempo modes—he made both brilliant records that are instantly gratifying and others that ratchet up the more difficult pleasures of frustration and anticipation.

In the first category, there's Levan's tight, concise production work on Logg's "I Know You Will" (Salsoul 12", 1981). A collaboration between Levan and Black Ivory's Leroy Burgess, "I Know You Will" is a boogie landmark. The song is built around a single bass, drum, and synth groove, and if it were an instrumental, this rhythm's repetitive looping would build tension. But Burgess's vocal frees the listener of pressure with every burst of his "I know you will" chorus. His singing seeds the song with many brief liberating moments of relaxation, which recur throughout the track. Even Levan's nine-minute, thirty-second 12" extended mix of "I Know You Will," while a bit slower and more digressive, preserves this build-and-release format—every time the groove pulls the cord tight, Burgess comes along and slackens its tension. "I Know You Will" is a record made to produce moments of joyful connection on the dancefloor. But even outside the club, it inspires a warm desire for togetherness, a need to break out of one's private thoughts and share the world with others.

On the other hand, there's *Padlock* (Garage EP, 1985), Levan's "special mix" of five Gwen Guthrie tracks. *Padlock* perpetually promises but always delays moments of listener transport. Borrowing a technique from dub reggae, Levan reworks Guthrie's original vocal tracks into an echo-laden, ghostly presence. This puts the emphasis on the heavy, insistent keyboard, bass, and drum rhythms (played by such luminaries as Wally Badarou and Sly & Robbie)—and forces the listener to lock into *Padlock*'s grooves. Using synth interstitials and beat matching to suture together "Hopscotch," "Seventh Heaven," "Getting Hot," "Peanut Butter," and "Padlock," Levan creates a unified whole. The overall effect is to drum up tension without ever providing catharsis—instead, the album generates more and more frustrated desire in the listener over time. This desire must be discharged elsewhere, and this forces the listener to go into the future with interest and engagement. Fittingly, this thirty-four-minute mini album doesn't culminate in a crescendo or conclusion of any sort so much as it just abruptly stops—after all, how can a record that seeks to prolong desire ever really end? The EP and other mid-tempo records like it leave this question to be resolved by the listeners in their "real" lives.

If "I Know You Will" provides many small bursts of joy in order to sustain our engagement with the world, *Padlock* defers such moments of release, building up potential energy in listeners to be activated later. Both mid-tempo modes heighten the lust for life—the first in the present, through epiphanic bursts of joy, and the second through a sharpening of our perceptions, an intensification of our desire for future fulfillment. This tension in Levan's mixes, between modes that generate pleasure in the present and those that heighten our taste for it in the future, are also at work within every dance genre that uses mid-tempo rhythms. The same divide can be found, for instance, in rhythm-heavy genres of the 1970s, '80s, and '90s—Italo, EBM, synthpop, house, techno, and modern soul. You can divide each of these genres into two types—records that bring immediate fulfillment and those that stoke our expectations for such satisfaction.

Nor is this divide limited to just dance vinyl—it's general to every mid-tempo genre. A canonical rock group like Fleetwood Mac, for example, uses mid-tempo in both of the ways described above. Tracks like "Dreams" (*Fleetwood Mac*, Reprise, 1975) and "Sara" (*Tusk*, WB, 1979) tease resolution without ever providing it, while songs like "Gypsy" (*Mirage*, WB, 1982) build to not one but two cathartic moments: Stevie Nicks's late vocal bridge and Lindsey Buckingham's incandescent concluding guitar solo. And the same dichotomy can be found throughout the classic rock canon—for example, on the records of Creedence Clearwater Revival. CCR's mid-tempo "chooglers" like "Run Through the Jungle" (*Cosmo's Factory*, Fantasy, 1970) and "Keep on Chooglin'" (*Bayou Country*, Fantasy, 1969) lock us into a tense, heightened state of mind. They're built on repeating riffs and grooves rather than strong melodies, and so never resolve. On the other hand, rousing anthems like "Hey Tonight" (*Pendulum*, Fantasy, 1970) and "Fortunate Son" (*Willy & The Poor Boys*, Fantasy, 1969) are made to release bursts of joy or righteous rage in the listener every time John Fogerty's gravelly choruses detonate.

Then there are the mid-tempo funk records. Both the Meters and James Brown and the JBs are unquestioned pioneers of the funk genre but do opposing things with a mid-tempo pace. The Meters work out minimal, self-contained forms using unbearably tight rhythms, on tracks like "Cissy Strut" and "Cardova" (both from *The Meters*, Josie, 1969), as well as "Chicken Strut" and "Joog" (*Struttin'*, Josie, 1970). Their arrangements are stripped down, their grooves insistent and repetitive. The Meters create closed systems, and our delight as listeners comes from the alert state of mind they elicit. By stirring desire they cannot satisfy, the Meters' records leave the listener always attentive and alive. They ask us to go into the future with hope and anxiety—with anything but apathy.

On the other hand, The JBs' mid-tempo tracks like "The Grunt" (King 45, 1970) and "Cold Sweat" (King 45, 1967) overflow with surprising new sounds and textures at every turn. Each measure of "The Grunt" is crammed with new notes from the JBs' horn section. And James Brown's expressive lead vocal, full of screams, grunts, and laments, dialogues with the horns in a different dynamic combination with every return of the main groove. This type of funk provides its pleasures in the present with no delay.

Finally, let's consider the operations dub reggae artists perform on their source material. Dub records are remixes—as a result, it's easy for us to "A-B," to compare a dub record with its source material. Dub "versions" decompose the traditional song structure of their originals, in the process turning songs that develop and grow into ones that loop and recycle themselves. Dub turns reggae from light into dark and moves it toward less immediately pleasing, headier forms. Take Scientist's *Scientist Rids the World of the Evil Curse of the Vampires* (Greensleeves, 1981), a contender for the best dub LP ever made.

Scientist created *Rids the World* using the records of just four roots reggae artists—the Wailing Souls, Wayne Jarrett, Michael Prophet, and Johnny Osbourne. And what he does to Wayne Jarrett's original "Love in Mi Heart" (*Chip In*, Greensleeves, 1982; Scientist's dub was made second but released first) typifies the difference between straight reggae and dub. "Love in Mi Heart" is an effervescent track, dominated by Jarrett's melodic, sweet tenor and sliding portamenti. Backed with staccato horn triplet, Jarrett's vocal gives the piece structure—a clear beginning, middle, and end. Scientist's version, "Blood on His Lips," though, strips out both Jarrett's vocal and the Roots Radics' horn lines completely—leaving only the basic "riddim" and an insectoid, tape-manipulated hi-hat click (which was subliminally low in the original mix). By doing so, Scientist has refashioned an expressive love song into a claustrophobic head trip.

The same goes for Scientist's transmutation of Wailing Souls' "Fire House Rock" (Greensleeves, 1981), *Rids The World*'s "The Mummy's Shroud." Here, Scientist takes out most of Wailing Souls' rootsy, impassioned vocals, preferring to focus on a minor rhythm guitar figure. He raises this figure in the mix and turns it into the new track's rhythmic center. While there are exceptions, roots reggae generally uses the mid-tempo for the release of emotion, and dub tends to cultivate a pleasurable tension, storing up frustration and expectation for the future.

Sample-based mid-tempo rap inherited this dichotomy directly from dub. For example, one major difference between East Coast and West Coast rap productions comes down to whether they work like traditional reggae to provide release or like dub to delay it. Compare the desublimated pleasures of Dr. Dre and DJ Quik's G-funk productions with the dynamic tension of New York ones by RZA (Wu-Tang Clan) and Havoc (Mobb Deep). West Coast productions tend to be jubilant, crackling with extroverted energy, while East Coast ones explore darker and tenser affairs. In his heyday, Dr. Dre often sampled exuberant party music from the 1970s and '80s like Parliament-Funkadelic, Kleeer, Zapp, and Michael McDonald, while RZA preferred moody, ruminative deep and crossover soul tracks like Wendy Rene's "After Laughter" (Stax 45, 1964) and the Charmels' "As Long As I've Got You" (Stax 45, 1967). If a good G-funk record seeks to turn the listener into a live wire, spilling free-flowing current everywhere, a good East Coast rap record treats them like a capacitor, caching their power for later use.

## TIME ALTERNATIVE 3: ACCELERATION

According to French theorist Paul Virilio, we're all victims of speed. If Virilio's 1977 book *Speed and Politics* is to be believed, accelerative military technology has taken over our lives and disempowered us in the process. The nuclear weapon is Virilio's central example of this phenomenon—in the atomic era, total war can break out in a single instant. In *Speed and Politics*, the "bomb" erases the boundary between civilian and combatant, rendering us all its unwilling subjects. Modern speed leaves us in an "aimless and permanent state of emergency."[2] Within this new existential state, Virilio claims, we trade "life" for "survival."[3] Dominated by a regime of militarized speed too fast for us to control, economic and political transformation seems impossible. According to *Speed and Politics*, the motors that once drove history—mass movements and group ideologies—have been left in the dust by a newly sovereign war machine.

Clearly, the penetration of speed into our daily lives has been thorough. The systems that shape our perceptions have only grown faster and more chaotic since *Speed and Politics* was published in 1977. The nuclear threat still looms. The destruction of our environment is picking up speed at a nightmarish rate ("the slowness of climate change is a fairytale" warns David Wallace-Wells on the first page of *The Uninhabitable Earth*[4]). Catastrophe and violence bubble up in new forms on a regular basis around the globe. More than ever, speed kills.

But if *Speed and Politics* remains a compelling account of contemporary ills, it fails as a prescription for the future. It does nothing to help us imagine a life beyond the limits of today's system. For Virilio, modern speed is fundamentally all-powerful. His argument itself leaves no room for resistance. It imagines speed's victory over us as total, final, and irrevocable.

Now, records alone will never dismantle the war machine, halt the pace of global climate die-offs, or bring justice to a world foundering on thoroughgoing systemic inequalities. We just can't be as sanguine as master cellist Pablo Casals, who mused in 1961 (in the home nation of Hiroshima and Nagasaki, no less)—"Perhaps it is music that will save the world."[5] But records that push our boundaries, that seem to move too fast for us to keep up with, do make space for hopes for a breakthrough. Listening to the best "acceleratory" records, it seems impossible to return to slower forms of life. Unlike slow and mid-tempo records, fast records use musical speed to counter the militarized speed of the world at large. Some genres, like punk, hardcore, and thrash, do this directly—trying to destroy one form of speed with their own. Others, like post-punk, use speed as a sort of diagnostic tool to allow us to catch up with fast-moving times and then critique them. Post-punk's jerky, off-kilter rhythms show the fault lines implicit within even the sleekest and smoothest forms of life. And genres like house, techno, free jazz, and rap model future forms of unalienated speed.

Guitarist Günter Schickert is not a household name, even among many fans of krautrock and *kosmiche* music. He's known as much for his association with Berlin school pioneer Klaus Schulze as he is for his own solo records. Recent Bureau B reissues of Schickert's first two LPs, *Samtvogel* (orig. self-released, 1974) and *Überfällig* (orig. Sky Records, 1979), have brought him back into the collectors' consciousness, but just barely. While these records are uneven, their best tracks equal the heights reached by Manuel Göttsching, Schickert's more celebrated contemporary and closest musical analogue.

One of these tracks is "Puls," *Überfällig*'s fifteen-minute opener. We've chosen it to introduce our section on fast records because, in an almost schematic way, it uses speed in its three main forms—as a blunt weapon, as a tool for subversion, and as a model for new practices of speed. Since krautrock came from the intersection of rock, jazz, contemporary classical, and electronic music— it's fitting that one of its works would contain three separate uses of speed within its fifteen-minute run time.

"Puls" begins with the sound of water gently lapping against a pier. After a few moments, a child's voice echoes in the background; birds chirp and winds blow overhead. Four divers plunk into the water one after the next, followed by the sound of breath being drawn through a scuba regulator. An insistent drumstick on metal pattern starts up but abruptly stops, and then resumes in earnest. This ticking pattern remains a constant throughout the song. A looping, relentlessly circular electric guitar figure begins, and a heartbeat-like kick drum enters alongside it. Meanwhile, strange textures begin to creep in around the margins. A second "echo guitar" begins wandering off from the main guitar line, as the song picks up in violence and intensity. Environmental sounds from sky and water are mixed in throughout—gulls squawking with liquid rushing, a faraway voice with scuba breathing—leaving you uncertain whether you're on land, at sea, or in the air. The main electric guitar continues pummeling forward on a straight path, while the second chiming "echo guitar" continues interrupting at unpredictable intervals, wobbling away from the more aggressive lead guitar pattern. More children's noises, now slightly distorted, are added, while all builds in intensity. We hear water pouring, still unsure of our relation to land, sea, and air. Harsh drones from the echo guitar join the main guitar, and then everything suddenly grinds to a halt, except the metronomic tapping and the sound of children giggling in play with their parents. Then even the ticking stops and finally we hear only the sound of the children at play.

In "Puls," then, three distinct forms of speed are embodied. The first comes with the insistent rhythms of the guitar and drums, the pounding kicks and metronomic ticking—these are an aggressive, driving form of speed. They never let up, dragging you along in their wake. This layer of the song comes closest to transposing into music the aggressive forms of speed Virilio describes—it bears a propulsive violence. The next layer, the more subtle "echo guitar" layer, often works to disrupt the main "pulse" of the song. This form of speed, a sudden interruptive force, uses speed for critique and commentary. If the listener hones in on this level, they find a more probing, improvisatory relation to acceleration. Finally, the ambient soundscapes allow a third form of speed to come into being. These found sounds are the only ones running throughout the track. They work to suture the track's pieces together. While not fast themselves, they allow us to link the two forms of speed in the song together, the directly aggressive with the indirect and disruptive, into a single coherent whole. Taken as a complete work tied together by ambient field recordings, we can hear in "Puls" the relentless main guitar and the experimental, debunking "echo guitar" as two parts of the same musical system.

When we consider "Puls" in this way, we can see it as a battleground for the interaction between two distinct forms of speed. It teaches a way of making music in layers, putting together alternate forms of the same sounds in order to build a larger whole. The work becomes an occasion to consider different forms of speed and their interactions. It spurs listeners to rethink their own approach to speed in both the world and in music. Unlike krautrock, most genres are not so polymorphous in their use of speed. Many genres double down on one of the three types of speed found in "Puls," expanding on the combative, interruptive, or alternative practice of speed to the exclusion of the others. Below, I'll detail some pertinent examples.

First-wave punk, hardcore, and thrash records use speed for combat. Right at the beginning of punk, there's the Ramones' first single, "Blitzkrieg Bop" (Sire 7", 1976), with its drums racing along at 172 beats per minute on the record and hitting 250 during some live shows. This inaugural 7" borrows its speedy form and subject matter from the military—more specifically, the Nazis' so-called lightning war, the blitzkrieg. Presumably, Tommy Ramone added "bop" to the end of the title to ironize the fascistic associations of "blitzkrieg," but the song's martial origins remain. From Motörhead's "fast and vicious" (Lemmy's motto for his band) LPs *Overkill* and *Bomber* (both Bronze, 1979) to the Weirdos' "We Got the Neutron Bomb" (Dangerhouse 7", 1978) and on to Slayer's "Chemical Warfare" (*Haunting the Chapel*, Metal Blade, 1984), punk and metal records are obsessed with the world of militarized modernity Virilio described in *Speed and Politics*. On the one hand, many punk and metal artists rightfully pride themselves on their anti-authoritarian politics; on the other, they take constant inspiration from the war machine's speed and power, often mimicking the violent rhythms of its weaponry. Even when groups like Discharge, Varukers, Corrosion of Conformity, and Napalm Death write explicitly leftist lyrics, the speed and intensity of their music often maintains an undeniably warlike feel. Add to this some metal and hardcore groups' "flirtation" with fascist imagery and their fans' taste for crew cuts, fatigues, and jackboots, and the connection seems clear.

But the relationship between the two is not predetermined—fast, aggressive music does not automatically lead to warmongering politics. The outright fascist idiocy of Rock against Communism, Screwdriver, and Mayhem is part but not all of the story. The brutal speed of hardcore and thrash can just as easily open up consideration of violence—critiques of militarism, rage, and resentment—as it can encourage it. These records are not pacifist—they insist on centering the role of rage and anxiety in modern life. And while this has led some collectors to reject these genres as somehow fundamentally tainted, such moralism is no substitute for actual analysis of the records themselves.

The best "fast and vicious" records only ask us to recognize the central roles of modern violence and leave it up to us to decide which forms of this violence are legitimate. Speed in this form does not further the militarization of the world; rather, it turns it from a supposed fact of nature into an open political question. These records confront you with the reality of violent speed. They get you in touch with your feelings of rage and resentment. As a result, they can be a first step toward distinguishing between war and revolution, crime and justice, repression and liberation. They are a provocation, a tool to draw decision out from neutral, indifferent, and complacent listeners.

Thrash and hardcore particularly force a confrontation with the world of speed and violence. But like *Speed and Politics*, these records offer no answers to the questions they raise. The classic thrash records, for example Metallica's *Master of Puppets* (Elektra, 1986) and Slayer's *Reign in Blood* (Def Jam, 1986), seek to overwhelm the listener with extended attacks of speed and power. Metallica's "Battery" and "Damage Inc," like so many of their early '80s monsters, assault you with all its instruments pounding and wailing at a breakneck speed. They search and destroy—and often explicitly sound like an army charging into war. Slayer's 220 beats per minute "Raining Blood" follows the same blueprint, but if anything ups Metallica's speed with its album-capping guitar solo. When thrash works, it takes over your senses—producing an extended feeling of whiplash and incredibly intense feelings of rage. It aims to impress the listener with its lightning-fast riffs, mechanically speedy blast beats, and/or jackhammering drums. And its musicians are usually self-serious enough to build epic worlds of speed, to demand awe from the listener through heavy, fury-filled workouts. But when the raw emotion of listening fades, listeners are left to sort through their own more visceral reactions and start making distinctions between them.

Hardcore has similar effects, but while thrash tends to build overstuffed epics of speed, hardcore packs everything into the briefest forms possible. Hardcore builds concise miniatures out of speed, aiming to do the most in the shortest amount of time possible. Negative Approach's "Pressure" (Touch and Go 7", 1982) slams seven lines of lyrics into eight seconds of song, dramatizing the intense frenzy that comes in an unrelieved bout of high anxiety. Clocking in at just over a minute, Bad Brains' "Fearless Vampire Killers" (*Bad Brains*, ROIR, 1982) races past you, a would-be thrash track compressed into a short shock wave of energy. The title track of the "first" hardcore record, the Middle Class's one-minute-flat "Out of Vogue" (*Out of Vogue 7″*, Joke Records, 1978) doesn't develop so much as explode and then disappear—dueling vocalists briefly bat the song's chorus back and forth while the drums and guitar charge and halt, and then it's over. Unlike thrash epics, these songs are unadorned—their lyrics are spit and shouted without the vocal staginess that plagues even the best metal, and they rarely ever indulge in guitar solos. If Metallica and Slayer albums are full military campaigns, hardcore singles are guerilla raids. Thrash songs present a vision of a world dominated by violent speed; hardcore songs present brief moments of this speed's eruption.

Thrash and hardcore, then, attempt to port the violent speed of modernity directly onto records. This blunt approach has its limitations. After a while, sheer speed gets dull for both musicians and listeners—there are only so many tricks in the kit bag, and the records all start to sound the same. This, something hardcore punk and thrash share with some of the ultra-fast dance genres (one of which is also, a bit confusingly, called hardcore), makes it difficult for a genre to grow and develop. Ironically, at the speed of light everything starts to run together. At times, it seems like all that can be done in hardcore and thrash has already been done, and that the genres' high-water marks are terminal statements never to be topped.

In contrast, when post-punk gets fast, its rhythms loosen up. Speed is used more obliquely in post-punk than in hardcore and metal. As it accelerates, it becomes more herky-jerky and chaotic—it's as if post-punk groups no longer believe in the connection between speed and authority. Bands like This Heat and Essential Logic use speed less as a bludgeon and more as an experimental device. As a result, the records often sound more like works in progress than finished pieces, as attempts to use speed without falling into the outright aggression of their punk predecessors. At its best, post-punk is vibrant fast music that's at the same time intelligent and self-critical; at its worst, it manages to somehow be both less exciting and more pretentious than the music that preceded it.

This Heat's use of speed on records like the *Health and Efficiency* 12″ (Piano, 1980) and the *Deceit* LP (Rough Trade, 1981) is quite complex. The title track "Health and Efficiency," for example, begins as a muscularly drummed, aggressive, anthemic punk track. But about two and half minutes in, the band segues into a strange open hi-hat groove, in which the drum and guitar rhythm mutates alongside found sound samples, tape-manipulated echoes, and aleatoric clanging on metal. This five-minute section gives way to an equally fast but sparer coda, in which metal scrapings and fragmentary rhythms continue until the song fades out. In its three sections, the song probes three linked but distinct forms of musical speed—the first represents traditional punk and the second delivers an industrial breakdown, while the coda offers a loose free jazz rendering of the track's opening. Not settling on any one version of the song, it presents three fast modes turned inside out and each on the verge of falling apart. *Deceit*'s anti-imperial tour de force "S.P.Q.R." represents the paradox of life in our imperial age—it feels both repetitive and terrifyingly out of control at the same time. The jerky gallop of the song represents a chaotic system managing to keep itself going loop after loop. Speed on this track (and on *Deceit* more generally) is used to represent the mad race of life lived within imperial time— to present a world moving so fast the wheels feel like they could fall off at any moment. This captures the energy and frustration of daily life lived within the boom and bust cycles of overlapping empire, spanning from ancient Rome to imperial Britain to the "new imperialism" of United States hegemony—like the imperial system, "S.P.Q.R." keeps moving even though it threatens to fall apart at every moment. This Heat use speed to show the cracks and fissures in the systems that dominate the modern world.

Post-punk saxophonist Lora Logic's Essential Logic uses fast and chaotic arrangements for a similar deconstructive effect. While listening to records like "Aerosol Burns" (Cells 7", 1978), "Wake Up" (Beat Rhythm News 12", Rough Trade, 1979), "Quality Crayon Wax O.K. Horn" (same), and "Born in Flames" (7" with Red Krayola, Rough Trade, 1980), you hear two levels of music at once. First, there's the songs' spiky energy—music and words rush by, leaving you straining to catch every detail. But at the same time, there's also a disruptive, satirical spirit at work—this is carried in the records' stop-start arrangements and above all in Logic's disjunctive sax playing and singing. Her horn on "Wake Up," for example, is a funk line played with free jazz abandon—it grooves, but in a dissonant, off-kilter cadence, which always keeps the listener on edge. On "Born in Flames," Logic's vocals range from soprano lilts to arpeggiated chants to frenetic screams, always keeping the listener guessing and alert. In general, post-punk records like these subdivide speed down into many forms. They dissolve the unitary aggressive approach to speed found in earlier punk and metal to expose a variety of possible speeds, often within the space of a single song.

Most electronic dance records use speed for less aggressive purposes. Unlike thrash and hardcore, they avoid trying to use the master's violent speed to dismantle its war machine. Nor do they tend to employ the deconstructive approach of post-punk. Rather, genres like Chicago house, acid house, techno, synth pop, and EBM seek to produce new forms of speed as alternatives to those currently existing. There are of course exceptions to this—genres like the aforementioned gabber, dubstep, breakbeat, and the 300–1000+ beats per minute nonsense of speedcore and extratone—but they are not particularly collectible or broadly appealing genres. The best dance records don't use speed for one-trick novelty effect, and you don't have to be in the club (or rewatching *The Matrix* or *Blade*) to enjoy them. As with punk and metal, when tempos get too fast and unvarying in dance music, the listener stops registering them as speedy. They may be technically fast, but they feel anything but. So while literal tempos and BPM mean something, they're not decisive. In this section, then, we're concerned more with songs that give the feeling of acceleration and speeding.

Speedy dance records are by their nature sleeker and use more fixed rhythms than the ones made with plucked, strummed, and drummed instruments. Even when drum machines and synths are broken and reprogrammed in irregular ways, they produce more regular, consistent patterns than instruments played by humans. Stripped of the fills, flourishes, and flubs (which you find on even the most *motorik* live records), fast dance music provides steadier grooves around which to orient one's thoughts, feelings, and movements. Its predictable but speedy pulsings leave less chance for the spell to be broken, for distraction to jump in between the beats. This steady drive, noted even in dance songs' titles like Doctor's Cat's Italo classic "Feel the Drive" (Il Discotto 12", 1983), rather than leading to a robotic slavishness to the rhythm in the present, opens up a different sort of creativity in the listener. It drives them into the future, on and on in anticipation toward the next beat. The best fast dance records produce an almost mystical orientation to the present, charging it with the future desire. They generate the feeling that the future is open to change—and conjure up premonitions of new ways of being.

Though Chicago house, Detroit techno, and experimental synth pop are three distinct genres, they all use speed for the purposes described above. All deploy the steady pulse of drum machines to drag the listener forward. Unlike the mid-tempo dance records we discussed above, these faster records leapfrog the whole dialectic between tension and release. They attempt to take you to a place beyond pleasure and pain. Through both the speed of their synthetic rhythms and the layered, estranging atmospherics, they lead you into an inherently science-fictional relation to time. Their rhythms are not always assaultive—they work as much as speculative representations of future worlds as they do as straightforward "bangers." Frankie Knuckles and Jamie Principle's Kraftwerk-influenced house classic "Your Love" (Trax 12", 1987), for example, pairs a pounding rhythm track with an otherworldly-sounding arpeggiating synth—it feels like the future, or at least a possible future we missed the chance to realize. While you follow the steady beat, the synths (one lead and one accompanying) open a feeling of something ineffable, forever racing past your understanding. Phuture's "Acid Trax" (Trax 12", 1987), while it now sounds a bit played out, still holds the charge of synthetic speed's power to drag both your body and mind into considerations of what the future could be.

By the time we get to Detroit techno, the music's become even more future-oriented and rhythmically streamlined. For example, Juan Atkins's Model 500's "Testing 1-2" (Metroplex 12", 1986) mixes a driving beat with skittering, chopped-and-sped vocal samples that echo throughout the track. The song is the feeling of human time being stretched and accelerated to find new possibilities for experience. Drexciya's catalog is filled with such experiments with speed. "Positron Island" (Underground Resistance *Bubble Metropolis* 12", 1993) represents a world of wiggly, slippery acceleration; "Triangular Hydrogen Strain" (*Neptune's Lair* LP, Tresor, 1999) manages to race and calm at the same time, like a submarine journey; and "Black Sea" (*The Journey Home* 12", Warp,

1995) is as close as they got to a straightforward dance tune but nonetheless manages to put one in a meditative, premonitory state. And though they came out of Sheffield and Philadelphia rather than Chicago and Detroit, fast synth pop songs like Cabaret Voltaire's "I Want You" (Some Bizarre 12", 1985) and Experimental Products' "Glowing in the Dark" (Short Circuit 12", 1984) have similar effects on listeners, pushing them to break with their old habits and perceive the world in newer, faster ways.

When jazz and rap records move fast, they also orient the listener to the future. They explicitly model new practices for budding musicians—you can slow down, repeat, and play along to these records until you crack the code. This applies to all genres (think of young George Harrison playing along to his favorite R&B 45s slowed down to 33⅓ speed), but particularly to the intricate, dense, and improvised performances found on rap and jazz LPs. Without recordings, it would be impossible to emulate certain speedy, off-the-cuff rap and jazz playing. Whether it's John Coltrane's famous 300 beats per minute modulation through three keys on "Giant Steps" (*Giant Steps*, Atlantic, 1960) or the Notorious B.I.G. and Bone Thugs-n-Harmony's rapid fire rhyming on "Notorious Thugs" (*Life after Death*, Bad Boy, 1997), dramatic uses of speed in rap and jazz records raise a challenge for the listener. They call out to be decrypted and unpacked. This can lead to either a note-by-note, word-for-word breakdown or more abstract analysis of a record's construction and method. Either way, the miles-per-minute runs and rhymes of fast jazz and rap teach and model potential futures. As recorded artifacts, they inspire analysis and active learning from all listeners, especially aspiring musicians. While this has long been understood and put into practice for jazz at elite musical academies like Juilliard and the Berklee College of Music, it remains less explored in regard to rap records.

Fast rapping is divisive: Some heads hate it; others love it. When it's bad, it certainly feels less like a skillful display of artistry and more like a monotonous school exercise. Listening to some of the technically fast rapping out there can be about as exciting as watching paint dry. As with the fast but dispiriting metal riffs of Yngwie Malmsteen, speedy rapping is no guarantee of exciting music. In fact, speedy rap in the form of rote, mechanical exercises does nothing to maintain a feeling of acceleration in the listener. But when fast rap works, it really works. Though a recording, its speed makes it feel out-of-control, improvisatory, and off-kilter. On first listen, your senses struggle to catch up. The best fast rap records keep us on our toes, inspired to follow them in all their velocity.

Generating such thrilling speed was integral to early rap coming into its own. Disco rap like the Sugarhill Gang, for example, was locked into singsong nursery rhyme flows. To modern ears, their records sound stilted and corny. The innovation came with songs like Spoonie Gee and the Treacherous Three's "The New Rap Language" (Enjoy 12", 1980). With one foot in the old disco rap style (for example, they still reference nursery rhymes), the Harlem group introduced a faster, more breathless rap style into the mix. The song's a sort of relay race—the first rapper passes his verse to the next, who completes and extends it without a pause, and then himself hands the track off to a third rapper. The result is still a thrilling, relentless performance. It's filled with inventive flows that are fun to both analyze and memorize. Wild Willie's sought-after acetate from 1982 (Sterling Sound Incorporated) follows in Treacherous Three's footsteps, while introducing a chaotic element into the mix. A boogie rap party cut, "Wild Willie" uses a rushing, off-kilter delivery to keep things interesting. A comic song, replete with Willie's Tom Thumb persona and an affected speech impediment, the track uses an imprecise form of speed to break up the expectations we have of disco rap. It's still an infectious record, compared to the many exhausted ones of Sugarhill Records. Like "The New Rap Language," it encourages the listener to run it back to figure out how it works.

Rapping's acceleration itself accelerated as the 1980s ended. Public Enemy, of course, upped the speed and aggression of both their vocals and production on tracks like "Rebel without a Pause" and "Fight the Power" (both on *It Takes a Nation of Millions to Hold Us Back*, Def Jam, 1989) along with "Burn Hollywood Burn" (*Fear of a Black Planet*, Def Jam, 1990). Rappers became more adept at delivering complex rhymes over fast production. Ultramagnetic MCs' "Kool Keith Housing Things" (*Critical Beatdown*, Next Plateau, 1988) condensed a sped-up "Cold Sweat" sample and a riff from "Giving Up Food for Funk," setting the template for both mainstream and "random" rap in the coming decade. Kool Keith's ability to deliver coherent lines and pithy put-downs at high velocity remains stunning. Random rap gem Lonnie O's "Dream On" (Hot Comb Hits 12", 1992), with its heliumnated Everly Brothers sample and hyper Big Daddy Kane flow, stays in the same lane. One of A Tribe Called Quest's breakthrough tracks, the posse-cut "Scenario" (Jive 12", 1991) features especially lightning-fast rapping from Busta Rhymes, inspiring a generation of *Yo! MTV Raps* viewers to buy ATCQ records in order to crack the code of what they heard. Miami bass and LA electro-rap took the electro genre's speedy 808 beats and started rapping over them—a rap like Willie Wil's "Rap Terminator" (Franki Flight 12", 1989) coasts over a minimal electro-style beat. Records like Egyptian Lover's "Egypt, Egypt" (Freak Beat 12", 1984) paved the way for hit records in a similar electro style— Ice-T's "Power" (*Power* LP, Sire, 1988), and crossover hits JJ Fad's "Supersonic" (Dream Team 12", 1988), Salt-N-Pepa's "Push It" (Next Plateau 12", 1987), and L'Trimm's "Cars That Go Boom" (Time-X, 1988). These tracks became pop hits because of their speedy energy, the infectious way they taught listeners how to keep up with fast flows over electro beats.

In the 1990s, speedy flows became even more intricate, more exciting objects for listeners to decode. The previously mentioned "Notorious Thugs" showcased Bone Thugs-n-Harmony's innovative, particularly cryptic, blazing tongue-twisting delivery, which they may or may not have patterned on early Three 6 Mafia tracks. While slower than the rappers in Bone, Big Pun tracks like "The Dream Shatterer," "Twinz," and "Fast Money" (*Capital Punishment*, Loud, 1998) feature breathless, rapid-fire bilingual flows that are tough to crack on first listen. Outkast's hit "Bombs over Baghdad" (*Stankonia*, LaFace/Arista,

2000) finds André 3000 and Big Boi bobbing and weaving around a hyperspeed electronic dance track, taking things in a more digital, less sample-oriented direction in the process. In the same year, Binary Star's "alternative" rap classic LP *Masters of the Universe* (Subterraneous, 2000) found MCs Senim Silla and One Be Lo spitting rapid-fire, dense lyrics filled with complex internal rhymes, setting the pattern for the 2000s and its indie labels like Definitive Jux. More recently, tracks like Frank Ocean's "Comme des Garçons" (*Endless*, Def Jam, 2016) and Vince Staples's "War Ready" (*Prima Donna* 10" EP, Def Jam, 2016), the latter not coincidentally featuring a sample from André 3000, use syncopated, speedy rapping to keep listeners off-balance and straining to understand the lyrics encrypted in their rappers' delivery.

The best fast raps call for fans to memorize them. In this, the record aids them—a record that can be stopped and started, played slowly for easier parsing. Here the record provides a two-part experience—the first, in which one is overwhelmed by the virtuosic speed of rappers like Big Boi and Bizzy Bone. The second comes in replay, in breaking down a rap and figuring out how it works. In this circuit, between the experience of sublime speed and the pleasure of analyzing it, a whole world opens up. You get both the magic and mystery of a work that challenges your understanding, and then the opportunity to understand it and transform it in your own future work. In the old days, schoolchildren used to be forced to memorize poems, which enhanced not only their powers of memory but also their faculties of language and structure. This exercise not only made them better students of poetry; it also made them potential poets. Unfortunately, it was also often a tool of social control—a way to beat ideology into students in their very ways of perceiving. Set texts, set messages, replaced creativity. The DIY experience of listening to rap records, especially on fast records, keeps the benefits of this process while remaining completely voluntary and free. It instills a love for aesthetic form free from institutional education. Like jazz and poetry used to, speedy rap records still have the power to inspire new music by modeling old forms still exciting to decode.

## EXPERIENTIAL ZONE 2: VOICE

"Find your voice," the self-help refrain goes. If advertisers and marketers are to be believed, each of us has a unique voice just waiting to be discovered. We must only cut through the buzz and hum of daily life to find the singular voice we secret within. After doing so, we can be assured the world will take to this voice as an authentic contribution to the annals of the human spirit.

Of course, this view assumes we possess an inborn voice and, by extension, a fixed identity. But our voices and senses of self are works in progress, or at least they should be. Even though the singing voice can seem as if it's emanating directly from the body, even the most powerful vocal performances are the products of both craft and accident. For example, American rockers Robert Pollard, Alex Chilton, and Chris Bell made brilliant records using completely invented British accents. Singers shape their voices—and so their recorded identities—in reaction to social norms and musical conventions, a wide range of the world's taboos and enticements. People are *born* with singing voices, but the singing voices we hear on record are *produced*. As critic Edward Said wrote, the effect on the listener is "a paradox": "[S]omething as impersonal as a text, *or a record* [emphasis mine], can nevertheless deliver an imprint or a trace of something as lively, immediate, and transitory as a 'voice.'"[6] In the case of vinyl specifically, this means that while recorded singing voices are the product of technique, they can nevertheless genuinely feel "lively, immediate, and transitory." Said goes on to argue that all artistic choices are made with past and future audience expectations in mind. This, I am arguing, extends even to the recorded singing voice, the most seemingly natural and unconditioned of all musical instruments. But in this, it's not just a singer's technique that determines the final sound of their vocals.

In recorded music, the style of production applied to the singing voice is decisive. Because production fundamentally alters the way a voice sounds and comes across to a listener, it can be used to denature a voice for an imagined audience and specific sectors of the consumer base. Vocal production works as a mediating filter between singers and their intended audiences; it is the site where audience expectations are imagined and catered to within the recording itself.

The current taste for vocal production seems to favor broadly palatable voices. This is not because singers are more or less unique than they were in the past, but because they are all being produced in a more homogenous and standardized way than they used to be. As a result, the most popular voices are the ones that sound like other already successful voices within their genre. Whether it's rap, pop, or country, contemporary vocal production has the effect of making all vocalists sound similar to one another. This is because digital vocal production applies the same regime of techniques over and over: compression, pitch correcting, and chorus vocal effects produce a sweetened, loud, and monochromatic effect. This applies both within genres and across them. And while there's more room for aesthetic outliers and swerves from the dominant paradigm in independent music, the same phenomena can be found on Bandcamp as on corporate radio—the range and variety of vocals heard on record seem to have fundamentally narrowed. Now, this is not to say that music is worse now than it was in the past—just that digital recording techniques and the taste for them has obscured the range and variety of things that can be done with the recorded singing voice. Both trap producers and post–Max Martin (Britney Spears, Backstreet Boys) pop producers tend to apply one-size-fits-all production regimes on all their vocalists, and both create highly enjoyable and innovative music. But sometimes it's hard to tell one vocalist from another.

The vinyl past offers a far richer range of voices than top 40 or even contemporary Bandcamp currently provides. These recorded voices of the past were no less manufactured than today's, but they vary from one another dramatically. This is because multiple combinations between production style and vocal performance were still being experimented with, and no single approach had yet congealed as an industry standard. The more time you spend in the vinyl archive, the more you expand your idea of the possibilities for the human singing voice in and out of the recording studio. The voices of the past were produced more heterogeneously than they are today: lo-fi and hi-fi, with heavy reverb and echo treatments and with no treatments, with vocoders and naked, on porches and in fields and in Abbey Road Studios, by professional singers and by hobbyists and children. In relation to the dominant digital productions of today, these voices sound singular. In the current era, the relation between vocal production and the voice has become fixed. As a result, it seems of vital concern to go back in the vinyl archive and unearth singular vocal recordings. By doing so, we can unearth many past unique vocal production and vocal performance combinations, still viable for future recorded music.

## VOICE ALTERNATIVE 1: SINGULAR

Singular recorded voices are, by definition, unique—no one example can stand for their whole. So, unlike the section on time above, I won't be singling out any one recording to introduce this section. Some singular voices produce feelings of melancholy, others of mystery, while others charge us with power. All are instantly recognizable yet impossible to imitate. Going beyond vocal gimmickry, they build complex, intense worlds of feeling for the listener.

### EXPRESSION OF DAMAGE

Some voices express and induce feelings of damage. By damage, we mean socially and institutionally inflicted suffering, as opposed to "pain," the more generic common lot of all living creatures. To express damage, singular recorded voices can be divided into two categories. They either mimic traumatic experience with atonal and abrasive singing or they represent traumatic states of mourning and melancholy. The first grapple with damage in its immediacy while the second plumb its long-term effects.

In the first category, there are the voices that actively assault the conventions of harmony and melody in order to render the rawness of tragic experience. On records like *The Litanies of Satan* (Y, 1982), *Masque of the Red Death* (Mute, 1988), and *Plague Mass* (Mute, 1991), Diamanda Galás decomposes her own virtuosic natural singing voice (she has a three-octave range) into a series of shrieks, wails, whimpers, and whispers. Galás embodies the horrible suffering of life in order to break through to a world content to deny its existence. Her voice carries the pains of being exploited, tortured, and driven mad by a system indifferent to its sufferers' individuality and needs.

Patty Waters's take on the folk and jazz standard "Black Is the Colour of My True Love's Hair" annihilates all previous recordings of the track. The traditional narrative and sentiment of the song are stripped away, leaving only Waters's anguished riffs on the word "black," punctuated with distressing birdcall-like noises. The Rolling Stones, of course, wrote a famous pop song about painting everything black—but Waters's performance actually does it. "Black Is the Colour of My True Love's Hair" (*Sings*, ESP-Disk', 1966) seems to be sung from the colorless center of a desolate void.

Alan Vega's singing on "Frankie Teardrop" (*Suicide*, Red Star, 1977), ranging from ghoulish narration to piercing screams, depicts what it feels like to wander through an earth turned manmade inferno. Scott Walker's "late" voice (on albums like *Tilt*, Drag City, 1995, and *The Drift*, 4AD, 2006) is a baritone of the undead. These voices—whether shrieking, screaming, or croaking—force us to confront the abysses of modern life. When everything else human is stripped from us, only bare cries of dread and horror distinguish our unaccommodated lives from those of the dead. Such excessive, scarifying voices penetrate our powers of denial, exposing the depths of abjection possible in this world. They map out the barriers to liberation in agonizing detail. As such, you will probably never hear these singers through a Starbucks PA.

While such fraying and flaying of the human voice is understandably rare, singers capturing the long-term effects of damage are more common. The record archive of course has no shortage of sad songs—we've been overexposed to the standard sounds of the ballad and lament. Both virtuosic and "just plain folks" styles fail to penetrate anymore. The only records that still have the power to communicate mourning and melancholy are the strangely broken, excessive, singular ones. To quote the late David Berman of Silver Jews, "All my favorite singers couldn't sing." Only eccentric voices have the blasting power to cut through the deadweight of tradition. This goes for the popular singers as well as the obscure. For example, Roberta Flack and Donny Hathaway have sorrow-laden voices, totally singular despite their high sales. And Billie Holiday's inimitable voice still conveys damage in every line—we feel her hurt in the alternation between her precise, blunt assertion and distinctively weary warbles. Her unpredictable phrasing undercuts even happy sentiments with blue notes.

More obscure voices, like those of Waheeda Massey, Robbie Basho, Robert Wyatt, Kath Bloom, and Vic Chesnutt, are all uncannily broken in their own unique ways. Their styles of singing convey damage only by breaking sentimental vocal clichés. On an album dedicated to the "children of Vietnam," Hannibal Peterson's *Children of the Fire* (Sunrise, 1974), eight-year-old Waheeda Massey's singing on "Forest Sunrise: Song of Life" cuts us to the quick. Her untrained, pitchy paean to childhood joy contrasts absolutely with Diedre Murray's weeping cello and the sound of postapocalyptic winds. Massey's is the voice of a child trying to hold on to an innocence besieged from all sides. Her unpolished singing about simple joys set against an ominous backdrop lets us measure what stands to be lost in the fire. A professional jazz singer would have been incapable of such a performance.

On "Florida" (*West of Rome*, Texas Hotel, 1992), Vic Chesnutt's singing is as "volatile" and "wobbly" as the situation he describes. Within the space of a single line, Chesnutt's voice can metamorphose from a dark croak to a shakily lyrical tone to sardonic half speech. The song, a tribute to a friend after his suicide, never holds to a straight line—it has the power to pierce us because it represents the flux and constant churn of loss. Kath Bloom's voice on "The Breeze My Baby Cries" (*Sing the Children Over*, Ambiguous, 1982) falters, cracks, and soars at various points in the track—like all affecting voices, it is a broken vessel, far from technical precision and polish. Bloom's is a voice grappling with the reality of annihilation, asserting its right to expression in rough and raw fashion.

Robert Wyatt's singing on "A Beautiful War" (*Comicopera*, Domino, 2007), as on his earlier classics *Rock Bottom* (Virgin, 1974) and *Ruth Is Stranger than Richard* (Virgin, 1975), conveys an immense fragility. A song written in the midst of the "War on Terror," his straight-toned falsetto plays with the utopian jargon of hawks and generals—of the "total success" and absolute freedom that supposedly comes from "daring raids." If the lyrics supply the war in the title, Wyatt's voice (and Karen Mantler's sampled voice) provides the beauty. There's a gap between the Orwellian military double-speak of the lyrics and the tender, straining way Wyatt elongates the phrase "we'll all be free." Through the heartrending power of his vocal, Wyatt wrests the concept of freedom away from its cynical deployment during Operation Enduring Freedom and back toward a loving and collective vision of liberation, of a true freedom yet to come.

Robbie Basho is known primarily as an "American primitive" guitar virtuoso, but "Orphan's Lament" (*Visions of the County*, Windham Hill, 1978) finds him uncharacteristically singing and playing the piano. He should have done both more! His voice is an affected but affecting baritone. Mixing mock-operatic and Anglo-American ballad forms into an unstable compound, Basho conjures the sound of a raw youth alone in a large and cold world. Basho's odd voice, amateur and theatrical at once, captures perfectly the alienated, disconnected life of an orphan. He sings in a voice of desperate need, unsure of the best way to put itself across and be heard.

Each of these angry or sad singers has a voice that can't be copied—insofar as it is sui generis, each represents a particular experience of a specific place and time. And paradoxically, this is what draws us in—with these voices, we identify by witnessing difference, something we haven't gone through, but emotions to which we can still connect. Traditionally, people tend to think they can only identify with experiences that they can personally relate to their own life. These voices ask for more difficult but rewarding acts of connection between singer and listener. Rather than ask for identification, they convey damage we can't immediately relate to and ask us to use our imaginations in order to understand circumstances outside of our own.

## BUILDING MYSTERY

Some singers craft a singular voice for more circuitous, cryptic purposes. Singers like Mark E. Smith, U-Roy, Keith Hudson, Carolanne Pegg of Mr. Fox, Sister Ann, Comus's Roger Wooten, Van Dyke Parks, Peter Ivers, Karen Dalton, David Thomas, Abner Jay, and Dillinger all manipulate their voices to make their songs obscure and difficult to interpret. With apologies to Sarah McLachlan, these vocalists "build mysteries." They introduce an abstraction into their performances that makes them difficult to parse. The effect of this on us is to denature our sense of the everyday—to defamiliarize our daily round.

The Cleveland punk scene's interest in the British Isles folk revival has mystified some, puzzled by the incongruity between Cleveland's aggressively weird rust belt outfits like Pere Ubu and the bucolic British works of the "electric Eden" musicians. But the link makes more sense when you consider the use of "encrypted" voices by both David Thomas of Pere Ubu and the more enigmatic UK folk singers. What the singing on Pere Ubu's "Chinese Radiation" (*The Modern Dance*, Blank, 1978) shares with Carolanne Pegg's on "Mr. Fox" (*Mr. Fox*, Transatlantic, 1970) and Roger Wooten on Comus's *First Utterance* (Dawn, 1971) is a mysteriousness that treats the material world as a cover for what lies beneath—a netherworld of ambiguous signs and wonders. Pere Ubu described themselves as "industrial folk," I suspect, because both they and the weirder bands of the British folk revival sensed that the surfaces of life were flat and dull, and that to capture the depths of what was really going on, you needed to develop new singing styles.

On "Chinese Radiation," for example, Thomas begins singing in a creepy, shaky vocal, capping this first section off with a difficult-to-understand, half-mumbled cry. He then punctuates his slurred, shaky vocal with hard-to-scan yelps. The lyrics, written in the wake of Chairman Mao's death, sketch the contours of a romantic relationship between the "Red Guard" and the "New World," using the political jargon and touchstones of the Cultural Revolution, gray caps and little red books and all, to mix up the personal and the political. But it is Thomas's voice that produces amazing effects. In the track's middle section, over a 1950s-style rave-up and some canned crowd noise, his tone becomes more hyper, even hysterically high-pitched at times. And during the bridge, Thomas sings with a spikier but ironizing (he's no fan of Maoism) tone over a more rocking backing—that is, until the noise of crowds begins to drown him out. After this, with only a piano and drum coda remaining, Thomas starts whispering in a deadpan. Without knowing exactly what the referents are and what's at stake, Thomas's voice, alternating between nervous warble and enervated undertones, turns the everyday world into the site of a grand conspiracy. In the modern world of "Chinese Radiation," it's nearly impossible to gain your footing and impossible to hold it for too long. Thomas's is a voice that keeps shifting, dragging us from states of paranoia to mania to calm without revealing the relative value of any of these conditions.

Mark E. Smith of the Fall's voice is often caricatured down to its most obvious gimmick—his pronounced additions of "ahh" as a perennial suffix to many words. But it's much more than that; it unmistakably blends a wailing, thin singing voice; a machine-gun spoken word chest-voice; and moments of electrifying screams that often accent the speech of his characters. His best recordings, like the BBC Peel session version of *Hex Enduction Hour*'s "Winter" (Kamera, 1982), show him using every trick he can to occult the known world in mystery. The lyrical kernel of the song is the stuff of socially minded naturalism. It describes a run-down slum environment (presumably Smith's home in Manchester) of deferred dreams, childhood disability, and rampant alcoholism. But Smith's surreal lyrics and vocals turn "Winter" into something miles away from the kitchen sink tradition. Smith works out his own vocal rhythms, in semi-autonomy from the rest of the band's straightforward rhythm. As his voice weaves in and out of sync with the band, we struggle to predict what Smith will do next. In Smith's presentation, outlandish inventions spring from the profitless chill of a Manchester winter—secret street signs and hidden portals, the transmigration of souls, and a host of other murky goings-on. On "Winter," the sky holds both doves and krakens, and every character's plot takes a turn toward the grotesque or surreal. Sometimes written off as an arch-ironist, Smith uses his voice here to pump desire and empathy into what would in others' hands have been a seemingly dull sociological scene. Smith's voice takes an encrypting approach to the daily occurrences of life in order to reinvest our desire in them.

While common to punk and post-punk, this encrypting effect of the voice is not exclusive to it. While some reggae dubs were made for parties and good times, Keith Hudson's more sinister-sounding records, like "Darkest Night on a Wet Looking Road" (Spur 45, 1971), "Satan Side" (Duke 45, 1972), "No Friend of Mine" (*Flesh of My Flesh, Blood of My Blood*, Mamba, 1974), "Turn the Heater On" (*Torch of Freedom*, Atra, 1975), and "Troubles" (Nuh Skin Up Dub, Joint, 1979), use his throaty, croaky baritone and echo effects to lead the listener down obscure winding paths—rides on metaphorical dark nights on wet-looking roads. A master producer as well as singer, Hudson perfectly situates his voice midway between clarity and obscurity, half-submerged under the track's heavy backing "riddims." We feel the meaning that's there to fish out, but find it hard to grasp. One is never quite sure of the full scenario Hudson is describing. Stress, vexation, and haunting are being hinted at, but never fully fleshed out. These songs are darkly enchanting because they hide as much as they reveal, showing us the effects of duress without elaborating its causes.

Such secretive vocal effects can just as easily be used to enchant as they can to imply dark workings beneath the surfaces. Some voices draw you into puzzling out their meaning for playful rather than sinister designs, so as to superimpose a game upon the surface of life. Whether it's the arch camp of Brian Eno's Bryan Ferry impersonation on "Dead Finks Don't Talk" (*Here Come the Warm Jets*, Virgin, 1973), Abner Jay's "aww shucks" faux naïveté on *The Backbone of America Is a Mule and Cotton*'s title track (Brandie, 1975), or the Raincoats' tongue-in-cheek cover of "Lola" (*The Raincoats*, Rough Trade, 1979), parodic singing asks you to figure out the object of criticism. The joy here comes in being part of the community that understands both the text and subtext of such vocal emulations. On other tracks, the playfulness results from a vocalist playing with their own private language and imaginative figures, building out worlds of surreal nonsense—like Bob Marley's carnivalesque "Mr. Brown" (Upsetter 45, 1971), U-Roy's mumbly, echo-y 1970s toasts on records like *Rasta Ambassador* (Virgin, 1977), Peter Ivers's outrageous helium-laced singing on *Terminal Love* (WB, 1974), and the goofy harmonizing of the Roches. The listener's pleasure springs from overhearing uses of the voice participating in a form of private play. Such records express a disinterest in the listener's need for meaning in favor of the singer's or singers' own nonsensical sense of fun.

## COMMANDING VOICES

Still other voices command us to believe with a sovereign force beyond the normal range of expression. They radiate authority in the nuances of their phrasings and very timbre and tone. This does not mean that they are authoritarian, as they don't demand submission from listeners. Rather, singers like Nina Simone, Evangelist Maria Scott, Ken Boothe, and Karen Dalton, to name just four, overwhelm us with their intensity. They produce an excess of feeling in us, whether rage, melancholy, joy, or some combination of these. By doing so, they disclose to us moments in which aesthetic feeling seems to take over all that blocks its fulfillment. They inspire us to put the quotidian in its place and start to wonder why the freedom their voices manifest can't become a permanent state of being.

Recorded live only three days after Martin Luther King Jr. was assassinated, Nina Simone's "Why? (The King of Love Is Dead)" (RCA 45, 1968) expresses power in mourning and majesty in tenderness. A live performance, Simone's voice captures both the present grief of her audience and the need to actively resist the white supremacy that killed Dr. King. The obscure gospel singer Evangelist Maria Scott possesses a more assured, sweeter voice than Simone, but on her standout track "I've Got a God That Is Real" (*I've Got a God That Is Real,* Champ, 197x) her vibrato syncs with the piano and drum groove in a way that projects absolute mastery. Her voice bristles with the force of true belief and manifests her faith in action. The song abandons the traditional verse-chorus-verse structure entirely and has only a few lyrics. Yet the track is electrifying, with Scott drawing shades of meaning from the word "God" every time it recurs. A voice like this works a miracle and puts you inside the space of absolute assurance for the duration of its run time.

Ken Boothe's cover of Syl Johnson's "Is It Because I'm Black" (Splash 45, 1972), a song like Simone's also written in response to the killing of Dr. King, has richness in its every line reading. In just its first moments of singing, Boothe proves himself a master of phrasing. He projects a dense, full-throated power that Johnson's equally amazing original lacks. Boothe's phrasing swerves from the elegance of Johnson's original, replacing it with raw, emotive power. Omitting Johnson's aspirational conclusion about being somebody and Cadillacs, Boothe ends without even Johnson's conditional statement of hope, leaving the listener in a state of waiting and expectation. Boothe sometimes used a lovely, higher register on records like the beguiling "Everything I Own" (Trojan 45, 1974), but here he goes for deeper, more resonant tones. He particularly lingers on the lyrics about the body and soul, elongating phrases, dramatizing the weight of his oppression. As tears and doings in town come and go in the song, the agents of white supremacy keep pushing, an unnamed force that's always holding the singer back. Boothe's voice both makes us believe his pain and strikes at the root of its causes.

And while Karen Dalton's voice sounds fragile at times, particularly on her first LP, *It's So Hard to Know Who's Going to Love You the Best* (Capitol, 1969), and some of her subsequently released tapes, her voice always carries an absolute authority. This is part of why it's hard to take seriously Peter Stampfel's description of Dalton as a "Hillbilly Holiday." It denies the unique sovereign force of her voice so palpable on tracks like "Something on Your Mind" (*In My Own Time*, Paramount, 1972). In an instructive way, both Dino Valenti's original and subsequent covers by Jackie-O Motherfucker and St. Vincent pale in comparison with Dalton's. They don't command your attention, and they raise no intense feelings of struggling against real difficulty. They are stakeless, diffuse, and bland. All they can muster up is self-pity, the beautiful soul's obsession with its own suffering. What Dalton's voice on "Something on Your Mind" has that all others lack is power—an ability to put across emotional vulnerability with booming authority. While the other versions take "Something on Your Mind" in the direction of downer and easy listening, there's struggle and fight in Dalton's rendition. Beyond the solipsism of the folk paradigm, this is a singular voice battling to make itself heard and respected in all its glorious tenderness.

## VOICE ALTERNATIVE 2: DOUBLE

The preceding singular voices are not more meaningful or compelling than others, but they can feel that way. Through the use of technique, they manage emotionally direct, raw, and intense effects. This can lead us to believe that these performances spring immediately from the life of the singer, without a filter between life and art. These voices make us believe in the unitary, strong identity of the singer we're hearing and make us forget the editing process and craft that goes into representing a voice and persona. But other singers take a more abstract, theatrical approach to their own singing and personas.

The technological capabilities of record production are conducive to such abstract, stagey effects. Unlike in live performance, a recording artist can multiply, distort, and generally manipulate the sound of their voice. And while vocal processing is usually just used to "sweeten" or "beef up" the normal singing voice, even a close listen to tracks like the Beatles' "And Your Bird Can Sing" (*Revolver*, Capitol, 1966) uncovers the two distinct John Lennon performances blended together to create the choruses. Inherent in its practice of multitracking is a certain estrangement of the singer's spontaneous voice into an object to be experimented on, played with, and tinkered with in the studio.

Since the early days of Abbey Road multitracking, many records have accentuated rather than hidden the artifice implicit in recording one's singing voice. They play up the fact that recordings are productions rather than reproductions of a voice—emphasizing the differences between multiple takes of their own singing. Take, for example, Deloris Ealy's barn-burning funk 45 "Deloris Is Back with Jerome and His Band" (Big Vick Hammond, 1973). What seems at first glance to be a stripped-down collaboration between vocalist Ealy and teen drummer Jerome becomes stranger as the track goes on. While it's impossible to know for certain if the vocal doubling on the song was intentional or accidental, two distinct, out-of-sync vocal takes by Ealy crisscross one another on the 45, and it sounds amazing! One vocal is louder than the other, so the quieter one functions like a ghostly echo of the first. At times, this second vocal reproduces the tenor of the louder voice, while at others it is wildly out of sync with it. This opens up a rich listening experience—you can simultaneously enjoy two versions of the track at once, depending on where it draws your focus—either to the divergence or confluence of the two vocals. The fact that the song works like a time-lapse photography, superimposing two versions of the same song on top of one another, does nothing to diminish our enjoyment. In fact, it heightens it. The vocal persona Ealy offers is fragmented, and the song draws our attention to the fact that personhood is a process rather than an end result.

Listening to songs like this can be liberating, insofar as they teach us the joys of change and transformation. When two versions of self by the same singer are presented in the same song, we are freed to listen in an experimental and active way, rather than literally and passively.

Records like "Jerome," whether it was Ealy's intent or not, remind us of the mediation of the recording technology itself, how even the most natural voices and personas we encounter on record are as much produced as captured. But "Jerome," like the rest of the double-voiced records we'll discuss here, does not represent the exhausted pastiches of identity we associate with the postmodern—the predictable blankness of Cindy Sherman photographs and Kenneth Goldsmith's anhedonic celebrations of "unoriginal writing." I have chosen songs that more jubilantly let us break out of the tyranny of the self, and the joy that comes in recognizing you can experiment with your identity. The technology of the recording studio literalizes what the poets and the philosophers had long argued, that the self is a crowd of possibilities—it's what happens when Rimbaud's "Je est un autre" moves from opium-soaked, speculative fancy to a reality for everyone with a four-track. The possibility of experimenting with one's recorded voice, making it multiple, frees us from the prison of being one thing until death.

These records bring not postmodern ennui but jubilant recognition of the fact that we all include many possibilities within us, and that these are amenable to our own experimentation. "Jerome," for instance, lets us chart the similarities and differences between two performances of the same song on the same day, and lets us track both what remains common to both and what changes. Such songs show the potential for experimentation against the clichés and conventions of vocal persona hardwired into the modern recording studio. By definition, a multitrack recording allowed singers to outsource parts of their voice and then respond to this with a doubled version of that voice. As we will see, this ability to treat one's own voice as a conventional object to improvise with has led to many explosions of the concept of identity—both what it means to have a self, and what one can do with that self.

Take Kate Bush's "Suspended in Gaffa" (*The Dreaming*, EMI, 1982). A song about the frustrations of failed transcendence, its lyrics are beautiful but tread familiar Romantic ground. The story told by the relation of the song's voices, however, is dramatic and captivating. Breaking down the form of Bush's four distinct voices on this single song, one realizes this is a song that dramatizes the subject of identity formation. Bush's first voice is that of a playful but grounded, reasonable narrator; the second's a witchy voice that periodically screams "I want it all." The third's a barely audible wisp of a voice, given over to dreams of the ineffable, and the final voice is that describing the state of suspension the narrator feels ("gaffa" is what Americans would call gaffer tape, so the image is of one's arms and legs being bound tightly in duct tape).

Each voice bears a distinct persona, but the voices are intermeshed. They are not represented as separate parts of the singer's persona—as in misreadings of Freud where the superego fights the id and so on. Here all the voices bounce off of and reinflect one another. Lines that begin in the mouth of the endlessly demanding, high-pitched voice show up later in the resigned narrator's voice. Later in the song, roles reverse and the hysterical voice repeats the grounded voice's lines. Bush's production layers them over one another, as if to suggest the ideas of the song are in circuit from one form of identity to another, without any one providing decisive control. The process of identity formation here is represented as an open-ended conflict between interconnected means for achieving understanding and wisdom, rather than a situation in which there is reason on one side and folly on the other. In "Suspended in Gaffa," there's an entire allegory of the psyche implicit in the relation of its voices.

One of Bush's admirers, Prince, wrought many changes on his singing voice over time. He most notably pitch-shifts his voice, distorting it into both lower and higher registers. His most radical experiment with double-voiced tracks perhaps came on *Camille* (unreleased by Paisley Park, 1986), the forerunner to Prince's infamous and now better-known *The Black Album*. Three tracks from *Camille* later became part of the double LP *Sign o' the Times*. The record was intended to be released without Prince's name on it, attributed only to Camille, a feminine persona who shows up as the main character of the record's "Shockadelica." But the record was scrapped, maybe because Prince didn't think the world was ready for his Camille persona.

On *Camille*, his pitched-up feminine persona's voice allows him to say some things that would sound shocking in the voice he used on *1999* and *Purple Rain*—this is a record about the vertigo of desire, and the way one's identity gets uncomfortably mixed together with the object of one's affection. Prince uses the Camille voice on these songs to vent about the emotional sadism and masochism that strong desire entails, and this desire's power to blur the lines of individual identity.

On "Shockadelica," for instance, Prince describes Camille as a sadist who demands total submission from those she beguiles. For those in her thrall, the lust she inspires is indistinguishable from suffering—using golden ropes, she keeps whom she commands from playing his guitar. But tellingly, on "Strange Relationship" it is Prince who plays the sadist, taking more pleasure out of his love's pain than her joy—and gloats that he has taken control of her body and soul and destroyed her "self-respect." But on this track he too slips into a higher register—whereas the earlier 1983 piano demo uses his natural singing voice. And even *Camille*'s "If I Was Your Girlfriend," the best known of its tracks, is not the straightforwardly sensitive track a gloss of its surface conceit suggests. Insofar as the song uses the Camille voice to imagine total access into the life of his love, it seems less like a sympathetic attempt to understand his lover and more a fantasy of taking over the place her female friends have in her life. Like Roger Troutman's talk-box voice or Q's vocoder "Voice of Q" (Philly World 12", 1982), the Camille voice allows Prince to invent a character based on his better-known persona but one with important differences. On *Camille*, Prince, one of pop's premier theorists of desire, dramatizes the risks that come with love and lust. Behind every romantic cliché about "losing yourself" in love, Prince dramatizes a more complex, potentially more disturbing possibility—that in love you will lose control of your own voice and identity, so taken over you will be by desire. Whether you are a seducer or the seduced, on *Camille* you never know where your voice and identity ends and your lover's begins.

Though Annette Peacock shares Prince's interests in the workings of desire, the way she doubles her vocals strikes a different emphasis. One of the first to process her singing voice through a Moog synthesizer (she got a prototype from its inventor, Bob Moog himself, in the late '60s), her vocal doubling on *The Bigger the Love the Greater the Hate* (since reissued as *Revenge*) and above all on 1972's *I'm the One* explores the effect of high tech itself on identity. In 1965 the playwright Samuel Beckett made an experimental movie with Buster Keaton, simply titled *Film*. It told, in allegory form, the story of an individual's various failed attempts to evade a camera eye. *Film* makes just one point, but forcefully— that with the advent of modern photography and film, our identities will always be constructed for us by the technologies that capture and distribute our doings. Annette Peacock's late '60s and early '70s records can be said to explore the same subject matter for audio technology, but with more verve and less fatalism than the perennially melancholic Beckett.

Rather than give a simple answer to a complex question—"How does new media shape our identity and the perception of that identity?"—Peacock's performances work out a variety of possible answers. At times in "I'm the One" (*I'm the One*, RCA, 1972) Peacock overdrives her voice through the Moog box so much that it squelches into pure noise, before she then pulls it back into a form recognizable as singing. On "Seven Days" and "Been Gone" (same), this voice-turned-signal for the most part is kept in the background, as a low-volume stalker of Peacock's ballad voice. But even here it occasionally jumps to the foreground, reminding us of its presence. At times the distorting effects the Moog setup has on Peacock's voice feel intentional; at others they give the impression of a machine gone haywire and acting free from human control. Sometimes Peacock's straight vocal improvises with the technologically altered form of her own voice, and at other times noise overwhelms the single. No record better allegorized the productive push and pull between organic and technological music than *I'm the One*, though Peacock has yet to be acknowledged for the extent of her achievement.

Finally, others double their voices for less intellectualized, more action-oriented effects. On "Gimme the Loot" (*Ready to Die*, Bad Boy, 1994), the Notorious B.I.G. duets with a higher-voiced version of himself, a younger alter ego. In the action of the song, he and his mischievous double maraud their way through New York City streets, one-upping each other as they trade gleeful, antisocial verses detailing their exploits. The song is a highly stylized, stagey treatment of a life of crime—and nothing illustrates this more than the doubling. The splitting of B.I.G.'s persona lets him turn the city into a site for masquerade and allows him to take things in a surreal, comic direction. While literal-minded critics have often missed this, criticizing B.I.G. and others' violent lyrics, many rappers have used personas to distance themselves from stereotypes about rap, the street, and authenticity. Rappers as varied as Tupac (Makaveli), MF Doom (real name Daniel Dumile), T.I. (T.I.P.), and Nicki Minaj (Roman) have all used vocally altered personas to highlight the creativity and the release that comes from role playing. Such personas provide a third form to explore between literal-minded (the recent wave of rappers releasing songs about actual crimes, like Tay-K and Tekashi) and absolutely nonsensical (e.g., many mumble and SoundCloud artists) rap.

## VOICE ALTERNATIVE 3: COLLECTIVE

The final mode in which musicians experiment with voice and identity is the collective, through groups of two or more singers. Unlike with single or double voices, groups of singers must collaborate. These multiple-voiced songs necessarily imply a social situation, a simple allegory of the relation between band members. When we listen to a group of singers we bring with us an imagined idea about the dramatic context in which the singers relate to one another. A group's singing always explores, whether implicitly or explicitly, the relationship between the singers. This group relation is often, of course, made explicit in a band's name—the Louvin Brothers, the Beach Boys, Buckingham-Nicks, the Source Family.

But even when the names aren't so explicit, vocal relationships suggest interpersonal ones—romantic duets project a couple even if the two singers have never met one another before recording. Others dramatize the relation between family members, between a group of friends, a gang, a cult, or a flock of believers. But all project their experiments in collective being outward—when groups sing together, they necessarily play around with transpersonal forms of shared life.

And while such collective articulations seem to be on the wane since the 1980s (the era of the individual megastar—Madonna, Michael Jackson, Prince, Springsteen), the history of recorded music is rich in a variety of group singing outfits. In an era when it has become harder and harder to imagine collective life, our desire for collective voices in music seems to be on the decline. While experiments in group singing continue along the margins, popular tastes seem to run in the contrary direction.

Country singers Charlie and Ira Louvin's close harmonies, like their greatest influence, the Delmore Brothers, achieve a nearly perfect vocal blend. Though they had a completely dysfunctional relationship off record (read Charlie's autobiography *Satan Is Real* for the gory details), their voices fit together so well that their songs project a shared voice and vision. The closeness of their harmonies lends authority to their unanimous, unbreakable bond of brotherhood. Records with righteous heroes and tragic sinners, their duets project a moral center from which Ira and Charlie can judge the men and women of this world. On tracks like "Broadminded" (Capitol 45, 1953) and "Wreck on the Highway" (*The Great Roy Acuff Songs*, Capitol, 1967) and whole LPs like *Nearer My God* and *The Family Who Prays*, the Louvins manufacture a union that, for better and worse, lets them sharpen their moral vision.

By contrast, Kevin Coyne and Dagmar Krause's *Babble* (Virgin, 1979) measures how far the duet form can be taken from the Louvin Brothers' two-become-one moral assurance. Coyne and Krause sing in the personas of the most notorious killer couple in twentieth-century English history—the "Moors murderers" Myra Hindley and Ian Brady. Coyne and Krause use the duet format not to consolidate an iron-clad set of judgments on the world, but to suspend them. Singing from the identities of two child murderers, of course, has a way of scandalizing your audience, and *Babble* was rejected by the English press and record buyers alike.

But the record is no endorsement of Brady and Hindley; the lyrics mention none of the grisly particulars of the couple's actual crimes. Rather, it is a record about codependence, the antisocial form that partnership can take in the alienating crucible of modern life. If the Louvins beautifully blend their voices, Coyne and Krause jarringly clash with one another. Derby, England, native Coyne's voice is English blues, a gravelly speak-sung instrument that moves from mumbled oaths to cries of disgust. The German Krause, of Slapp Happy, Henry Cow, and Art Bears fame, is perhaps now best known as the preeminent modern interpreter of the Brecht, Weill, and Eisler songbook. Her voice is, to reuse a term from above, singular. Even at its quietest, it booms and overwhelms. It is a stagy, operatic voice that unnerves at any volume. On more unhinged performances, like *Babble*'s "Sweetheart," she sings with the absolute self-assurance of an exterminating angel bent on universal destruction.

Together, their singing captures the nihilism at the heart of a Bonnie-and-Clyde, us-against-the-world myth. When the two sing together on "Stand Up," "The Sun Shines Down on Me," "Shaking Hands with the Sun," and "It Doesn't Really Matter / We Know Who We Are," their joint singing never resolves into tight harmony. Rather, you hear again and again two voices straining for a oneness they never quite achieve. It is the sound of two deranged individuals attempting to unite into a single shared madness, only to find that even their madness is incompatible. On *Babble*, the attempt to carve out a moral world free from any external strictures results only in shared paranoia and delusions of grandeur. If the Louvin Brothers duets are the sound of two voices becoming one in order to establish moral authority, *Babble* is the sound of the dissolution of such a project under the pressure of darker times. But as a record, it is a bracing, invigorating work.

Vocal groups and bands with multiple vocalists of course bring an entirely different energy to a record than duos. While singing duos dramatize the relationships of couples, larger singing groups work through big group dynamics. The 1960s were the last time a large number of us shared collective dreams and nightmares, before going our own separate ways into 1,001 microcultures and taste niches. This was, not coincidentally, also the last time vocal groups held sway over solo singers. Coming out of R&B, doo-wop, and barbershop group singing traditions of the 1950s, the 1960s were a fertile time for groups that articulated collective identities through their singing.

In this context, we'd be loath to forget the Beach Boys, a band often celebrated as the pinnacle of harmony singing. But while Brian Wilson has, since 1966, been marketed as the "genius" behind the group, as if he alone led the band to execute his teenage symphonies to God, the music tells a more complicated story. Though Wilson was an incredible songwriter, what records like *Today!* (Capitol, 1965), *Pet Sounds* (Capitol, 1966), and *Smile* (recorded 1966–1967) project is not the work of a genius and his willing followers. Rather, these records, starting with the B-side of *Today!*, are made of systems of harmonies that simultaneously incorporate a variety of individual voices and depersonalize them all, including Wilson's. Though Wilson's jump falsetto and Mike Love's hectoring whine sometimes stand in relief, when listening to these LPs it's often hard to tell who's singing what when. It's as if the background and foreground have switched places. The group harmonies and countermelodies are mixed so high as to envelop the lead in a current of overlapping layers of vocals. On songs like "I'm So Young," "Kiss Me Baby," "I'm Waiting for the Day," "Sloop John B," "Good Vibrations," and "Heroes and Villains," we hear the production of a kind of musical oversoul, a group singing together to spiritualize and dematerialize the real world of distinct individuals and things.

And small differences in tone and timbre aside, there's clearly a homogenous Beach Boys "house voice" ideal for which all the band members aim. This overlapping of similar voices produces a depersonalized, decentralized vision of interconnected beings with no clear leader. This effect had been so perfected by the time of *Surf's Up* (Brother/Reprise, 1971) that the Beach Boys manager Jack Rieley and Van Dyke Parks could sing the downer "A Day in the Life of a Tree" and the production could still sell them as Beach Boys–esque. In other words, the Beach Boys' production regime is no respecter of individuals.

Beach Boys contemporaries the Impressions (in their '60s soul incarnation of Curtis Mayfield, Sam Gooden, and Fred Cash) took a much different approach to their shared vocal recordings. If the Beach Boys sought to manufacture a collective unconscious, the Impressions sought to model something more grounded, a cadre that can collaborate on a picture of contemporary life. If Beach Boys vocals ask you to spin out to the astral plane, the Impressions' movement-minded tracks ask you to engage with your material here and now. As a result, they project a much different relationship between their voices than the Beach Boys. On songs like "People Get Ready," "Choice of Colors," "Keep on Pushin'," "We're a Winner," "Mighty Mighty," and "This Is My Country," Curtis's tenor takes the lead at the highest volume, with Fred Cash's supporting his, and Sam Gooden's baritone popping in for a line here and there. Unlike the free-flowing nature of the Beach Boys' singing, the Impressions' is structured and precise—they establish rules and singing patterns that other groups did and can emulate. They present a tight-knit band with one clear leader and distinct vocal specializations. They make direct, forcefully beautiful songs that exhort action and declare catchy slogans such as *get ready, keep pushing, we're going to fight, this is my country*. These songs became Black Power anthems because of Mayfield's powerful unifying lyrics. But they also provided an example of these lyrics in action—a group coming together to generate the shared voice of a movement, a participatory structure that lets individuals each contribute what they're best at to produce something more powerful than they could create themselves. In doing so, they model a type of collective action. While the group's politics never reached the radicalism of the Black Panthers or Malcolm X (if they had, Barack Obama would never have been able to use "Keep on Pushing" to endorse John Kerry in 2004), their singing style has proved a lasting example for resolving the tension between the one and the many that plagues all bands hoping to make a statement.

If duos and group vocal records have fallen somewhat out of fashion, full-on choral records represent a fully exhausted tradition. Whether in gospel or classical, vinyl featuring ensembles of singers seems to have little to do with contemporary life or music. The kitsch of Gregorian chant and the Langley Schools, Music Project aside, choral music seems irremediably linked to the declining authority of the church and high culture alike. The contemporary revival of interest in gospel records has for the most part passed over choral gospel in favor of soulful, funky, and jazzy sounds made by solo vocalists or small bands. Choral classical records, on the other hand, are only exciting nowadays if they actively attack the conventions of the nineteenth-century tradition. Such records are few and far between, as most contemporary composers have just avoided the form altogether. If the decline in our feel for collective expression has pushed small group singing to the background, it has sent choral singing to the brink of extinction.

This being the case, my examples of exciting choral records will necessarily be a little esoteric and out-of-the-way. They are not staples you find in every collector's stacks. I have chosen two choral records that radically experiment with tradition in order to articulate a universalist vision, a powerful sound of a multitude of voices coming together to produce an imposing group ethos. In an era in deep need of a reinvention of international identity, as opposed to the prevailing military and corporate ones, experiments in choral sounds hold to visions of communal expression, in which every member has an equal voice and everyone can be counted among the whole. These are songs that, even as they falter and fail, push to grasp a truth that could hold true for us all.

English composer Cornelius Cardew famously gave up a respectable career as an avant-garde composer to make Marxist-Leninist music for the masses drawn from simple folk and choral forms. Most classical critics and fans have lamented this transition as a fall from sophistication into vulgar political sloganeering. And while his pre-Marxist work remains fascinating and enjoyable, the critical rush to trash the entirety of Cardew's later work has obscured his unique revival of the choral form on "There Is Only One Lie, There Is Only One Truth" (*Memorial Concert*, 1985). Yes, by 1980 Cardew had passed down some preposterously strident political condemnations (David Bowie is a fascist; the Clash and all punks are reactionary; Stockhausen serves imperialism), but that does nothing to diminish the fascination of "There Is Only One Lie, There Is Only One Truth."

The song is at once a history lesson, a straightforward celebration of the spirit of the oppressed, a critique of "Soviet social-imperialism" since Lenin, a winking travesty of socialist realism, and a work of strange beauty. What could be perceived as its weakness—its looseness and mischievous sense of humor—is actually its strength. The singing jams far too many words per line, and its ragtag vocal arrangement means many voices with their own rhythms overlap one another, sometimes making it hard to even understand the lyrics. Only on the refrain does the choir sing with one voice, pitting a vision of true justice against the Soviet (and Maoist) betrayals of the revolution since 1924. The joy of this song comes from the way it inverts the monumental tradition of nationalist art while also affirming hope in true democracy. It comes together and falls apart because these are everyday people singing alongside a few professionals. Rather than a well-wrought urn, it is a rough-hewn deconstruction of the choral form's epic pretensions. Against a cluttered catalog of Soviet Russia's betrayals of Marx and Lenin, beauty emerges only when the choir sings Cardew's title lines about the coming of a future truth. As a result, Cardew provides us with a positive picture of a community to come by demolishing the epic choral form and the chauvinism that comes with it.

Andrew Brown and the National Baptist Convention Choir's "Lord, Lord" (*Lord, Lord*, Mark, 1974) holds to the monumental form Cardew rejects, but with a twist. Christianity, like Marxism, professes to a total explanation of the world. And like Cardew, Brown and company seek to replace the past's faulty universal visions with their own, rather than dispense with the universal perspective altogether. The innovation in "Lord, Lord" comes in the interplay between two large sections of the choir and the female soloist. Yes, the undeniably funky drums and cascading piano keep things vital throughout, but it's the mass choral effects that make the track so special (and the parts that Just Blaze sampled for Drake's "Lord Knows," *Take Care*, 2011).

The NBCC singers begin and end the track with the same booming of "Lord, Lord" sung in unison. The full voice of the choir is used as a runner through the track, as a massively loud and concentrated blast of sound. This sheet of sublime noise alternates with a counter-refrain, detailing the ways God provides for and protects his flock. While also sung by a large number of vocalists, the tone in these passages shifts from imperious to tender. After being exposed to the raw power of the Godhead in the exclamations of "Lord, Lord," we are then shown the divine effect on the community of believers. God's power is quickly presented in two aspects, its external might as a constitutive force touching everyone and everything, and then as an agent of inner transformation in the spirit of all who have ears to hear. Only after the interchange between this sovereign power and the sea of believers has been run through multiple times are we introduced to a soloist (uncredited), who reinterprets the refrains of the believers in her own voice. In this staging of voices, the individual voice is only given space after the voice of God and the voice of the flock dialogue. And even when the soloist sings, her voice is enmeshed by these two louder, more upfront groups of singers. Taking the gospel choir beyond what we've come to expect from the call-and-response form, we get an allegory of the collective flock's dependence on the universal power of God, and the individual's dependence on them both for meaning.

What Cardew and Brown's works share is a commitment to representing life in common, the will to express multitudinous vision to which each participant contributes. But the democratic visions of the two themselves are different. Cardew uses mostly amateur singers in accordance with his political first principles; Brown's choir are the professionals needed to represent the sublime majesty of God's power. Cardew and his singers make a historical critique of twentieth-century collectivism in a collective voice, while Brown and his choir express a revelation of our eternal dependence on the divine. Cardew builds his community around satire in the name of a future ideal, while Brown's group is deadly serious throughout. Taken together, they prove there's still life in group singing to keep us in touch with our collective dreams (and nightmares, though we've focused here on the dreams). Whether it takes the forms of shared critique (as we find in Cardew) or in expressions of shared might (as we find in Brown), the future's going to require such new forms of collective expression to survive.

## EXPERIENTIAL ZONE 3: SPACE

Though Muzak no longer exists under its original name, its spirit lives on. As more and more spaces are taken over by the homogenizing forces of gentrification, our ambient environments have increasingly become decorated with so much sonic wallpaper. Seemingly everywhere you go in gentrified space, you hear inoffensive, low-volume background music intended to lubricate your navigation through the world. And now the contemporary workplace has its own form of Muzak, which comes in the form of corporate playlists designed to elicit specific moods and responses from the listener. These playlists have the stated or implied goal of increasing a laborer's productive capacities—to boost their concentration ("Find Your Zen"), to lengthen their attention span ("Lo-Fi Hip Hop Beats to Study To," "Work Jazz"), to help them sleep, and so on. Even new popular music these days often resembles such sonic wallpaper and works when you don't pay too much attention to it. This is music that makes few demands on the listener, either intellectually or emotionally. More and more, such edgeless music, benign instrumentals, polished pop, and overfamiliar oldies overlay vague soundscapes onto the literal spaces of our material lives.

All records, not just the explicitly "atmospheric" ones we discussed in a previous chapter, produce an imagined soundscape. This built-in spatial dimension is what led Joni Mitchell to term music "fluid architecture."[7] You need not subscribe to Mitchell's definition as complete to recognize that it has the benefit of emphasizing an underconsidered dimension of an art form so obviously made of time. And records, because they allow repeated play, help us build up an image of this "fluid architecture," which would otherwise remain only "fluid," an ephemeral one-off experience. All the recorded genres produce a sonic space for the listener—an environment, mood, and ambience. As opposed to tempo, which of course develops through time, the space of a recording is a more gestalt experience, an overall pattern, mood, or tone. In this sense, all music is atmospheric or environmental. Every work produces a sound world of its own through its use of texture, relative volumes, panning, microphone placement, spacing of instruments in the mix, and so on—these are structural elements that produce the overall architecture of a record. For example, consider the effects of the extensive vocal and guitar overdubs on a record like My Bloody Valentine's *Loveless* (Creation, 1991). Independent of the action of its main harmony and melody lines, *Loveless* contains an immersive sound world that persists throughout the LP that can only be conceived as spatial. This spatial dimension, *Loveless*'s maximalist architecture and the lush mood-space it creates, leaves as strong an impression on us as the record's individual songs and moments.

The three types of sonic space we'll discuss here can be described as alienating, defamiliarizing, and immersive. All three represent alternatives to the gentrified soundspace of streaming sites, utilitarian playlists, and even many new releases that increasingly cover our public and private space. As the name I've chosen indicates, alienating sound worlds are aggressive, off-putting, and abrasive. They seek to distance the listener by creating a world of sound that is forbidding and uninviting. Defamiliarizing records, on the other hand, are ones that take some part of our known world and seek to help us hear and think differently in relation to it. And finally, immersive sound worlds seek to generate wholly other worlds of sound that transcend our own sound world. The variety of new sonic spaces records can create is profound: Some records are ruins, others are haunted houses; some remodel real space, while others build stately mansions of the mind in inner or outer space.

# SPATIAL ALTERNATIVE 1: ALIENATING SPACE

In many ways, records that produce alienating sonic spaces are a contradiction in terms. Genres that produce alienating atmospheres—harsh noise, industrial, power electronics, free jazz, and improv—depend on live performance. But records by their nature preserve even the most aleatoric, spontaneous, and off-the-cuff sounds for posterity. Sound and noise meant to terrorize, antagonize, or disturb the listener loses its shock value with repeated listening, and records aid pattern-seeking habit in turning even the most chaotic, violent noise into music, albeit a still threatening and forbidding one. In this context, then, alienating records seek to produce antirepresentational noise that can never be assimilated and tamed. In other words, this music seeks to break our habitual patterns of imagining through shock and awe.

This is music that confronts the listener. It is a cacophonous assault on the very assumption that music can conjure imaginative space for the listener. Rather, it forces the listener to focus on the ugly materiality of sound. Like all avant-garde products, it attacks the possibility of representation as illusory. Tellingly, the title of one noise compilation featuring such noise "names" as Whitehouse, Ramleh, and Incapacitants is *Even Anti-Art Is Art...That Is Why We Reject It* (Statutory Tape [awful name], 1991). Spatially speaking, harsh noise targets the very idea that music should create a sense of atmosphere at all. The ideal noise work would create no space in the hearts and minds of listeners. Instead, it would function like a tsunami or earthquake, materially devastating the listener.

But no work can dispense with the representation of sonic space. Or it can, but we stop recognizing it as music. At that point, it becomes just another unmotivated piece of our sound environment. Even the most brutal Merzbow record needs to create a space for the listener in order not to be confused with sounds from, say, a randomly chosen construction site or recycling center. What's more, record listeners will infer a sonic atmosphere even where none was intended. This being the case, outré records tend to create ruins, demolished spaces in the imagination.

Take a record like Hanatarash's *3* (RRRecords, 1989). Japan is home to many of the world's most limit-pushing experimenters with noise (Merzbow, Incapacitants, KK Null), and Hanatarash held their own among such company. The band often created literal ruins when they played—after forcing attendees to sign waivers, they would attack the clubs they were performing in with backhoes and electrical saws during their performances. Hanatarash's *3* creates the sonic analog to such destruction—a sound world in which nothing works anymore. It's filled with malfunctioning machinery and steam pipes, tapes running the wrong way, horrible metal scraping, blown-out amplifiers, and distorted voices chanting from within vortexes of noise. It creates a sound world out of sonic debris: an assemblage of wrecked and malfunctioning technology. The soundscape it projects is that of an annihilated world, forbidding, polluted, and inhospitable to human life. At their best, such sonic ruins can shake us out of our complacency and instill in us a sense of how wrong things can go and how terrifying life can get. At a time when the alienations of the world daily outstrip those to be found on record, it's an open question whether we need to be reminded that the apocalypse is on its way.

Perhaps more compromising in their sonics are the noise rock and industrial groups. Noise rockers like New Zealand's the Dead C, England's the Shadow Ring, and the US's Sonic Youth incorporated avant-garde disruption into more recognizable song structures, though still minimal and damaged. Industrial groups like Einstürzende Neubauten, Throbbing Gristle, and Coil, on the other hand, worked recognizable rhythms between the clangs and hisses, with Throbbing Gristle even producing a few skewed dance tracks like "Hot on the Heels of Love." The records of these groups all generate dark, forbidding atmospheres, but ones more aesthetically varied and layered than more avant-garde works. Because of this, they make space for desire, mystery, and occasionally even hope to surface out of the sonic wreckage. No matter how scarifying an experience listening to *Harsh 70s Reality*, *Put the Music in Its Coffin*, *Bad Moon Rising*, *Kollaps*, or *Horse Rotorvator* becomes, one still feels the pulse of an alternative atmospheric subcurrent. Not content simply to destroy, these artists provide glimpses of humor and juxtapositions of noise with more recognizable musical forms. As a result, they transcend the chaotic despair blowing through the heart of pure noise.

## SPATIAL ALTERNATIVE 2: DEFAMILIARIZING SPACE

French historian Pierre Nora's concept of a *"lieu de mémoire"* (place or site of memory) is not one usually thought of as particularly relevant to music. A *lieu de mémoire*, according to Nora, is an imagined "site" in which the collective memories of a community are embodied: "a *lieu de mémoire* is any significant entity, whether material or nonmaterial in nature, which by dint of human will or the work of time, has become a symbolic element of the memorial heritage of any community."[8] Nora's examples for French culture range from material objects (the Eiffel Tower) to more figurative entities (Joan of Arc)—but sites of memory tend to be where the real and symbolic meet and combine to create the shared memories of a community. According to Nora's definition above, American examples of the phenomenon would no doubt count Washington, DC; the Lincoln Memorial; and the American flag as *lieux de mémoire*.

In this section, we will examine how records produce atmospheres and moods that reshape our collective memory and its symbols. These records create counter-spaces of memory that attempt to pin new moods and concepts to preexisting *lieux de mémoire*. In doing so, they defamiliarize the commonplace versions of acceptable memory by investing the listener with new associations and feelings about the symbolic spaces that help constitute our communal sense of identity. Just as W. G. Sebald's *The Rings of Saturn* transforms the stereotypically bucolic English countryside into a zone of future ruins, its manors populated with history's ghosts, records can transform our sense of the spaces important to us by re-atmosphering them, so to speak. Music, more than any other art, sutures together inner emotional space with external public space to create powerful *lieux de mémoire*.

A record indicates its spatial context in many ways—through its title, song names, album art, liner and back cover notes, and of course sounds and forms within the music itself. In this way, we never come to a record without preconceived ideas and aesthetic expectations. The Lloyd McNeill Quartet's *Washington Suite*, which we are about to discuss, indicates this in its title and song names. Chester Lewis's "Wade in the Water / Precious Lord" is a live record, and we're able to hear the crowd's reactions to Lewis's playing, which clues us in that he's playing in a small Southern church. The tiny private label's name on the 45, Eternal Gold Ltd., also alludes to this context. The liner notes of Abdul Wadud's *By Myself* speak of the record's inspiration in the twin concepts of "Mother Africa" and the "natural world"—a context necessary to understanding the sonic space created by the album's centerpiece, "In a Breeze"—as do the pictures, which show Wadud with his cello in a forest, beside and almost within an enormous tree. By reshaping our sense of three sites of memory—Washington, DC; the archetypal American black church; and Africa—McNeill, Lewis, and Wadud prove the power of a musical atmosphere to tap into the building blocks of our collective memory.

As its title suggests, Lloyd McNeill's soul jazz masterpiece *Washington Suite* (ASHA, 1970) takes America's federal city for its thematic center. *Washington Suite* creates a conceptual mapping of black Washington, DC, in the late 1960s. Recorded at the National Collection of Fine Arts (now part of the Smithsonian) and Corcoran School of the Arts (now part of George Washington University), the record was commissioned by the Capitol Ballet Company of DC, the United States' first predominantly African American professional ballet troupe. Composed for dance trailblazers Doris Jones and Claire Haywood, *Washington Suite* began as the musical accompaniment for a black ballet performance. Its song titles are up-to-the-moment references to different aspects of black DC life, ranging from the minutely personal to the broadly political. The land of "taxation without representation," the District of Columbia has long called for home rule, real autonomy from the US federal government, hence the title of the opening song "Home Rule." At the time of the album's recording, DC was widely known as "chocolate city"—it was 71 percent black in 1970—hence the punning title of the LP's second piece, "Just 71% Moor." Although limited home rule was granted by Lyndon Johnson in the year of *Washington Suite*'s recording, most of the white fear about granting DC full political autonomy had to do with the city's blackness. The song title "The Black Mayor" refers to Walter E. Washington, then the city's mayor. Though he originally held his office by President Johnson's appointment, Washington was the first black mayor of a major American city. "Sandra Is the City" refers to the lead dancer of the Capitol

Ballet Company, Sandra Fortune, then only nineteen, pictured on the LP's back cover. The scene around the fountain at Dupont Circle, then a bohemian enclave and countercultural hub for artists and outsiders, is conjured up in "Fountain in the Circle." The album's third track, "2504 Cliffbourne Pl.," names the address of a residence in the Adams-Morgan neighborhood—presumably McNeill's own while he taught at Howard University.

The record, then, takes as its symbolic center of gravity an empowered, creative black DC—in the arts, in politics, in personal life. To account for the varying registers of black experience in DC, *Washington Suite* shifts modes from song to song. It moves from pounding, funky self-assertion ("Home Rule") to urban fantasia ("Just 71% Moor") to extended jam ("City Triptych"), only to slow things down for stately neoclassical conclusion ("Fountain in the Circle"). It keeps two scales in play at once—the rising hope for black autonomy to be found at every turn (as hinted at in the titles) and the more varied, tension-filled unstable political makeup of the city as it then existed. The music pits the dreams embedded in the titles against representing the struggle to achieve them in the music itself. By pairing different spaces in DC to different genres of music, the record seeks to define particular neighborhoods as enclaves of black DC. In McNeill's version of DC life, the federal city's grid is broken up into distinct zones of experience. Black DC can't be represented by one genre alone. It requires an odyssey of styles.

The complexity of the work as it flows from genre to genre, from one emotional atmosphere to another, mirrors the heterogenous, divided realities of the city. Even the most spiritually unifying track, "Imani (Faith)," speaks to the political divisions of DC along lines of race and class—Imani is the seventh and final day of Kwanzaa, which was then a nascent holiday (created by Maulana Karenga in 1966). Not yet the established holiday it is today, Kwanzaa was then an inherently political flashpoint for the time because of its origins in the Black Power movement and the pan-Africanism of founding intent. If the titles taken together point to the contemporaneous reality of Black Power as it existed in every pore of that city's life, then the music itself, in its variety and genre shifting, embodies the technical search and political struggle necessary to fight for its realization. *Washington Suite* is the sound of a virtuoso flautist and his band searching for representation of black DC through form after form, of an achieved black cultural power in a city still seeking to realize its political, collective power. If one has spent time with *Washington Suite*, one today moves through that city haunted by the record. At every turn in DC's cityscape, snatches of McNeill's soundtrack fill your head. A *Washington Suite* listener measures the city against McNeill's dream image and finds it unrealized.

Few symbolic spaces are more important to the American imagination than the black church. In contrast to the staid, formalized religious practices of WASPy Protestantism, Americans tend to think of the black church as freer, more passionate, and more expressive in its worship. Historically, the black church functioned as a refuge for black life during slavery and as a cornerstone of black civic life in a country built on white supremacy. Furthermore, the black church is rightfully celebrated as a wellspring for American popular music—a crucial influence on the blues, R&B, soul, rock, and more.

But while the black church's centrality to American life cannot be denied, it can and has been systematically misrepresented. In our postmodern times, Americans lean on a stereotyped battery of clichés about the black church. These, for the most part, have replaced the more complicated, living reality. These clichés should be close to mind for anyone half-familiar with contemporary American popular culture—in which the black church represents authentic, soulful worship. In the American imagination, the black church too often gets reduced to a primitivist stereotype. It becomes the site where black folk do what comes naturally (as opposed to reflectively and rationally) and express raw joys and pains.

These white-friendly clichés come dressed as tributes to the vitality of black life but are double-edged. They laud the black church and its worshippers as a monolithic expression of spirit, denying the actual variety of expression to be found within existing black communities. The clichés emphasize the passion of black church music while glossing over the technique and musicianship that went into its creation. This celebration of gospel music's raw immediacy rests on the belief that such fervor only comes out of a more naïve, less-than-modern culture. In summary, the popular image of the black church works more to comfort and entertain white voyeurs than it does to represent what goes on in the many real, diverse spaces of black worship.

But if you listen to the gospel records that have come out of the black church, it becomes impossible to keep thinking in such clichéd terms. These records explode the belief that the black church represents one thing. After exploring gospel records in depth, you can no longer see the black church as a symbol for the "heart" of the American nation, nor can it be considered an organic whole that espouses any one theological doctrine. Below, we examine the way three versions of the spiritual "Wade in the Water" produce distinct, even contradictory soundspaces for the listener. By doing so, we will see that gospel music provides a richer, more complicated vision of what goes on in black churches than American mythopoetics currently allow. Using the same content as their starting point, each of these records produces a profoundly different sound map of what goes on in the black church. Chester Lewis gives us a funky, intimate space in which the crowd actively participates; the Staple Singers create a broadly appealing, transracially populist space; while Kenneth Moales constructs an intimidating space in which a God who is no respecter of persons rules.

A single 45 like Chester Lewis's "Wade in the Water" (Eternal Gold Ltd., 197x) goes a long way in disabusing anyone with the above clichés about the black church still stuck in their head. Sometime in the 1970s, this sacred steel guitar recording was made as part of a church convention, with Lewis and band representing the parishioners of the Ebenezer Missionary Baptist Church in Rocky Mount, North Carolina. "Wade in the Water" is a famous spiritual, dating back to the Civil War, and is even alleged to have been sung on the Underground Railroad. It was first commercially recorded by Sunset Four Jubilee Singers for Paramount Records in 1925 and then by many others, but its best-known version is the Staple Singers' 1960s take, which became an unofficial Civil Rights anthem.

Perhaps one way to measure Lewis's achievement, then, is to note the ways in which his "Wade in the Water" creates a radically different sonic space than the Staple Singers' version. The Staple Singers' version is a catchy studio recording, with a sturdy groove and tasteful electric guitar accompaniment. It's a showcase for Mavis Staples's incredible voice and built around a familiar call-and-response form, which puts an emphasis on its lyrics and the voice of the lead singer. It features a single lone handclap keeping time with the band, a muted token of the song's origins in the field and church. It is Mavis Staples's voice that makes the song, and that carries its broad message of liberation. It's a traditional studio recording and is radio friendly. The Staple Singers' "Wade in the Water" has an easy appeal, and it's no wonder that it became an anthem. It is a well-recorded, polished studio track made to be played in large public gatherings.

Chester Lewis creates a more intimate, testimonial version of the spiritual. His radical rearrangement puts the emphasis on the voice of his sacred steel guitar as it rides above a funky minimal bass and drum backing. Lewis turns the spiritual, famous for its lyrics, into an instrumental. This alone makes his version a more intimate affair. Lewis's "Wade in the Water" is a believer's prayer, but one shared with an audience. And this audience actively participates in the sound of the song—their loud, enthusiastic claps keep time with the drums, and various crowd members applaud and voice their appreciation for particularly funky, intense moments of Lewis's playing. The recording is slightly lo-fi and sounds almost like an audience bootleg, and because of this, it captures the room tone of the performance space. As a result, the listener feels as if they are one of many in an audience of believers. But the recording is not churchy in the sense that it sermonizes; rather it equates an audio equivalent for the space of belief and demands the listener to feel within it. Far from the anthemic populist soundspace created by the Staple Singers' version, Chester Lewis's recording of "Wade in the Water" is the stripped-down, heavy-grooved sound of one believer sharing his wordless testimony, and an audience rejoining him with their own. It is the sound of an aesthetic experiment finding confirmation from an audience in the moment. And because of the fly-on-the-wall fashion in which it was recorded, we the listeners are drawn close to its space of belief.

Finally, we come to Kenneth Moales and the Kenneth Moales Ensemble's "The Waterside" (*Serve the Lord* LP, Glori, 1972). This version of "Wade in the Water" interpolates original verses from congregation member Jimmy Mitchell and projects a radically different sonic space. While the Staple Singers produced a secularized radio- and crowd-friendly studio version of "Wade in the Water," and Lewis dramatized an intimate scene of spiritual connection between audience and performer, Moales created an apocalyptic vision. "The Waterside" presents the space of God's judgment of the world—replete with gothic lyrics about children dressed in red and the end times. This version presents "God troubling the waters" as a cataclysm of divine judgment. With creepy choral and wind sound effects and above all an insistently spooky piano riff, the song asserts the voice of God's authority. The sonic space created by this version of "Wade in the Water" is haunting, intimidating, and overwhelming. It's a completely depersonalized expression of the divine's transcendence of human space. It presents a vision of the black church as trans-individual, the vessel for God's awful, inscrutable sovereign will.

The theorist Achille Mbembe begins his work *On the Postcolony* with a meditation on the West's inability to rationally think and speak about the African continent: "Africa is never seen as possessing things and attributes properly part of 'human nature.' Or when it is, its things and attributes are generally of lesser value, little importance, and poor quality. It is this elementariness and primitiveness that makes Africa the world par excellence of all that is incomplete, mutilated, and unfinished, its history reduced to a series of setbacks of nature in its quest for humankind."[9] It's telling that *On the Postcolony* was crucially inspired by Mbembe's experience of Congolese music.[10] We find in the music of the Black Arts Movement in the West, and in spiritual jazz in particular, an attempt to create sonic spaces from within the West that critique colonial concepts and provide imagined alternatives to them. Much of the best spiritual jazz sought to redeem the image of Africa from negative superstition and replace it with a sonic space in which Africa and the rest of the world could be interconnected on equal terms.

Because this section is conceptually of a piece with the last one, we'll discuss just one example of the way music can create a sonic counter image of "Africa" from within the heart of America. Cleveland-born bassist Abdul Wadud, long-time collaborator with Julius Hemphill, has backed such avant-jazz luminaries as Frank Lowe, George Lewis, and Charles "Bobo" Shaw. Wadud's 1977 masterpiece *By Myself* (Bishara), as its title suggests, is a solo work, featuring just Wadud and his bass. The record is "dedicated to my parents and Mother Africa. For if it were not for them I would not be able to speak the *Music* the way I speak it." In this dedication, Wadud links his American family to "Mother Africa"—treating them as twinned sources for the music on *By Myself*. In Wadud's own conception, his music comes from a shared, generative zone connecting his American family with his spiritual family and "Mother Africa." *By Myself* attempts to give this trans-Atlantic zone of the imagination a musical form. This zone, which Wadud elsewhere in his notes calls a "world of possibilities, fresh and new," would correct the centuries of Western misprision of Africa Mbembe discusses above.

Nowhere does *By Myself* do this better than on "In a Breeze," the B-side's standout track. Given Wadud's notes, we think of the title's breeze as Atlantic in nature, a force that bridges the division wrought by the forced separation of the African slave trade and centuries of historical change in the two regions. A delicate piece, "In a Breeze" positions the listener between two musical zones—one made up of sustained bass notes, the other of quick bass runs. The rapid alternation of these two gives the piece its structure. Built this way, "In a Breeze" represents the gusts and lulls of a wind connecting two spaces, with its sprightly runs mimicking blasts of air and its droning moments of calm. A delicate piece, "In a Breeze" puts the listener in perpetual motion, caught in transit between two spaces without ever arriving at either of them. It is a musical figure for the shared past and a dream of a shared future between America and Africa, a vision of reconciliation through the symbol of a natural creative force that blows between them both. It creates a musical zone of shared life, love, and mutual respect in advance of its realization in politics and economics.

## SPATIAL ALTERNATIVE 3: IMMERSIVE SPACE

In this final section on recorded space, we turn to records that cut themselves off from the real world entirely. Rather than represent chaotic postindustrial hellscapes (alienating music) or shape new perceptions of real spaces (defamiliarizing music), these records try to build hermetic worlds sealed off from the material plane. Intended as wholly other spaces than those we encounter in waking life, these records tend to work in three forms of soundscape. The first can be analogized to the worlds created by science fiction novels and stories, the second to those found in fantasy works, and the third to a hybridization of sci-fi and fantasy. At the risk of oversimplifying, the first create otherworldly, alien emanations from deep space—these are the science-fictional works we associate with futuristic journeys through hitherto unexplored regions of space. Their opposite number create fantasy worlds, warmly immersive, in which magic, not alien high tech, detethers the listener from the real world. The third type mixes these immersive sound worlds together with unpredictable results. As you would expect, most records that create immersive sound worlds are instrumental: Singing and lyrics both tend to ground a song in our material reality. These three major types of immersive records draw you in, seeking not to represent the world but to replace it.

The difference between cold and warmly immersive records is the difference between the austere vasts of records like Klaus Schulze's *Timewind* (Brain, 1975) and *Moondawn* (Brain, 1976), Tangerine Dream's *Phaedra* (Virgin, 1974), and Abdur Razzaq and Rafiyq's rare "Reflections from the Grave" (*The Night of Power* LP, Green Essence, 1983), on the one hand, and the immersive warmth of Steve Tibbetts's *Northern Song* (ECM, 1982), Dollar Brand's "Jabulani–Easter Joy" (*African Space Program*, ENJA, 1974), Arthur Russell's *World of Echo* (Upside, 1986), and Suni McGrath's *Cornflower Suite* (Adelphi, 1969), on the other. The first often use synthesizers and sequencers—musical high tech—to immerse the listener in icy sound worlds beyond human scale and human meaning. The second type also immerse the listener, but within delicate, mystical, and internal landscapes. Though they sometimes use tape loops, synthesizers, and computers, synthetic sounds never dominate the overall aesthetic as they do on records in the first category. They provide an imaginary realm of escape not through the production of alien soundscapes, but through a mystic investment in realms of enchantment and magic. The third type alternate between the two approaches to connect alien outer worlds with mystical inner ones.

Berlin school pioneer Klaus Schulze's near forty-minute opus "Echoes of Time" (*Timewind*) provides a paradigmatic example of cold but immersive musical space. As far as we can tell, it contains no organically produced sound—nothing that is not sequenced or left untreated by the studio mixing board. It is a heady ride into another zone, all arpeggiating loops and durational synth washes. While the loops give one the sense of being immersed in an unnatural realm saturated by the chirping routines of machines, the washes simultaneously produce the feeling of floating through the endless blackness of deep space. Together, they forge a transhuman sound world—while listening to "Echoes of Time," there is no sense that anything living could meaningfully intrude into its space. It is a realm complete and impenetrable by humans. *Timewind*'s cover art, in which three giant metallic alien-angel hybrids toweringly prance over a small human skull, represents the total effect. Like Tangerine Dream's *Phaedra* (Virgin, 1974) and so many records that followed, *Timewind* is a record tired of the puniness of the human-sized world and its follies. Such frigidly immersive music indulges a powerful but dangerous fantasy—that one day, the difference between humankind and its machines will be erased. This will let us leave behind the limitations of earthly existence and merge with the unhuman things of this cosmos.

Compared to the bracing chill of *Timewind*, Steve Tibbetts's *Northern Song* is a warm bath of a record. Though sparely rather than lushly immersive, *Northern Song* creates a warm, hypnotic soundscape conducive to the expansion of inner space. By this, we mean it creates an edgeless, gentle, and calming utopian sound world. The song titles are elemental—"The Big Wind," "Form," "Walking," and "Aerial View"; with the record's focus on producing and inner space, these simple titles are just sketched placeholders for the intricate musical worlds they name. With only Tibbetts's guitar and kalimba playing and Marc Anderson's percussion (and yes, tape loops, though so inconspicuously deployed as to be unnoticeable), the record makes everyday things shimmer with overwhelming beauty. Every song turns basic facts of existence into an occasion for self-discovery. Records like *Northern Song* allow the listener to bracket out all inessential worries and concerns through an immersion in a profoundly peaceful sound world. Through hypnotic effect and precise playing, this record creates a space in the imagination where only reflective thought and care for the delicate enchantments of existence matter.

But most records that immerse the listener in total sound worlds are hybrids—they mix or alternate the tendencies above. Take the sound world created by Detroit techno legends Drexciya. In their track titles, interviews, and writings, Drexciya self-consciously invented a mythos for themselves and their music. According to a Discogs summary, Drexciyans are "a race of underwater dwellers descended from pregnant slave women thrown overboard during trans-Atlantic deportation."[11] Their records represent a "dimensional jumphole between their black African roots and the contemporary USA" and combine science-fictional narrative with the structuring historical tragedy of the United States, the slave trade.

With such an ambitiously conceived mythos, it's been easy for critics to get lost in the group's self-descriptions and avoid deeply listening to the music itself. As Philip Sherburne's fine review of *Journey of the Deep Sea Dweller* Volume 1 compilation notes, "It's easy to remember Drexciya primarily for their shtick."[12] While Sherburne contrasts this "shtick" with the more "cryptic" sound of the music, it seems more parsimonious to consider that the music produces and sustains the imagined underwater mythos of Drexciya. Their music creates a full sound world, mixing cold techno (e.g., "Hydro Cubes") with warm piano lines (e.g., "Davey Jones Locker") and campy vocal samples. The completeness and variety of the sound world Drexciya creates—its outlandish sci-fi excess paired with occasional beauty and hard techno spaciness—is one carved away from the terrors of history. By creating such a slippery, immersive, variegated sound world in which you can find your own way around from track to track, Drexciya provides an inspiring critique of the actual by providing a better alternative in imagined space. By alternating between cold and warm, high-tech and fantasy, Drexciya holds in stark relief the difference between what black life has been and what it could be.

While Drexciya builds a world stunning in its completeness, a group like Cocteau Twins are up to something different. Their version of immersive space is a gentler, more pastoral one. It is narrower, but perhaps more focused than Drexciya's. But that's because they intend different things with their music. Like Virginia Astley's *From Gardens Where We Feel Secure* (Rough Trade, 1983), Cocteau Twins' *Blue Bell Knoll* (4AD, 1988) aspires to reinvent an enchanting second nature in sound. Against the backdrop of global ecological collapse in the actual world, dream pop like that of Cocteau Twins tends to consciously rebuild green spaces of the mind. In this, *Blue Bell Knoll* works within an established British Isles aesthetic tradition, in the William Morris garden utopia variety. The difference, however, is that a record like *Blue Bell Knoll* is self-consciously a fictive space with little to do with actual nature. It is sung in an invented language of "nonsense" phrases: singer Elizabeth Fraser says she created by just going "with the sound and the joy." It aims for an epiphanic sense of pleasure, beyond the structures of human language. In every song, the tension comes from Fraser's warm, lush voice overcoming their colder guitar and synth backing.

*Blue Bell Knoll*'s song titles, making occasional oblique concessions to the English language, are drawn from the lexicon of infancy, folk tradition, fairy tales, and natural life: "Athol-Brose" is an old Highlander's grog, "Suckling the Mender" and "For Phoebe Still a Baby" gesture toward the utopia of infancy, and "The Itchy Glowbo Blow" conjures up visions of garden sprites.

The music of a song like "Carolyn's Fingers" projects a vegetal calm, serene and peaceful. It is music of an achieved utopia, in which human life has transcended the perpetual struggle for existence. It projects a vision of existence that has outgrown its humanity and become again part of a placid nature. Anything but "red in tooth and claw," nature here becomes the suspension of all motion, drive, competition. What remains is the free-floating warm expression of Fraser's voice enveloping everything around it in a dewy mist.

In the same time period as Cocteau Twins, shoegaze took a more aggressive, overloaded maximalist approach to dreampop. As a result, the listener is immersed in a hybrid space, alternately soothing and alien, where one can't tell quite what's going on at all. Though the two genres are often conflated, the sonic space that shoegaze groups like My Bloody Valentine, Medicine, and Slowdive produce can be considered anti-pastoral. It's overloaded with pedal effects and endless layers of sound that have nothing to do with the natural world. Works like Medicine's "One More" (*Shot Forth Self Living*, Def American, 1991), My Bloody Valentine's "What You Want" (*Loveless*, Creation, 1991), and Slowdive's "Souvlaki Space Station" (*Souvlaki*, Creation, 1993) generate disorienting, confusing soundscapes. In shoegaze, the pastoral can no longer be rendered even in imagined space—like contemporary rave music of the time, shoegaze records work entirely within the limits of the technologically dominated world.

Recently, record compilers have coined the neologism "personal space" to describe lo-fi, bedroom experiments with synths and drum machines, made predominantly by African Americans. "Electronic soul" is the subtitle of *Personal Space*, Dante Carfagna's 2012 compilation on Chocolate Industries. Tracks from Guitar Red, Makers, and Deborah Washington are standouts, but Jeff Phelps's *Magnetic Eyes* LP (Engineered for Sound, 1985), the only LP featured twice on the comp, most clearly generates the sound of its own "personal space." As opposed to the full virtual world of Drexciya, the garden fantasias of Cocteau Twins and Virginia Astley, and the controlled chaos of shoegaze, Phelps and his vocalist Antoinette Marie Pugh create a mesmerizing toy world, more fascinating than warmly immersive. A DIY synth record, it has a tiny, dinky sound not made for the dancefloor. Yet it features great drum programming and a unique sense of timing. The result is a vision of artists reinventing the sound of the home and hearth. Listening, you never quite get lost in the undermixed music, so what remains is a romanticized vision of Phelps and Pugh in a Missouri City, Texas, home studio, making the best they can on a shoestring budget. It is the sound of the artists trying to create a warm, immersive sound world out of the lifeless presets of budget musical technology. *Magnetic Eyes*, like the best "personal space" records, creates a homemade sonic space. It tries and fails to immerse the listener—and in the process leaves them fascinated, in a cold world always on the verge of heating up.

## EXPERIENTIAL ZONE 4: DYNAMICS

In our everyday conversations about music, we automatically slip into the language of dynamics. We like how one song builds and how another trails off into silence. We grow attached to the way certain songs mutate, disintegrate, or explode. Calling a track "dynamic" is for many a general term of praise. The Pixies and Nirvana built a whole subgenre of indie rock, around soft-loud-soft verse-chorus-verse dynamics, and a genre like jazz fusion borrows its name from elementary nuclear physics. Galaxie 500's Damon Krukowski has argued that digital has subtracted the noise out of recordings in favor of pure signal, impoverishing our sense of "spatial hearing" in the process.[13] Whether we're talking about production, songwriting, or genre, the way music changes in energy over time is integral. A whole theory of recent musical history depends on a claim about music production dynamics. According to those fighting the "loudness wars," like writer Greg Milner, digital engineering via compression has been "reducing the dynamic range of the music"[14] since recording's halcyon days in the 1960s and '70s.

For critics like Milner, modern record techniques have sacrificed a balance variation between quiet and loud for just plain loud. At the centerpiece of his argument is a study by software engineer Chris Johnson, who has plotted dynamic variation versus commercial success (number of sales), in order to argue: "The most commercially important albums, [Johnson] wrote, featured lots of 'high contrast' moments, when 'the transient attacks of instruments'— very brief outbursts of high energy—were allowed to stand out against 'the background space where the instruments are placed.'"[15] Milner's takeaway from Johnson's study was: "Loudness has its place, but most of us like our music to have breathing room, so that our eardrums are constantly tickled by little sonic explosions. In a tight, compressed space, music can get asphyxiated."[16] A balanced recording, where loudness makes brief appearances to "tickle our eardrums" and then returns to the background, represents the ideal for Milner, Johnson, and many others. But dynamics, whether social or musical, cannot be reduced to simple $x$-$y$ plots: Interpretation of individual works is still necessary. For example, Johnson takes pride in the fact that the record he calculated to be most sonically dynamic, The Eagles' *Their Greatest Hits*, is also "the single most commercially important album in R.I.A.A. history."[17] But sales do not equal musical importance. Whether a work is dynamic or not depends on more than statistical analysis of a soundwave: for every Eagles lover, you will find an Eagles hater. Numbers that would show great numerical contrasts between the Eagles' *Their Greatest Hits* and Metallica's *Death Magnetic* obscure the fact that they are both unlistenable to wide swaths of music lovers. And maybe some genres use compression differently than others: Soul records made in the 1970s can't necessarily be compared to trap rap made in 2019. When we talk about "dynamics," form, genre, and historical context still matter; if we ignore them, we end up cherry-picking the data, often reinforcing our musical biases rather than challenging them.

What's more, the ideal for balance in all things has no basis in material reality. I suspect it comes from a more general unconsidered assumption that a balance of forces is always positive. For example, in politics, we're taught to respect compromise between Democrat and Republican; in economics, we're taught that peaceful relations between labor and capital will lead to the fairest system; on television, "equal time" for points of view is the norm. While compromise in the service of balance is sometimes necessary, it can often have disastrous effects.

Balanced dynamics in music tend to result in listener boredom, "little sonic explosions" aside. Balance is predictable: the best records present music that is unbalanced, or complicated enough to seem so. In this section, we discuss records that break with expectations of harmonious balance by creating their own unique dynamics—by breaking down, recycling, or transforming their musical energy.

## DYNAMIC ALTERNATIVE 1: BREAKING DOWN

One of the hoariest clichés about jazz holds that it is a conversation between its players. Well, if Cecil Taylor's *Unit Structures* is a conversation, it's like no conversation I've ever had—it's certainly not comparable to a free-flowing exchange of pleasantries. The interplay between instruments on *Unit Structures* has little to do with the polite give-and-take the jazz-as-conversation metaphor implies. It is filled with divergences, breaks, moments of the musicians not listening to one another, and bursts that are the equivalent of yelling, screaming, and screeching. It contains the musical equivalent of sentences broken off midway, unexpected monologues, and digressions. Here conversation, if the metaphor still applies, does not mean consensus building—one person sharing their point of view, the other replying with theirs, ending with a harmonizing agreement between all parties.

In fact, it's best if we dispense with the conversational metaphor for something better. As its title suggests, *Unit Structures* works to break existing jazz forms into their constituent parts, their unit structures. Its aesthetic frisson comes, even now, from the energy released as it subdivides jazz's larger forms into often dissonant micro-figures. Its dynamics come from the unbalancing of the traditions that preceded it: modal, bop, downbeat, and big band. What emerges on *Unit Structures*, as with the best free jazz, is not absence of all form, but *new* forms. In the liner notes, Taylor asserts that "each instrument has strata." *Unit Structures* finds these strata everywhere, breaking apart the balance of established forms. In the process of breaking apart conventional jazz notions of melody, harmony, and interplay ("the conscious manipulation of known material"), Taylor and band draw attention to the "strata," the layers of texture, tone, and rhythm hidden underneath. This is what happens when you explode the idea that jazz is a balanced conversation between instrumentalists. Taylor describes it as a "group chain reaction"—jazz fission rather than fusion.

On *Unit Structures*, as elsewhere, Cecil Taylor's piano often works as a decomposing agent. By this, I mean that it often functions to take apart the lines presented by the other instruments on the record. The more organized one player sounds at any moment, the more "out" Taylor's percussive playing will sound. The title track starts with a traditional drumbeat from Andrew Cyrille: Taylor fills the spaces between Cyrille's beats with a herky-jerky, discordant counter-rhythm. When Eddie Gale's trumpet line and Jimmy Lyons's alto become momentarily "skronky" and dissonant two and a half minutes into "Enter, Evening (Soft Line Structure)," Taylor goes into a rare, brief lyrical run. If something begins settling into a pattern, Taylor will often break that pattern into fragments. But if the rest of the band starts playing atonally and that threatens to become a pattern of its own, Taylor will swerve briefly into a mellifluous run over the keys. The function is to produce a constant double image: an expression by one of the players, and an analysis of it by Taylor. Even on the level of the individual line, performances will decompose from consonance to dissonance, from expression to its dismantling. The musicians perform a sort of self-criticism in the moment. On "Enter Night," a straightforward, beautiful solo sax solo begins over a scrambled Taylor piano line. Gradually, this solo mutates into something more aggressive before fading out completely.

At other moments, all five players seem to be pursuing parallel paths at once. Rather than synthesize into a single, indivisible sound, the record sounds like five individuals racing in the same direction, each with their own peculiar gait and style. Much of the record's opener, "Steps," works this way. From the jump, the track gives equal sonic space to Cyrille, Lyons, and Taylor. They race to catch up with one another, maintaining the same basic speed. But the sound of their playing works independently from one another. It's as if three distinct solos have been overlaid on top of one another, and each would make its own fine track independent of the other two.

Alex Ross writes that "the twelve-tone method was really an expression of Schoenberg's horror of repetition."[18] *Unit Structures* too studiously avoids repetition, but in the moment of improvisation. Even when Taylor plays the same basic line in the middle of "As of a Now," the volume and rhythm slightly vary from version to version. Taylor didn't need to generate a rigid system of rules by which notes would be mathematically avoided; he and his band proved that you could invent new things through interactions that upset the balance of existing conventions in the moment. Thus, they hold on to the freedom Schoenberg sacrificed in his systematizing but also hold on to the power of breaking clichés that free jazz shares with twelve-tone.

This musical avant-gardism required extreme creativity and intelligence ("idea precedes experience," as Taylor puts it) but not a PhD in musicology (though Taylor, Cyrille, and Lyons were all talented teachers, training undergraduates at Antioch College in the 1970s). While free jazz has a reputation for being difficult, even among supposed music fans, it's really nothing to be afraid of, especially when compared to the arch music of system builders like Schoenberg and his Second Viennese school. All you need to do to start enjoying a record like *Unit Structures* is to abandon your belief in a theory of dynamics that holds that harmony, melody, and balance are universal fundamentals of good music.

In *Unit Structures*, we are presented with a world in which the war on convention ends not in chaos and nihilism, but the release of new energy and the production of new forms. Gone are the broad clichés of the past and instantiated are newer "structures" which still have the power to excite us. It is the sound of a group testing what still works from the past, throwing out what doesn't, and adapting what still does for the future. It maps an active future, full of testing, searching, and experimenting. *Unit Structures*, like the best free jazz LPs, teaches us not only that balance is boring, but that treating it as a desired outcome for every circumstance will end in tears. It asks us to evolve, and to chase change like Lyons's sax trails Taylor's piano.

## DYNAMIC ALTERNATIVE 2: RECYCLING

If one were to believe the common sense that has crystalized around minimalism, it can be reduced to a set of formulas. Look in any musical encyclopedia, and you'll find a description of essentially the same basic parts:

The repetition of short musical figures.

Pieces that slowly change over time but are, as Kyle Gann puts it, "cleansed of goal-oriented European associations."[19]

An American postmodern intent to return to simple, pleasing tonal expression, away from the complex abstractions of chromatic European modernism.

The most famous practitioners of the genre are Philip Glass and Steve Reich, and their music has been used to develop the standard definition of minimalism. As Gann notes, they and minimalism became famous, while the many musicians who expanded and diverged from their blueprint into post-minimalism, totalism, rock, and dance did not.[20] But the fame of Glass and Reich (and to a lesser extent John Luther Adams) has also obscured the contemporary practice of other minimalists like Jon Gibson, Alvin Lucier, and Frederic Rzewski, all three of whom appear on Rzewski's *Attica/Coming Together/Les Moutons de Panurge* (Opus One, 1972). Though Lucier's *I Am Sitting in a Room* has inspired a thousand half-baked undergraduate imitations and William Basinski's overly praised *The*

*Disintegration Loops* is perpetually name-dropped, Rzewski's *Attica* does not have the same currency. Like Cornelius Cardew's *Four Principles on Ireland and Other Pieces* (1975) or Julius Eastman's work all through the 1970s, the radical politics associated with the music seem to have put off the sniffier classical types. Thus, it is often written off as a genre for MOR ("middle-of-the-road") listeners, for those who like the modest pleasures of gradual change and prefer modest tinkering to revolutionary transformation (in both music and politics).

Rzewski's subject matter, however, is explicitly political: the Attica prison rebellion of 1971. The prisoners of Attica protested for an improvement in their squalid conditions. They took hostages to secure their demands, and four days later, New York governor Nelson Rockefeller sent in the state police to end the strike. More than forty people died, most of them inmates. This was a cause célèbre at the time, a flashpoint for Black Power, and resistance to mass incarceration. The details of the case now are less remembered than *Dog Day Afternoon*'s reference to it, Al Pacino's chant of "Attica! Attica!" having had an enduring afterlife in popular culture.

The standard lists of minimalism's attributes, like the one above, are light on the political dimension: Its criteria focus on its formal dynamics. To both its detractors and celebrants, minimalism is usually considered an apolitical genre. It was for the Europeans to deal with the heavy tragedies of their twentieth century, while minimalism was about bringing a post-political enjoyment back to classical music. It's pleasing because it's all surface. There are no depths to plumb in minimalism. It's exactly as it seems, an engine for simple, easy consumption. Even when minimalists take up political subjects, like Steve Reich's *Different Trains* or *WTC 9/11*, it is to chop up and reprocess and rearrange existing responses to political tragedy, not to produce a political interpretation of them. For most critics, minimalism at best cites politics without being political.

But on a record like *Attica/Coming Together/Les Moutons de Panurge*, political dynamics and aesthetic ones are inextricably intertwined. While Reich's work on 9/11 and the Holocaust was done at a remove of a decade and a generation respectively, *Attica* was made in 1973 and released the next year, while the event was still fresh in peoples' minds. So, to the question "Is minimalism political?" it answers, "How could it not be?" The only question is, "How is it political?"

"Coming Together" is built around a long excerpt from a letter from New Left militant Sam Melville, one of the prisoners shot and killed during the Attica uprising. And the title track, "Attica," is constructed using just one line of dialogue, taken from Richard X. Clark, described in his obituary "as head of the inmates' internal security"[21] during the uprising: "Attica is in front of me." Rzewski isn't just name-dropping here: What happened in Attica is the inspiration and the guiding passion at the center of Rzewski and company's music here. This would seem to be a scanty amount of raw material with which to make a political statement. Yet it works, and to recognize how we first need to reconsider its use of "repetition."

While "Attica," like most other minimal works, depends on the repetition of short figures, it would be more accurate to say it "recycles" short figures for a particular purpose. This purpose is to keep Attica in front of the listener. It does this by spacing Steve Ben Israel's recitation into individual words:

Attica

Attica...is

Attica...is...in

Attica...is...in...front

Attica...is...in...front...of

Attica...is...in...front...of...me

Attica...is...in...front...of...me

Is...in...front...of...me...

In...front...of...me...

Front...of...me...

Of...me

Me

Ben Israel's phrasing is strict, nearly identical with each reading. And the music, beginning with Rzewski's piano against a quiet drone from viola player Joan Kalish, cycles through the same figure throughout the piece. As it rises to the full expression of the sentence, Jon Gibson on alto sax, Karl Berger on vibes, and Alvin Curran on piccolo trumpet thicken the sound, reproducing the initial drones and piano melody established at the outset. We call this recycling rather than repetition, because each subsequent line is expressed with a surfeit of energy carried over from the last cycle. The effect on the listener is to keep their mind locked both on each individual cycle, which has its own energy, and the forward direction of the piece, which swells as the complete sentence assembles over time. And once the complete sentence is put together at the midpoint of the song, the sentence starts to be taken apart again, terminating in a single "Me."

This dynamic puts an emphasis both on each fragment and the complete sentence. It evokes a string of questions from the listener: What is Attica? What does it mean for Attica to be in front of someone? What is this concluding "me" that is remade by the experience of Attica being constantly before them? Each word accretes its own power through Ben Israel's incantations and the dynamic recycling energy of the song. While "Attica" is a song concerned with a notorious historical tragedy, the music induces pleasure and a sense of questioning after mystery in the listener.

This pleasure in the recycling of energy implants a desire in the listener to go back and research the events that inspired it. If "Attica" is successful, it sticks with you: As we said before, it puts Attica perpetually in front of the listener. The event begins to live for you as present, at least for the moment of listening. And so, you will journey back into the past, which feels newly present because of the energy of this song, and you will uncover your own relation to the names Richard X. Clark, Sam Melville, Attica. The pleasure provided by this song's dynamics are an inducement to reanimate the events of the past from the boring and motionless dustbin of history. Records instill a desire for the past and a desire to find its lineages in our present, a desire without which it would be totally irrelevant to us in the present. It brings to life the past not as a settled thing but as the problems that we still have yet to solve, and keeps Attica in front of us all: mass incarceration, racism, exploitation, and state violence, to name just a few.

## DYNAMIC ALTERNATIVE 3: TRANSFORMATION

Longer recordings aim for epic sonic dynamics, but often fail. For every dramatic, larger-than-life song of transformation, every "Here in the Year" (Cold Sun's *Dark Shadows*), "E2-E4" (Manuel Göttsching's *E2-E4*), and "Been This Way Before" (Roger and the Human Body's *Introducing Roger*), there are a thousand prog rock and jazz records that lay claim to epic grandeur without ever delivering it. Critics have long debated whether the epic form is still possible in modern society. Longer recordings, rather than establishing the form's continuing vitality, tend to suggest the eclipse of the epic in modern life. For my example of "transformational" dynamics, I've intentionally chosen a song that's only four minutes, thirty seconds in length, Milton Nascimento's "Ponta de Areia" (*Minas*, EMI Brazil, 1975). It's not an epic. It makes no claims to a complete description of a world, it does not feature a full orchestra, and it aims for nothing so pretentious as a Wagnerian *Gesamtkunstwerk* (total work of art).

Yet it is constantly metamorphosing: its dynamics are never stable. The relation between the elements that make up "Ponta de Areia"—between loud and soft sounds, simple and complex forms, joyous and sad tones—never resolves into a balanced relation. It is a song forever becoming something else, which makes it a nearly inexhaustible record for the listener. Even in its lyrics (sung in Portuguese), the balance between the past and present plays out through its own unstable dynamic. The song gives form, in proto–magical realist style, to a lost world of Nascimento's childhood—the state of Minas Gerais, its towns and cities newly networked by the Bahia-Minas train line. Nascimento and his co-writer Fernando Brant describe a utopia, in which even the modern technology of the "Maria Fumaça" locomotive serves to unite Minas Gerais in a joyous communal celebration of flowers, beaches, and natural roads. But the song is retrospective, sung after the military dictatorship of Brazil tore up the tracks—leaving empty public space, once stately homes falling into disrepair, and weeping widows behind. In telling the tale of radical development and an equally radical disintegration, "Ponta de Areia" conjures a world subject to the constant flux of historical change.

But it is the music itself that brings about the feeling of constant transformation in the listener. "Ponta de Areia" opens with a brief, discordant soprano sax intro, which just as soon as it appears gives way to the singsong chanting of a group of untrained young children. Their voices then dramatically fade out, and after a brief pause, Nascimento's falsetto appears, taking over the vocalizations begun by the children. Nascimento almost immediately drops the falsetto and begins singing in Portuguese, using his full-throated voice. An electric piano follows his lead, underscoring his phrasing. Then an incredibly heavy-sounding bass and drum rhythm struts in as the vocal gathers in volume and intensity. The time signature they're playing in is 9/4, so just when you expect a standard 4/4 measure to end, an added beat from either the rhythm section or Nascimento is thrown in. This keeps the listener perpetually on guard and leaves space for an improvisatory moment at the conclusion of each musical phrase. As the song builds in power, the drums become more complex, featuring some elegant cymbal work that leaves the opening's drum pattern (modeled on a simple *bump-bump* imitation of a train whistle) far behind. The soprano sax then returns for a solo, Nascimento joins it one more time, and abruptly, the music stops. There's a smash edit back to the children's choir, reprising their introduction, a fast fade-out, and the song's over.

Such rapid musical transformations are awe-inspiring. If *Unit Structures* shows us how to take apart the dull, balanced forms of everyday life, and "Attica" how to alter those forms to produce new meaning, "Ponta de Areia" shows that new forms are still possible. Out of old forms, surprising new sounds can emerge. We are not doomed to the endless repetition of the world's norms; we are not locked into an iron cage of rationality or predetermined by our genes, our politics, or even global capitalism itself. At least for the time we're listening to such records, we are free and open to imagine other worlds. Records like "Ponta de Areia" promise listeners the chance for metamorphosis, which I take to mean another word for hope.

HE CARES / LUTHER BARNES AND THE RED BUDD GOSPEL CHOIR

YOU BRING THE SUN OUT

THE BEST OF THE PILGRIM TRAVELERS / LIGHT RECORDS

I'M TURNING AWAY (THE SENSATIONAL...)

THE YOUNG SUPREME...

WE CAN MAKE IT

CONCLUSION

# Records of Our Climate

If you haven't already noticed, our forests are on fire and the seas are rising. For record collectors, climate change (a euphemism if there ever was one) probably conjures up specific apocalyptic images—of melted vinyl and inundated record archives. If things continue at the rate they are going, the record world could be facing existential crisis sometime this century.

What does it mean, then, to collect records under the signs of potential annihilation? In the preceding pages, we've examined the past and present of vinyl's life. While we had occasion to discuss records' power to project us into imagined futures, the primary focus has been on the then and now, not the yet to come.

It's often assumed that the future is wholly unpredictable—the English language contains many sayings on the "unknowable," "unwritten," and "mysterious" state of the future. To deploy but one of these, the future can seem like a blank slate, a time in which anything can happen. Of course, this is technically true—implausible scenarios, whether science fictional like David Bowie's "Five Years" (*Ziggy Stardust*, RCA Victor, 1972) or theological like Dorothy Norwood's "Time Is Winding Up" (*Jesus Is the Answer*, Atlanta International, 1982), may come to pass, but are unlikely to do so, and I prefer here to examine the most probable future paths for record collecting.

What does seem clear is that the current model is unsustainable. If the climate continues to become more and more inhospitable to human life, even the most weatherproofed record vault will ultimately provide no protection for the records within it. Or if it does, humans will be so cut off from one another that there will be no social world to speak of, and so no one left to impress. The futility of hoarding and flipping records, as opposed to listening to and loving music, will become even more pronounced. The vinyl market itself may collapse. As Graham Steele and Gregg Gelzinis wrote in their recent Bloomberg op-ed "Climate Change Is a Financial Crisis, Too," "the planet is not a contract that can be restructured, and there is no bailout for a climate catastrophe."[1] Record wealth accumulation for its own sake, undertaken regardless of its costs, may soon be revealed as the fiction of a past age no longer relevant and perhaps bewildering to future generations.

Given vinyl's propensity to warp and scratch, some readers at this point may be thinking, *Thank God for streaming and downloading.* After all, physical media like vinyl seems much more susceptible to the wrath of sun, sea, and air than files and streams. But digital music won't save us: In fact, it may be making things worse. Not only does it gravely underpay musicians, the digital music industry is probably more damaging to the environment than any previous mode of production. According to Kyle Devine's *Decomposed: The Political Ecology of Music*,[2] the energy burned by streaming's data farms and consumers is anything but clean. As a précis of Devine's research in *Rolling Stone* summarizes, "the energy it takes to stream and download digital music has caused greenhouse gas (GHG) emissions to rise sharply: The study estimates that music consumption in the 2000s resulted in the emission of approximately 157 million kilograms of greenhouse gas equivalents; now the amount of GHGs generated by the energy needed to transmit music for streaming is estimated to be between 200 and 350 million kilograms."[3] What's more, streaming services rent rather than sell music. Unlike buying a record, you are paying for temporary access to a piece of music. This access can be rescinded at any time according to the prerogative of the rentier corporation, whether it be Apple Music or Spotify. And despite its immaterial appearances for the end user, streaming music still requires physical storage on servers and computers. This storage system is itself vulnerable. Personal hard drives can be corrupted, servers can suffer catastrophic data loss, and files can be paywalled, encrypted, and/or kept private. There's still no substitute for physical preservation of music on a record (or for that matter, CDs and tapes). Computers will probably prove no more climate-proofed than libraries and other repositories of "old media." Finally, it's a fallacy to think that everything analog has been migrated to a digital format: There are millions of vinyl records out there today that have never been digitized and probably never will be. For these reasons and more, it seems that vinyl is just as likely to persist far into the twenty-first century as streaming.

For this reason, we record collectors need to think long and hard about the future of our culture. We are faced with a choice: Do we persist in the old ways as if nothing has changed or work to imagine alternatives before it's too late? It seems clear to me that the first response would be inadequate, even disastrous, for the reasons I've elaborated above. But there's reason to believe, many will continue in the ways of the status quo: As critic Jeff Chang wrote, history so far has shown that consumers follow rather than lead revolutions.[4] As a result, many collectors will no doubt be tempted to pretend like nothing's changed and that records have nothing to do with the world at large. We've experienced the comfort and calm records can provide, and so understand the appeal of such vinyl quietism. But such self-soothing is not the basis for a long-term strategy— if climate change destroys the financial, social, and physical infrastructure that sustains record culture, no one will be safe.

So before it's too late, we have to again become open-hearted sharers and caretakers of recorded music. If our ecological future threatens a thousand burnings of the library at Alexandria, we need to do all we can to save the records that form our musical history. We need to abandon ostentatious shows of prestige and accumulation and start listening and communing again. As the world burns and floods, the old forms of status seeking will start to seem increasingly silly. Our relation to records will have to be revitalized. We need to get back in touch with the power of records to reeducate our senses and imagine new horizons for earthly existence.

Recorded music alone cannot save the world. But it can help us feel and think our way through new states of being. It represents modes of existence we hold in potential but have yet to realize in fact. This means we need to conserve vinyl records both as precious physical objects and as bearers of knowledge and wisdom. They embody the reasons life will remain worth struggling for in even the most dystopic future.

To build the collective life needed for our survival, we will need the passion, imagination, and method embedded in the vasts of the vinyl archive. We will need to cultivate new states of mind, sometimes meditative, like Steven Halpern's *Spectrum Suite* (SRI, 1976), and sometimes insurrectionary, like Crass's *Feeding of the 5000* (Small Wonder, 1979); both the old form breaking of Cecil Taylor and the new form building of Alice Coltrane. We will need to overcome our historical amnesia and the deceptions it enables, sometimes with secular memory projects like Lloyd McNeill's *Washington Suite* (ASHA, 1970), and sometimes with more mystical historical work like Burning Spear's *Garvey's Ghost* (Island, 1976). We will need to hold on to joy and continue to seek happiness, both through the pure ludic release of Cloud One and the more abstract pleasures of Drexciya. And we will need models in order to articulate new concepts and feelings, both as members of particular political movements, like Rex Harley's "Dread in a PRA" (Trex, 1979) and as universally minded internationalists, like Manuel Göttsching's *E2–E4* (Inteam GmbH, 1984). The recorded past both glimmers forth visions of a life still worth living and trains us to prepare the way for that life.

Here's hoping we can fulfill the promise latent in our records.

# ACKNOWLEDGMENTS

In a past life, I was an English professor. Inside academia, it seemed many assumed they had a monopoly on the "life of the mind." While not everybody thought this way, it wasn't uncommon to hear the "real world" condescendingly described as "merely" practical. When I started working for Carolina Soul in 2013, however, it didn't take me long to see the absurdity of this view. I was surrounded by a bright bunch of unpretentious, music-loving co-workers, each with their own areas of expertise and insight. In those early days of the company, when we were still operating out of Jason Perlmutter's house in Durham, I learned what an organic intellectual community could be. For this and much more, I'd like to thank each of my fellow workers at Carolina Soul Records, past and present: Our labor has built the business and kept it running.

I owe special debts of gratitude to the folks with whom I've worked the longest and talked the most about records. Some are quoted in these pages, and all have made them better through their intelligence, knowledge, and friendship: Grant Bisher, Jack Bonney, Kyle Borst, Nathan Bowles, Kyle Briggs, Ariane Ardalan Clarke, James Finnegan, Jake Xerxes Fussell, David Griffiths, Kat Kucera, Carley McCready Bingham, Zach Nusbaum, Katie O'Neil, Jason Perlmutter, Zack Richardson, Ian Rose, Geoff Schilling, Tayler Simonds, Nate Smith, and Groves Willer.

Carolina Soul's Nate Smith, my oldest music friend in North Carolina, ran all the numbers and conceived of many of the graphs and tables you'll find here. It was as DJs at Duke's WXDU radio station in the 2000s that Nate and I met fellow DJ Matt Tauch: Matt created the illustrations and graphics for *Vinyl Age*. One of the most rewarding things about writing this book has been getting to collaborate professionally with two fellow independent radio DJs on a project about records. They are both amazingly talented, and I'm grateful for both their hard work and inventiveness.

Over the years, I've learned much about music and critical method from many brilliant friends. Whether they realize it or not, their thoughts and tastes are always in the back of my mind as I listen, read, and write. As music and literature were often the means by which we became and stayed friends, I hope they can catch glimpses of our shared past in the present book. Nathan Hensley, Bill Knight, Erik Noftle, LaTarsha Pough, and Todd Schmidt: Thank you.

Next, I'd like to thank Becky Koh, publishing director at Black Dog & Leventhal. Becky's been all that I could have hoped for in an editor—judicious, patient, and professional. Her suggestions are always razor-sharp and helped this reformed academic find the right style. *Vinyl Age* wouldn't be what it is without Becky's guiding hand, but any remaining infelicities should be set at the author's feet alone. Melanie Gold, the book's production editor, provided everything an author could need and came through in the clutch. I'm also grateful to Lori Paximadis for her fine copyedits. Katie Benezra's book design elevated the text, and I greatly appreciate her work.

My agent, Sarah Bolling, and Chris Parris-Lamb, of the Gernert Company, deserve nothing but praise. Their early championing of this project, their efforts in finding the right home for it, and their support during the writing process have all earned my overwhelming gratitude.

Way back in 1982 my late father, Steve Brzezinski, played me my first record: the 12″ of Soft Cell's "Tainted Love/Where Did Our Love Go." Word is I danced like a child possessed on our living room floor. I remember him here for both his love and love of music, the latter of which he always discussed with passion and intelligence. My mother, Mary Brzezinski, has been a continual source of support during the writing of *Vinyl Age*—she has provided all the practical and emotional aid an overworked writer with a young child embarrassingly needs in this life. From Seoul, my brother Joe Brzezinski has always been there for me. Our Facebook chats, all jokes and commiseration, have kept me level and entertained over the past two years.

This book is dedicated to my wife, Sarah Harlan, and our son, Malcolm Brzezinski. Since our days as college radio DJs at Grinnell College's KDIC in the 1990s, Sarah and I have been in love with music and each other. Sometimes, it was hard to tell where the one passion ended and the other began. In the twenty-two years since we've met, Sarah has been my world, and I'm sure she always will be. She read every page of every draft of *Vinyl Age*, and her musical and stylistic acumen both can be sensed on every page.

Our son, Malcolm, inspired me to keep writing and has filled our lives with happiness since the day he was born. When even music can't cheer me up, Malcolm can—I feel blessed every day to have such a loving, playful, and intelligent child. And because he made our family listen to his favorite record, Steve Tibbetts's *Northern Song*, every day for the past year, he can be said to have inspired a large section of chapter 5.


MB

Durham, North Carolina

November 2019

# APPENDIX 1

The tables in appendix 1 ("Carolina Soul's Top Sellers by Genre") list the company's highest-priced record sales, broken down by subgenre and/or format. The 45 subgenres featured below are:

Northern Soul, '70s Soul, Sweet Soul, Crossover Soul, Modern Soul, Deep Soul, Funk, Disco/Boogie, Classic Rock, Blues, Psych, Popcorn, Latin, Punk, Rap, Hard Rock, Reggae/Roots, Doo-Wop, Garage, R&B, Gospel, Calypso, Rockabilly, Ska/Rocksteady, Folk, Jazz

These lists are followed by one charting Carolina Soul's fifty highest-selling LPs to date, and one detailing the top twenty-five highest-selling 12" singles. The sales data used to create this appendix spans 2012–2019.

| | NORTHERN SOUL › 45 RPM | PRICE ($) |
|---|---|---|
| 1 | Larry Clinton "She's Wanted" (DYNAMO) | 10,871 |
| 2 | The Four Bars feat. Bettye Wilson "I'm Yours" (EDGEWOOD ACETATE) | 6,099 |
| 3 | Jimmy Burns "I Really Love You" (ERICA) | 5,641 |
| 4 | Appointments "I Saw You There" (DE-LITE) | 4,840 |
| 5 | Soul Incorporated "My Proposal" (COCONUT GROOVE) | 4,741 |
| 6 | Nomads "Somethin's Bad" (MO-GROOV) | 4,611 |
| 7 | Gwen Owens "Just Say You're Wanted" (VELGO) | 4,494 |
| 8 | 4 Dynamics "Things That a Lady Ain't Suppose to Do" [sic] (PEACHTREE) | 4,450 |
| 9 | Grey Imprint "Do You Get the Message" (CLEAR HILL) | 4,371 |
| 10 | Combinations "I'm Gonna Make You Love Me" (KIMTONE) | 4,050 |

| | '70'S SOUL › 45 RPM | PRICE ($) |
|---|---|---|
| 1 | Hamilton Movement "She's Gone" (LOOK-OUT) | 6,643 |
| 2 | Ellipsis "People" (BRIARMEADE) | 4,550 |
| 3 | Faye Hill "Gonna Get Even" (BLUE DOLPHIN) | 4,494 |
| 4 | Kenyatta "Kick It Off" (NDUGU) | 3,578 |
| 5 | Soulfull Strutters "Let Your Feelings Go" (STRUT) | 3,575 |
| 6 | Wanda McDaniel & Ultimate Choice "Gangster Boy" (APPLERAY) | 3,506 |
| 7 | Seville "Show Me the Way" (KAYO) | 3,228 |
| 8 | Lynn Varnado "Wash and Wear Love" (GATOR) | 2,550 |
| 9 | Bobby Rich "There's a Girl Somewhere" (SAMBEA) | 2,255 |
| 10 | Mixed Feelings "Sha-La-La" (UNITED) | 2,125 |

| | SWEET SOUL › 45 RPM | PRICE ($) |
|---|---|---|
| 1 | The Scorpion "Keep On Trying" (SBP) | 2,850 |
| 2 | Soul Seekers "An Extrodinary Dream" [sic] (SOUL HEAD) | 2,025 |
| 3 | Soul Experience "Who's Lips You Been Kissing" [sic] (SMOKE) | 1,889 |
| 4 | Elvin Benjamin "I Knew" (FUNKY FEET) | 1,532 |
| 5 | Young Mods "Gloria" (GANGLAND) | 1,327 |
| 6 | Liquid Fire "Loving You" (FIRE) | 1,292 |
| 7 | Fantastic Soul Revue "Mama's Little Girl" (CRESCENT-CITY) | 1,247 |
| 8 | Willie Griffin "I Love You" (GRIP) | 1,225 |
| 8 | Tridels "This Thing Called Love" (SPEIDEL) | 1,225 |
| 8 | Soul Seekers "An Extrodinary Dream" [second copy, sic] (SOUL HEAD) | 1,225 |

| | CROSSOVER SOUL › 45 RPM | PRICE ($) |
|---|---|---|
| 1 | United Sounds "It's All Over (Baby)" (UNITED) | 6,766 |
| 2 | Syndicate of Sound "Make Believe" (SOUND TEX) | 6,338 |
| 3 | Sag War Fare "Don't Be So Jive" (LIBRA) | 5,655 |
| 4 | Chuck Cockerham "Have I Got a Right" (MALA) | 2,247 |
| 5 | Billy Byrd "Lost in the Crowd" (SCREAM) | 2,050 |
| 6 | Just Us "We've Got a Good Thing Going" (VINCENT) | 1,977 |
| 7 | August Tide "Far Away Places" (AUGUST TIDE) | 1,878 |
| 8 | Scott Three "Runnin' Wild" (MARCH) | 1,775 |
| 9 | Wayne Barnes "Peacemakers" (SALVATION IS FREE) | 1,691 |
| 10 | Young Mods "Who You Going to Run" (EVERBLACK) | 1,502 |

| | MODERN SOUL › 45 RPM | PRICE ($) |
|---|---|---|
| 1 | Ice "Reality" (ICE) | 5,367 |
| 2 | Chocolate Buttermilk Band "Head Games" (C.B.M.) | 5,139 |
| 3 | Mellow Madness "Save the Youth" (MEGA) | 3,427 |
| 4 | 5th Degree "You Got Me Hypnotized" (DEGREE) | 2,850 |
| 5 | Skull Sconiers "All & All" (EARTH & SKY) | 2,608 |
| 6 | Bee Vee & the Honey Bee "I'm Lost without Your Love" (STING) | 2,297 |
| 7 | Ritz Band "I Should Have Known" (RITZ) | 2,247 |
| 7 | New Xperience "Frisco Disco" (JOY RIDE) | 2,247 |
| 9 | Record Player "Free Your Mind" (GEM CITY) | 2,230 |
| 10 | Star Quake "Don't You Know I Love You" (MERIT) | 1,952 |

| DEEP SOUL › 45 RPM | PRICE ($) |
|---|---|
| 1 | Joe Walker "We Need Each Other" (SING SONG) | 1,392 |
| 2 | Elois Scott "Broadway Love" (CAROL G) | 1,030 |
| 3 | Jimmy Thorpe "Don't Let My Love" (TASK) | 998 |
| 4 | Lonnie Hill "Poverty Shack" (ASPEN) | 909 |
| 5 | Lee Bonds "I'll Find a True Love" (UNIDAD) | 897 |
| 6 | Joe Brown & the Soul Elderados "Vibration" (F.F.A.) | 867 |
| 7 | Richard Marks "I Can't Stand" (MIDTOWN) | 735 |
| 8 | Little Ronnie Mudd "A Teardrop Fell" (MALPASS) | 709 |
| 9 | Whole Truth "Can You Lose" (EFE) | 560 |
| 10 | Frank Tenella "You Came Along" (ODEX) | 519 |

| FUNK › 45 RPM | PRICE ($) |
|---|---|
| 1 | Ellipsis "People" (BRIARMEADE) | 4,550 |
| 2 | Deceptions "You're Gonna Run to Me" (PEACE) | 3,804 |
| 3 | Willie Wright "Right On for the Darkness" (HOTEL) | 3,661 |
| 4 | Kenyatta "Kick It Off" (NDUGU) | 3,578 |
| 5 | Soulfull Strutters "Let Your Feelings Go" (STRUT) | 3,575 |

| DISCO/BOOGIE › 45 RPM | PRICE ($) |
|---|---|
| 1 | Mellow Madness "Save the Youth" (MEGA) | 3,427 |
| 2 | Ritz Band "I Should Have Known" (RITZ) | 2,247 |
| 2 | New Xperience "Frisco Disco" (JOY RIDE) | 2,247 |
| 4 | Record Player "Free Your Mind" (GEM CITY) | 2,230 |
| 5 | Fifth Avenue "Do You Feel It" (FIFTH AVENUE) | 1,684 |

| CLASSIC ROCK › 33⅓ / 45 RPM | | PRICE ($) |
|---|---|---|
| 1 | Beatles "Ask Me Why" (VEE-JAY) | 3,050 |
| 2 | Beatles "Something New" *Jukebox* EP (CAPITOL) | 1,175 |
| 3 | Yoko Ono / Plastic Ono Band "Open Your Box" (NO LABEL) | 1,000 |
| 4 | Rolling Stones "Out of Our Heads" *Jukebox* EP (LONDON) | 647 |
| 5 | Rolling Stones "The Rolling Stones Now" *Jukebox* EP (LONDON) | 558 |

| BLUES › 45 RPM | | PRICE ($) |
|---|---|---|
| 1 | Hot Shot Love "Wolf Call Boogie" (SUN) | 2,247 |
| 2 | Doctor Ross "Chicago Breakdown" (SUN) | 1,275 |
| 3 | Binghampton Blues Boys "Cross Cut Saw" (X-L) | 998 |
| 4 | Tronquista "Hoffa's Blues" (TRONQUISTA) | 780 |
| 5 | Clarence Johnson & His Tom Cats "That's Not Right" (JEROME) | 609 |

| PSYCH › 45 RPM | | PRICE ($) |
|---|---|---|
| 1 | Moroccos "Union Depot" (CLEAR HILL) | 2,977 |
| 2 | Calico Wall "I'm a Living Sickness" (DOVE ACETATE) | 2,028 |
| 3 | Richard Marks "Purple Haze" (RSC) | 1,825 |
| 4 | Burning Star "Trip Horns" (WOW!) | 1,136 |
| 5 | Cave Dwellers "You Know Why" (JIM-KO) | 900 |

| POPCORN › 45 RPM | PRICE ($) |
|---|---|
| 1 | Priscilla Bowman "Sugar Daddy" (FALCON) | 1,613 |
| 2 | Joe Lewis "Teach Me Right Now" (NORTHERN) | 1,113 |
| 3 | Prince Conley "I'm Going Home" (SATELLITE) | 808 |
| 4 | Dick Ralston "Trouble" (NU-CLEAR) | 739 |
| 5 | Mike Lawing "In L.A." (HAWK) | 485 |

| LATIN › 45 RPM | PRICE ($) |
|---|---|
| 1 | Orquesta la Silenciosa "Me Gusta Mi Guaguanco" (LA SILENCIOSA) | 1,312 |
| 2 | Manny Corchado "Pow-Wow" (DECCA) | 810 |
| 3 | Sonny Bravo "Tighten Up" (COLUMBIA) | 787 |
| 4 | Tito Puente "Hit the Bongo" (TICO) | 575 |
| 5 | Unknown Artist "Latin Salsa" (STATLER) | 460 |

| PUNK › 45 RPM | PRICE ($) |
|---|---|
| 1 | Germs "Lexicon Devil" (SLASH) | 876 |
| 2 | The Exit "Who Asked You" (CITY ROCK) | 802 |
| 3 | Misfits "Night of the Living Dead" (PLAN 9) | 569 |
| 4 | AK-47 "The Badge Means You Suck" (PINEAPPLE) | 514 |
| 5 | Plugz "Move" (SLASH) | 493 |

| | RAP › 45 RPM | PRICE ($) |
|---|---|---|
| 1 | Breeze "Breeze Rap" (BLUE ROSE) | 1,303 |
| 2 | Manujothi "Shake Your Body" (MANUJOTHI) | 688 |
| 3 | Deacon Jones "Super Jamn" (FREEDOM) | 533 |
| 4 | Freedom of Culture "One of the Many" (RIGHTEOUS) | 504 |
| 5 | Jeff Jay Dog Scott "Burst Out" (J.D.) | 425 |

| | HARD ROCK › 45 RPM | PRICE ($) |
|---|---|---|
| 1 | Kiss "Let Me Go, Rock 'n Roll" (CASABLANCA) | 5,200 |
| 2 | TNS "Time's Up" (SOUND ASSOC.) | 876 |
| 3 | Black Ryder "Black Ryder" (NO LABEL) | 446 |
| 4 | Wrath "Warlord" (STONE COLD) | 405 |
| 5 | Mass Temper "Grave Digger" (KIX INTERNATIONAL) | 283 |

| | REGGAE/ROOTS › 45 RPM | PRICE ($) |
|---|---|---|
| 1 | Al & Freddy "Born a Free Man" (BLANK) | 3,650 |
| 2 | Orville Wood "You'll Lose a Good Man" (BLANK) | 1,913 |
| 3 | Dave Barker "Your Love Is a Game" (BLANK) | 776 |
| 4 | Rex Harley "Dread in a PRA" (TREX) | 735 |
| 5 | Bob Marley & the Wailers "Feel Alright" (BLANK) | 610 |

| | DOO-WOP › 45 RPM | PRICE ($) |
|---|---|---|
| 1 | Five Crowns "Keep It a Secret" (RAINBOW) | 3,350 |
| 2 | Henry Sawyer & the Jupiters "I Want" (PLANET X) | 2,551 |
| 3 | Mello-Harps "Love Is a Vow" (DO-RE-MI) | 2,550 |
| 4 | Buccaneers "Dear Ruth" (SOUTHERN) | 2,303 |
| 5 | Little Prince & the Freeloaders "Nursery Love" (M&M) | 1,200 |

| | GARAGE › 45 RPM | PRICE ($) |
|---|---|---|
| 1 | Fly-Bi-Nites "Found Love" (TIFFANY) | 2,805 |
| 2 | Alarm Clocks "Yeah" (AWAKE) | 1,650 |
| 3 | Paragons "Abba" (BOBBI) | 1,425 |
| 4 | Psychotrons "Death Is a Dream" (BCP) | 1,113 |
| 5 | Cave Dwellers "You Know Why" (JIM-KO) | 900 |

| | R&B › 45 RPM | PRICE ($) |
|---|---|---|
| 1 | Barbara Hall "Big Man" (TUSKA) | 1,890 |
| 2 | Priscilla Bowman "Sugar Daddy" (FALCON) | 1,613 |
| 3 | Zenobia Bonner "All Alone" (ACCIDENT) | 1,423 |
| 4 | Little Prince & the Freeloaders "Nursery Love" (M&M) | 1,200 |
| 5 | Family Jewels "One of These Fine Days" (ZEUS) | 1,136 |

| GOSPEL › 45 RPM | PRICE ($) |
|---|---|
| 1 | Silver Trumpeteers "Understanding" (CALVARY) | 1,759 |
| 2 | Wayne Barnes "Peacemakers" (SALVATION IS FREE) | 1,691 |
| 3 | Gospel Truth "He Can Do It" (MUS-I-COL) | 995 |
| 4 | Willis Sisters "He Rose" (REJO) | 968 |
| 5 | Converters "Live like the Lord Say Live" (ARK) | 898 |

| CALYPSO › 45 RPM | PRICE ($) |
|---|---|
| 1 | Bert Inniss "Slave" (NATIONAL) | 1,525 |
| 2 | Dutchy Brothers "Canadian Sunset" (EN CEE) | 669 |
| 3 | Mighty Sparrow "Under My Skin" (NATIONAL) | 623 |
| 4 | Cito Fermin Orchestra "Dark Eyes" (HUMMING BIRD) | 525 |
| 5 | Johnnie Gomez' Band "Venezuelan Waltz" (COOK) | 492 |

| ROCKABILLY › 45 RPM | PRICE ($) |
|---|---|
| 1 | Country G-J's "Go Girl Go" (VALLEY) | 2,037 |
| 2 | Mack Banks "Be-Boppin' Daddy" (FAME) | 1,113 |
| 3 | Bob Vidone & the Rhythm Rockers "Untrue" (SENTRY) | 1,077 |
| 4 | Hasil Adkins & His Happy Guitar "She's Mine" (AIR) | 1,052 |
| 5 | Carl Perkins "Movie Magg" (FLIP) | 997 |

| | SKA/ROCKSTEADY › 45 RPM | PRICE ($) |
|---|---|---|
| 1 | Joe Higgs with Carlos Malcolm "Goodbye" (UP-BEAT) | 709 |
| 2 | Keith & Tex "Stop That Train" (ISLAND) | 565 |
| 3 | Phil Pratt "Reach Out for Me" (BLANK) | 492 |
| 4 | Gaylads "Africa" (COXSONE) | 406 |
| 5 | Jackie Opel "I Am What I Am" (STUDIO ONE) | 380 |

| | FOLK › 45 RPM | PRICE ($) |
|---|---|---|
| 1 | Sebastian "I'll Still Be Loving You" (RIVERMONT) | 898 |
| 2 | Thomas Meloncon "400 Years" (JUDNELL) | 493 |
| 3 | Temptations "Call of the Wind" (CUCA) | 417 |
| 4 | Ellin Amos "It's a Happy Day" (THE MUSIC BANK) | 397 |
| 5 | Halflings of Minas Tirith "Synthesis" (WELHAVEN) | 247 |

| | JAZZ › 45 RPM | PRICE ($) |
|---|---|---|
| 1 | Rick Davis "Wonders of Antiquity" (ISIS) | 560 |
| 2 | Wooden Glass "Monkey Hips" (INTERIM) | 425 |
| 3 | Llans Thelwell & His Celestials "Jive Samba" (SOUL) | 415 |
| 4 | Roy Haynes "Dorian" (PRESTIGE) | 390 |
| 5 | Steve Grossman "Zulu Stomp" (P.M.) | 370 |

| | LP ALBUM | $ | GENRE |
|---|---|---|---|
| 1 | Mighty Ryeders "Help Us Spread the Message" (SUN-GLO) | 6,200 | Funk |
| 2 | Machine (with the Whatnauts) "S/T" (ALL PLATINUM) | 4,950 | Funk |
| 3 | Ricardo Marrero & the Group "A Taste" (TSG) | 3,550 | Latin |
| 4 | Prince Lasha/Clifford Jordan/Don Cherry "It Is Revealed" (ZOUNDS) | 3,050 | Jazz |
| 5 | Brief Encounter "S/T" (SEVENTY-SEVEN) | 3,049 | Sweet Soul |
| 6 | Cook County "Released" (GREEDY) | 2,700 | '70s Soul |
| 7 | Ray Gant *Unreleased Acetate* (VARIETY) | 2,618 | Funk |
| 8 | Misfits "Earth A.D./Wolfs Blood" [*sic*] (PLAN 9) | 2,550 | Punk |
| 9 | Abdur Razzaq & Rafiyq "The Night of Power" (GREEN ESSENCE) | 2,415 | Jazz |
| 10 | Isabelle Collin Dufresne "Ultra Violet" (CAPITOL) | 2,358 | Classic Rock |
| 11 | Tommy Flanagan "Overseas" (PRESTIGE) | 2,255 | Jazz |
| 12 | Lee Morgan "Candy" (BLUE NOTE) | 2,080 | Jazz |
| 13 | Equatics "Doin It!!!!" [*sic*] (NO LABEL) | 2,032 | Crossover Soul |
| 14 | M'Boom "Re:Percussion" (STRATA-EAST) | 1,913 | Jazz |
| 14 | Albert Ayler "Spiritual Unity," *Silk-Screened Cover* (ESP) | 1,913 | Jazz |
| 16 | Kenny Dorham "Quiet Kenny" (NEW JAZZ) | 1,901 | Jazz |
| 17 | Don Pullen & Milford Graves "At Yale," *Hand-Painted Cover* (SRP) | 1,895 | Jazz |
| 18 | Hank Mobley "S/T" (BLUE NOTE) | 1,894 | Jazz |
| 19 | Rhythm Machine "S/T" (LULU) | 1,824 | Modern Soul |
| 20 | Bobby Moore & the Rhythm Aces "Dedication of Love" (PHINAL) | 1,814 | '70s Soul |
| 21 | McNeal & Niles "Thrust" (TINKERTOO) | 1,800 | Funk |
| 22 | Moses Dillard & the Tex-Town Display "Now" (TEX TOWN) | 1,785 | Northern Soul |
| 23 | Music Emporium "S/T" (SENTINEL) | 1,740 | Psych |

| | LP ALBUM (CONT'D) | $ | GENRE |
|---|---|---|---|
| 24 | Maytals "Never Grow Old" (R&B) | 1,700 | Ska |
| 25 | John Coltrane "Blue Train" (BLUE NOTE) | 1,614 | Jazz |
| 26 | Beatles "Yesterday and Today," *2nd State Butcher Cover* (CAPITOL) | 1,602 | Classic Rock |
| 27 | Relatively Clean Rivers "S/T" (PACIFIC IS) | 1,580 | Psych |
| 28 | Hank Mobley "Peckin' Time" (BLUE NOTE) | 1,576 | Jazz |
| 29 | Turner Bros. "Act 1" (MB) | 1,560 | '70s Soul |
| 30 | Bernard Purdie "Lialeh OST" (BRYAN) | 1,536 | Funk |
| 31 | Lee Morgan "Vol. 3" (BLUE NOTE) | 1,481 | Jazz |
| 32 | Mystic Siva "S/T" (VO) | 1,430 | Psych |
| 33 | Beatles "White Album" (APPLE) | 1,423 | Classic Rock |
| 34 | Carl Holmes "Investigation No. 1" (C.R.S.) | 1,385 | Crossover Soul |
| 35 | John Coltrane "A Love Supreme" (IMPULSE) | 1,358 | Jazz |
| 36 | Freddie Hubbard "Open Sesame" (BLUE NOTE) | 1,358 | Jazz |
| 37 | Del Jones' Positive Vibes "Court Is Closed" (HIKEAH) | 1,356 | Funk |
| 38 | Beatles "Yesterday and Today," *3rd State Butcher Cover* (CAPITOL) | 1,326 | Classic Rock |
| 39 | Louis Smith "Smithville" (BLUE NOTE) | 1,324 | Jazz |
| 40 | C.A. Quintet "Trip thru Hell" (CANDY FLOSS) | 1,299 | Psych |
| 41 | Hank Mobley Sextet "Hank" (BLUE NOTE) | 1,257 | Jazz |
| 42 | Iveys "Maybe Tomorrow" (APPLE) | 1,246 | Power Pop |
| 43 | Douglass High School "Trojans Too Hot" (CENTURY) | 1,235 | Modern Soul |
| 44 | Rolling Stones "Big Hits" *Withdrawn Cover* (LONDON) | 1,246 | Classic Rock |
| 45 | John Windhurst "Jazz at Columbus Ave." (TRANSITION) | 1,181 | Jazz |
| 46 | Dave Lamb & Gye Whiz "I'll Be Alright" (SYMA) | 1,158 | Psych |
| 47 | Kenny Mann & Liquid Pleasure "S/T" (HEARTBEAT) | 1,150 | Modern Soul |

| | LP ALBUM (CONT'D) | $ | GENRE |
|---|---|---|---|
| 48 | 13th Floor Elevators "Psychedelic Sounds" (INT'L ARTISTS) | 1,145 | Psych |
| 49 | Stark Reality "Discovers Hoagy Carmichael's Music Shop" (AJP) | 1,126 | Funk |
| 50 | Octopus "Restless Night" (PENNY FARTHING TEST PRESSING) | 1,125 | Psych |

| | 12" SINGLE | $ | GENRE |
|---|---|---|---|
| 1 | Rammellzee vs. K-Rob "Beat Bop" (TARTOWN) | 1,727 | Rap |
| 2 | Fast Forward "Water Bed" (HI-IN-ER-GY) | 1,325 | Disco/Boogie |
| 3 | Miles Davis *Unreleased Acetate* (COLUMBIA) | 1,275 | Jazz |
| 4 | Misfits "Die Die My Darling" (PLAN 9) | 1,150 | Punk |
| 5 | Lo-Twon "Wicked Leaf" (PLAYER CITY) | 1,050 | Rap |
| 6 | Family Four "Rap Attack" (TYSON) | 922 | Disco/Boogie |
| 7 | Fronzena Harris "Lovetime Guarantee" (BALTIMORE-WASHINGTON INT'L) | 870 | Disco/Boogie |
| 8 | Mid Air "Ease Out" (FULL SCOPE) | 860 | Disco/Boogie |
| 9 | Le Cop "Le Roc" (K. SHAVONNE) | 811 | Disco/Boogie |
| 10 | Mad Drama "Raise Up" (BROKE RATT) | 800 | Rap |
| 11 | Al Mason "Good Lovin'" (AL THE KIDD) | 743 | Modern Soul |
| 12 | Lower Level "Top Notch" (QUEEN CITY) | 710 | Rap |
| 13 | Plush Bros. "City of Brotherly Hate" (PAY-HILL) | 653 | Rap |
| 14 | Private Pleasure "Close to the Heart" (UPTOWN) | 650 | Modern Soul |
| 15 | Ardonus "Got to Take a Chance" (LYON'S RECORD CO.) | 643 | Disco/Boogie |
| 16 | Subway "You Can Bet I'll Get You Yet" (SCORE) | 632 | Modern Soul |
| 17 | Determinations "Too Much Oppression" (DETERMINATION) | 627 | Reggae/Roots |
| 18 | Stevie "Sending Out for Love" (MID-TOWN) | 604 | Modern Soul |
| 19 | Skavengaz "10 Mill Stash" (CRE8IVE ENTERTAINMENT) | 585 | Rap |

| | 12" SINGLE (CONT'D) | $ | GENRE |
|---|---|---|---|
| 20 | Detroit Execution Force "Crack Attack" (ELOQUENT) | 580 | Electro |
| 21 | Lonnie O "Dream On" (HOT COMB HITS) | 565 | Rap |
| 22 | Bertman & the Bandit "S/T" (ALLEY 6) | 561 | Rap |
| 22 | Sharper LPH "Searching for Your Love" (TBS) | 561 | Electro |
| 24 | Wild Willie "S/T" Acetate (STERLING SOUND) | 560 | Disco/Boogie |
| 24 | Dark Forest "The Region (the Remix)" (JUSMIK) | 560 | Rap |
| 24 | King Ra-Sean "Powerful Impact" (STOMP) | 560 | Rap |
| 24 | Egyptian Lover "Dubb Girls" (EGYPTIAN EMPIRE TEST PRESSING) | 560 | Electro |
| 24 | Elements "Foodstamp Flavor" (INSOMNIA PROD.) | 560 | Rap |
| 24 | Lee Moore "Let's Get to It" (TEST PRESSING) | 560 | Disco/Boogie |

# APPENDIX 2

Appendix 2 ("Each US State's Top Record Genre") logs the top-selling genre/subgenre for each of the US's fifty states, according to Carolina Soul's 45 sales data. By "top" we don't necessarily mean the most frequently purchased genre for that state. Instead, we mean the genre most disproportionately purchased by that state's buyers relative to the national average for that genre. For example, when you see Alabama paired with gospel, that means that Alabamians buy both a high volume of gospel records from Carolina Soul and a higher percentage of gospel as compared to the nation at large. Readers of chapter 1 will recognize this appendix as a cousin to the US record sales chart featured there. The sales data used to generate this appendix spans 2012–2018.

# U.S. RECORD SALES
## 2012–2018

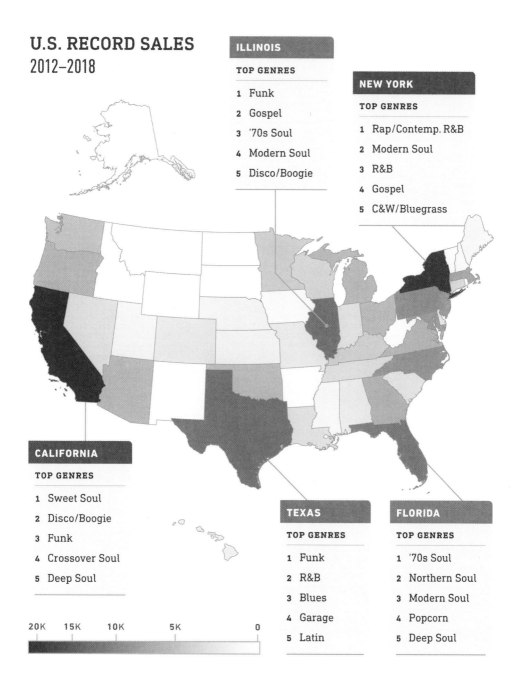

**ILLINOIS**

TOP GENRES

1 Funk
2 Gospel
3 '70s Soul
4 Modern Soul
5 Disco/Boogie

**NEW YORK**

TOP GENRES

1 Rap/Contemp. R&B
2 Modern Soul
3 R&B
4 Gospel
5 C&W/Bluegrass

**CALIFORNIA**

TOP GENRES

1 Sweet Soul
2 Disco/Boogie
3 Funk
4 Crossover Soul
5 Deep Soul

20K   15K   10K   5K   0

**TEXAS**

TOP GENRES

1 Funk
2 R&B
3 Blues
4 Garage
5 Latin

**FLORIDA**

TOP GENRES

1 '70s Soul
2 Northern Soul
3 Modern Soul
4 Popcorn
5 Deep Soul

| STATE | TOP-SELLING GENRE | STATE | TOP-SELLING GENRE |
|-------|-------------------|-------|-------------------|
| ALABAMA | Gospel | GEORGIA | Rockabilly |
| ALASKA | Classic / Alt. Rock | HAWAII | Reggae |
| ARIZONA | Rap / Contemp. R&B | IDAHO | Teen |
| ARKANSAS | Rockabilly | ILLINOIS | Funk |
| CALIFORNIA | Sweet Soul | INDIANA | Reggae |
| COLORADO | Punk / Post-Punk | IOWA | Mod/Beat |
| CONNECTICUT | Doo-Wop | KANSAS | Rockabilly |
| DELAWARE | Mod / Beat | KENTUCKY | R&B |
| FLORIDA | '70s Soul | LOUISIANA | Rock & Roll |

| STATE | TOP-SELLING GENRE | STATE | TOP-SELLING GENRE |
|---|---|---|---|
| MAINE<br>**Modern Soul** | | NEVADA<br>**Rap / Contemp. R&B** | |
| MARYLAND<br>**Funk** | | NEW HAMPSHIRE<br>**R&B** | |
| MASSACHUSETTS<br>**Gospel** | | NEW JERSEY<br>**Doo-Wop** | |
| MICHIGAN<br>**Gospel** | | NEW MEXICO<br>**Crossover Soul** | |
| MINNESOTA<br>**Blues** | | NEW YORK<br>**Rap / Contemp. R&B** | |
| MISSISSIPPI<br>**C&W / Bluegrass** | | NORTH CAROLINA<br>**Garage** | |
| MISSOURI<br>**Psych** | | NORTH DAKOTA<br>**Punk / Post-Punk** | |
| MONTANA<br>**Punk / Post-Punk** | | OHIO<br>**Classic / Alt. Rock** | |
| NEBRASKA<br>**Northern Soul** | | OKLAHOMA<br>**Garage** | |

| STATE | TOP-SELLING GENRE | STATE | TOP-SELLING GENRE |
|---|---|---|---|
| OREGON **Psych** | | VIRGINIA **Gospel** | |
| PENNSYLVANIA **Doo-Wop** | | WASHINGTON **Rockabilly** | |
| RHODE ISLAND **Reggae** | | WEST VIRGINIA **Psych** | |
| SOUTH CAROLINA **R&B** | | WISCONSIN **Rockabilly** | |
| SOUTH DAKOTA **Rock & Roll** | | WYOMING **Rap / Contemp. R&B** | |
| TENNESSEE **Classic / Alt. Rock** | | | |
| TEXAS **Funk** | | | |
| UTAH **Sweet Soul** | | | |
| VERMONT **Rock & Roll** | | | |

Appendix 3 ("International Genre Tastes") is the international version of appendix 2. The first table summarizes the largest international buyer bases for thirty-nine collectable genres and subgenres; the second lists the top three genres and subgenres for eighteen countries representing Carolina Soul's most active patrons. The sales data used to generate this appendix spans 2012–2018.

| GENRE | | TOP COUNTRY |
|---|---|---|
| '60's Soul/Motown | | Belgium |
| '70s Soul | | Great Britain |
| African | | Japan |
| Blues | | Japan |
| C&W/Bluegrass | | United States |
| Calypso | | Canada |
| Classic/Alternative | | United States |
| Crossover Soul | | Great Britain |
| Dancehall | | Australia |
| Deep Soul | | Japan |
| Disco/Boogie | | Norway |
| Doo-Wop/Girl Group | | United States |
| Electro/Bass | | Brazil |
| Exotica | | Belgium |
| Folk | | Russia |

| GENRE | | TOP COUNTRY |
|---|---|---|
| Funk | | Japan |
| Garage | | Germany |
| Gospel | | Netherlands |
| Hard Rock/Metal | | Greece |
| Instrumental | | Netherlands |
| Jazz | | Japan |
| Latin | | Spain |
| Mod | | Spain |
| Modern Soul | | Sweden |
| New Wave/Power Pop | | United States |
| Northern Soul | | Great Britain |
| Novelty | | Russia |

| GENRE | | TOP COUNTRY |
|---|---|---|
| Popcorn | | Belgium |
| Psych | | Germany |
| Punk/Post-Punk | | Italy |
| R&B | | Spain |
| Rap/Contemporary R&B | | Norway |
| Reggae/Roots | | France |
| Rock & Roll | | Netherlands |
| Rockabilly | | Spain |
| Rocksteady/Ska | | France |
| Surf | | Netherlands |
| Sweet Soul | | United States |
| Teen | | Sweden |

| COUNTRY | | #1 GENRE |
|---------|---|---------|
| Australia | | '70s Soul |
| Austria | | Gospel |
| Belgium | | Popcorn |
| Brazil | | Reggae/Roots |
| Canada | | Rap/Contemporary R&B |
| France | | Modern Soul |
| Germany | | Psych |
| Great Britain | | Northern Soul |
| Greece | | Psych |
| Italy | | Funk |
| Japan | | Modern Soul |
| Netherlands | | Gospel |
| Norway | | Disco/Boogie |
| Russia | | Disco/Boogie |
| Spain | | Mod |
| Sweden | | Modern Soul |
| Switzerland | | Rocksteady/Ska |
| United States | | Doo-Wop/Girl Group |

| #2 GENRE | #3 GENRE |
| --- | --- |
| R&B | Funk |
| Disco/Boogie | Modern Soul |
| Northern Soul | Teen |
| Electro/Bass | Rap/Contemporary R&B |
| Sweet Soul | Calypso |
| Disco/Boogie | Reggae/Roots |
| Garage | Disco/Boogie |
| '70s Soul | Crossover Soul |
| Hard Rock/Metal | Garage |
| '70s Soul | Mod |
| '70s Soul | Deep Soul |
| Rock & Roll | R&B |
| Modern Soul | Rap/Contemporary R&B |
| Modern Soul | Rockabilly |
| R&B | Latin |
| Disco/Boogie | Teen |
| Funk | Reggae/Roots |
| Sweet Soul | Gospel |

# NOTES

## INTRODUCTION: WHY VINYL NOW?

1. Bill Rosenblatt, "Vinyl Is Bigger Than We Thought. Much Bigger," *Forbes*, https://www.forbes.com/sites/billrosenblatt/2018/09/18/vinyl-is-bigger-than-we-thought-much-bigger, accessed January 10, 2019.

2. Dominik Bartmanski and Ian Woodward, *Vinyl: The Analogue Record in the Digital Age* (Bloomsbury Academic, 2015).

3. Michael E. Veal and E. Tammy Kim, eds., *Punk Ethnography: Artists and Scholars Listen to Sublime Frequencies* (Wesleyan University Press, 2016).

4. It's no accident that one of the most praised books on vinyl collecting treats the record as a sort of sacred object. See Evan Eisenberg, *The Recording Angel: Music, Records and Culture from Aristotle to Zappa* (Yale University Press, 2005).

5. Geeta Dayal, "A major reason why I like listening to vinyl has NOTHING to do with the sound quality, tactile feel or 'analog warmth.' It's because it's not networked. No service is tracking my listening, serving ads, or monetizing my experience. No one knows what I'm listening to, except me..." @geetadayal, Twitter, June 29, 2018, https://twitter.com/geetadayal/status/1012814479917133824.

6. Pauline Oliveros, *Deep Listening: A Composer's Sound Practice* (iUniverse, 2005), xxiii.

7. I don't mean to suggest here that "deep listening" is the best or only way to listen to music. For example, bumping music on your car stereo seems in many ways opposed to "deep listening," but is one of the most enjoyable ways to listen to a lot of music.

8. Piotr Orlov et al., *The Record: Contemporary Art and Vinyl*, ed. Trevor Schoonmaker (Duke University Press, 2010).

9. Better Records devote their entire business to finding, reviewing, and selling what they deem to be the best pressings of primarily rock LPs. "Hot Stampers: The Ultimate Analog LP," Better Records, https://www.better-records.com/gdept.aspx, accessed January 15, 2019.

10. "Scharpling & Wurster—New Hope for the Ape-Eared." Discogs, https://www.discogs.com/Scharpling-Wurster-New-Hope-For-The-Ape-Eared/release/2845432, accessed January 22, 2019.

11. Stephen Graham, *Sounds of the Underground: A Cultural, Political and Aesthetic Mapping of Underground and Fringe Music* (University of Michigan Press, 2016), 10–11.

## CHAPTER 1. PLAYING THE RECORD GAME

1. Simon Reynolds, *Retromania: Pop Culture's Addiction to Its Own Past*, 1st ed. (Farrar, Straus and Giroux, 2011).

## CHAPTER 2. DEVELOPING A COLLECTING METHOD

1. See Thorstein Veblen, *The Theory of the Leisure Class*, ed. Martha Banta, reissue ed. (Oxford University Press, 2009).

2. Walter Benjamin, "Unpacking My Library," in *Illuminations: Essays and Reflections*, ed. Hannah Arendt, trans. Harry Zohn (Schocken Books, 1969), 55–67.

## CHAPTER 3. COLLECTORS' GENRES AND SUBGENRES

1. Raymond Williams, "Dominant, Residual, and Emergent," in *Marxism and Literature*, rev. ed. (Oxford University Press, 1978), 121–127.

2. Private Facebook correspondence.

3. Peter Guralnick, *Sweet Soul Music: Rhythm and Blues and the Southern Dream of Freedom* (Back Bay Books, 1999).

4. Johannes Fabian, *Time and the Other: How Anthropology Makes Its Object, with a New Postscript by the Author* (Columbia University Press, 2014).

5. Michael E. Veal and E. Tammy Kim, eds., *Punk Ethnography: Artists and Scholars Listen to Sublime Frequencies* (Wesleyan University Press, 2016).

6. David Byrne, "Crossing Music's Borders in Search of Identity; 'I Hate World Music,'" *New York Times*, October 3, 1999, https://

www.nytimes.com/1999/10/03/arts/music-crossing-musics-borders-in-search-of-identity-i-hate-world-music.html, accessed November 23, 2019.

7. Veal and Kim, p. 147.

8. Brian Eno, *Ambient 1* (EG, 1978), liner notes.

9. Lance Scott Walker, *Houston Rap Tapes: An Oral History of Bayou City Hip-Hop*, new ed. (University of Texas Press, 2018).

10. Tim Lawrence, *Love Saves the Day: A History of American Dance Music Culture, 1970–1979* (Duke University Press, 2004).

11. Val Wilmer and Richard Williams, *As Serious as Your Life: Black Music and the Free Jazz Revolution, 1957–1977*, main-classic ed. (Serpent's Tail, 2018).

12. Thom Jurek, "Message from the Tribe: An Anthology of Tribe Records, 1972–1977," AllMusic, https://www.allmusic.com/album/message-from-the-tribe-an-anthology-of-tribe-records-1972-1977-mw0000557498, accessed November 23, 2019.

# CHAPTER 4. THE POLITICS OF RECORD COLLECTING

1. Nick Newman, "Gregg Turkington, the World's #1-Ranked Movie Expert, on Film Bloggers and 'Mister America,'" https://thefilmstage.com/features/gregg-turkington-the-worlds-1-ranked-movie-expert-on-film-bloggers-and-mister-america, accessed November 23, 2019.

2. Tressie McMillan Cottom and Stephanie Kelton, *Lower Ed: The Troubling Rise of For-Profit Colleges in the New Economy*, reprint ed. (New Press, 2018).

3. Keeanga-Yamahtta Taylor, *Race for Profit: How Banks and the Real Estate Industry Undermined Black Homeownership* (University of North Carolina Press, 2019).

4. Elspeth Reeve, "Why Does Marco Rubio Like Tupac So Much?" *The Atlantic*, February 5, 2013, https://www.theatlantic.com/politics/archive/2013/02/why-does-marco-rubio-tupac-so-much/318673.

5. Judy Berman, "The Uncomfortable Gender Politics of 'My Husband's Stupid Record Collection.'" *Flavorwire*, https://www.flavorwire.com/445998/the-uncomfortable-gender-politics-of-my-husbands-stupid-record-collection, accessed November 23, 2019.

## CHAPTER 5. EXPERIENCING RECORDS

1. George Lipsitz, *Footsteps in the Dark: The Hidden Histories of Popular Music*, 1st ed. (University of Minnesota Press, 2007), 105.

2. Paul Virilio, *Speed and Politics*, trans. Mark Polizzotti (Semiotext, 2006), 137.

3. Virilio, 85.

4. David Wallace-Wells, *The Uninhabitable Earth: Life After Warming*, 1st ed. (Tim Duggan Books, 2019).

5. Quoted in Karin S. Hendricks, *Compassionate Music Teaching: A Framework for Motivation and Engagement in the 21st Century* (Rowman and Littlefield, 2018), 55.

6. Edward W. Said, *The World, the Text, and the Critic*, reprint ed. (Harvard University Press, 1983), 33.

7. Stacey Luftig, *The Joni Mitchell Companion: Four Decades of Commentary* (Schirmer Books, 2000), 155.

8. Pierre Nora and Lawrence Kritzman, eds., *Realms of Memory: The Construction of the French Past, Vol. 3, Symbols*, trans. Arthur Goldhammer (Columbia University Press, 1998), xvii.

9. Achille Mbembe, *On the Postcolony*, 1st ed. (University of California Press, 2001), 1.

10. Achille Mbembe, "Achille Mbembe: The Value of Africa's Aesthetics," *The M&G Online*, https://mg.co.za/article/2015-05-14-the-value-of-africas-aesthetics, accessed November 18, 2019.

11. "Drexciya," Discogs.com, https://www.discogs.com/artist/1172-Drexciya.

12. Philip Sherburne, "Drexciya: Journey of the Deep Sea Dweller I," *Pitchfork*, https://pitchfork.com/reviews/albums/16175-journey-of-the-deep-sea-dweller-i, accessed November 18, 2019.

13. Damon Krukowski, *The New Analog: Listening and Reconnecting in a Digital World* (MIT Press, 2017).

14. Greg Milner, "Opinion: They Really Don't Make Music Like They Used To," *New York Times*, February 11, 2019, https://www.nytimes.com/2019/02/07/opinion/what-these-grammy-songs-tell-us-about-the-loudness-wars.html.

15. Milner.

16. Milner.

17. Milner.

18. Alex Ross, "Whistling in the Dark," *The New Yorker*, February 2002, https://www.newyorker.com/magazine/2002/02/18/whistling-in-the-dark-2.

19. Kyle Gann, "A Forest from the Seeds of Minimalism: An Essay on Postminimal and Totalist Music," kylegann.com, August 1998, https://www.kylegann.com/postminimalism.html.

20. Gann.

21. "Richard X. Clark," ObitTree.com, https://obittree.com/obituary/us/north-carolina/burlington/omega-funeral-service—crematory-llc/richard-clark/2238017.

## CONCLUSION: RECORDS OF OUR CLIMATE

1. Gregg Gelzinis and Graham Steele, "Climate Change Is a Financial Crisis, Too," Bloomberg.com, November 19, 2019, https://www.bloomberg.com/opinion/articles/2019-11-19/climate-change-is-a-financial-crisis-too.

2. Kyle Devine, *Decomposed: The Political Ecology of Music* (MIT Press, 2019).

3. Jon Blistein, "New Study Details Devastating Environmental Impact of Music Streaming," *Rolling Stone*. https://www.rollingstone.com/music/music-features/environmental-impact-streaming-music-835220, accessed November 20, 2019.

4. Jeff Chang, *Who We Be: A Cultural History of Race in Post-Civil Rights America*. Reprint edition, Picador, 2016.

# INDEX

(Illustrations are in **bold**.)

12" singles format, 2, 10, 14, 17, 18, 85, 91
13th Floor Elevators, 77, 80
45 rpm formats, 2, 10, 14, 17
4AD label, xiii
5th Degree, "You Got Me Hypnotized," 54
60s music, 48, 50, 74
70s music, 47, 50, 53, 74
80s music, 50, 53, 74
90s music, 74

# A

A Brother's Guiding Light, "Getting Together," 53
A.R.E. Weapons, *A.R.E. Weapons*, 36
Abdur Razzaq and Rafiyq, "Reflections from the Grave," 175
acceleration, 139–148
acid house, 144
active engagement, 135
Actuel label, 96
Adams, John, 70
Adams, John Luther, 182
Adams, Patrick, 53, 89
Africa, 174, 177
afrobeat, 136
Albach, Tom, 96
alienating space, 167, 168–169
All Day Records, Carrboro, NC, 9
Allen, Tony, 47
Allmusic guide, 14
ambient music, 69–71, 133
Andrew White's Andrew's Music label, 96
Animal Collective, 64
Appalachian music, 62
Apple Music, 190
Appreciations, "It's Better to Cry," 51
appropriation, 60

Archie Bell and the Drells, "Tighten Up," 52
Ardalan Clarke, Ariane, 61
Ardent Studios, 106, 107
Arhoolie catalog, 101
Art Ensemble of Chicago, 96, 97
"Art punk," 76, 79, 80
Ash Ra Tempel, 70, 81
Association for the Advancement of Creative Musicians (AACM), 97
Astley, Virginia, 130, 177, 178
Atlanta, 84, 86
Atlantic Records, 50, 95
atmospheric music, 46, 48, 69–73
    private-issue new age and library, 70–73
atonal and abrasive singing, 151
Au Pairs, *Playing with a Different Sex*, 78, 79
authenticity, 61
avant-garde punk, 78–79
Awesome Tapes label, 59, 61
Ayler, Albert, ix, 96, 97

# B

balance between quiet and loud, 179–180
Baltimore sound, 52
Banton, Buju, "Boom Bye," 68
Baobab label, 96
Barbadian Blue Rhythm Combo, *Magumba*, 66
Barnes, Ernie, xiii
Basho, Robbie, 152
Basic Channel label, 91
Basinski, William, *The Disintegration Loops*, 182–183
Basquiat, Jean-Michel, xiii, 33
Bauhaus (band), 36, 132–133
Beach Boys, 161, 163